The Things We Do and Why We Do Them

Also by Constantine Sandis

A COMPANION TO THE PHILOSOPHY OF ACTION (*edited with Timothy O'Connor*)
HEGEL ON ACTION (*edited with Arto Laitinen*)
HUMAN NATURE (*edited with Mark Cain*)
NEW ESSAYS ON THE EXPLANATION OF ACTION (*edited*)

The Things We Do and Why We Do Them

Constantine Sandis
Reader in Philosophy, Oxford Brookes University, UK

palgrave
macmillan

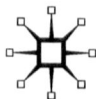

First published 2012 by
PALGRAVE MACMILLAN

Palgrave Macmillan in the UK is an imprint of Macmillan Publishers Limited, registered in England, company number 785998, of Houndmills, Basingstoke, Hampshire RG21 6XS.

Palgrave Macmillan in the US is a division of St Martin's Press LLC, 175 Fifth Avenue, New York, NY 10010.

Palgrave Macmillan is the global academic imprint of the above companies and has companies and representatives throughout the world.

Palgrave® and Macmillan® are registered trademarks in the United States, the United Kingdom, Europe and other countries.

ISBN: 978–0–230–52212–1

This book is printed on paper suitable for recycling and made from fully managed and sustained forest sources. Logging, pulping and manufacturing processes are expected to conform to the environmental regulations of the country of origin.

A catalogue record for this book is available from the British Library.

A catalog record for this book is available from the Library of Congress.

10 9 8 7 6 5 4 3 2 1
21 20 19 18 17 16 15 14 13 12

Printed and bound in Great Britain by
CPI Antony Rowe, Chippenham and Eastbourne

Αφιερωμένο στους γονείς μου

Contents in Brief

Illustrations

Tables

Figures

Preface

Caveat lector: this book does not offer any overarching explanations as to why we behave as we do. Such books are a dime a dozen: biologists, economists, historians, philosophers, psychologists, sociologists, and other theorists bombard us constantly with competing conjectures regarding the 'true' or 'real' reasons that lie behind our actions. In direct opposition to this trend, I shall be arguing that there is no one thing called 'action' or 'behaviour' which all action explanation aims at. What I offer, then, is not a theory of why we do the things we do, but an account of why all such theories are bound to fail. More positively, I present an investigation of the relationship between various theories of action explanation and our everyday accounts which yields some surprising results concerning human nature.

I proceed by pointing out various interrelated conflations shared by many theorists: between the things we do and the events of our doing them, between the reasons for which we act and the underlying factors which render us sensitive to them, between the motivation of action and its causal production, and so on (a list is provided on pp. xviii–xix). Such commonly held assumptions, I suggest, are collectively responsible for the rise of numerous irresolvable disputes across a range of disciplines. Once this is revealed, many questions which have long served to characterise intractable debates relating to the nature of action and its explanation begin to evaporate.

The theory of action explanation may be roughly divided into four parts whose boundaries and inter-dependencies are both blurred and contested: (i) meta-theoretical issues relating to ontology, meaning, and methodology; (ii) theories of why it is that we act as we do (e.g. Homeric, Humean, Nietzschean, Freudian, or Milgramian); (iii) practical applications of the aforementioned theories (e.g. in marketing, politics, psychotherapy and so on); and (iv) a philosophical psychology which cuts across the first three fields of enquiry, just as the study of moral psychology cuts across that of meta-, normative, and practical ethics. This book is *about* theories of human action and its explanation. It examines (i) with the further aim of casting doubt upon various accounts relating to both (ii) and (iii), and reaching a better understanding of how to best go about developing (iv).

In the first chapter, I distinguish between a plurality of things that may all legitimately be called action and/or behaviour and, similarly, numerous different things that we may wish to explain in relation to them – viz. different objects of action explanation. Chapter 2 presents some basic conflations that arise from the failures to make the sorts of distinctions highlighted in the previous chapter, followed by an exploration of their recent philosophical ancestry. Chapters 3–5 highlight further conflations whilst also advocating the theoretical benefits of abandoning them all. Chapter 3 does this in relation to debates between causalists and rationalists on how to best explain individual and social action; Chapter 4 turns to philosophical debates surrounding the nature of reasons and motivation; and Chapter 5 examines psychological theories that purport to uncover the 'real' reasons for our actions. The sixth chapter investigates the relation between the considerations we act upon and the explanatory statements that cite them. In the seventh, final, chapter I introduce some constraints between different spheres of action explanation previously delineated, with the further aim of clearing the ground required for collaborative cross-disciplinary progress.

Acknowledgements

I began working on the material for this book over a decade ago. Largely to blame for its slow progress are those commentators on earlier versions (including abandoned parts) who gave me good reason to extensively revise both my thoughts and their expression. I am thankful to all of them for making this a better book than it otherwise would have been.

My greatest debt is to Jonathan Dancy, who supervised the PhD thesis which begat the general argument of this volume. I do not know whether any sentence from that work bar its title has survived intact, but Jonathan's voice remains lodged in my head, reminding me that there is no proposition that cannot be rendered true by appending 'in a sense' to it. I am also hugely grateful to my thesis examiners, Michael Smith and Galen Strawson, for extremely sound advice and generous encouragement.

Drafts of various chapters were also read and commented upon at various stages by David Backhurst, Mark Bevir, David Charles, David Dolby, Giuseppina D'Oro, Fred Dretske, Geoffrey Ferrari, Hanjo Glock, Michael Lacewing, Maggie Little, Jack Marr, and Karsten Stueber. I thank them all for their invaluable advice. David Dolby, in particular, sent frequent feedback on numerous drafts and has saved me from more errors than I would care to point out.

Complete lists of those who, over the years, made helpful suggestions at conferences, seminars, coffee shops, or bars are rarely possible if ever welcome, but it would be callous not to mention Maria Alvarez, Nafsika Athanassoulis, Annette Baier, Jon Bishop, Reid Blackman, Emma Borg, Lisa Bortolotti, Stephen Boulter, Thom Brooks, John Broome, Gary Browning, Stephen Butterfill, Mark Cain, Beverley Clack, John Cottingham, Josep Corbi, Max de Gaynesford, Katerina Deligiorgi, Alice Drewery, Douglas Farland, Stephen Finley, Keith Frankish, John Glasbrook, Simon Glendinning, Rémi Clot-Goudard, Phil Goff, Martin Groves, Naomi Goulder, Peter Hacker, Natalia Waights Hickman, David Hillel-Ruben, Perry Hinton, Jeppe Høj, Brad Hooker, Stephen Houlgate, Rosalind Hursthouse, Kent Hurtig, Dan Hutto, John Hyman, Emma Jay, Tom Joyce, Mahmoud Kassem, Leonard Kahn, Javier Kalhat, Peter Kail, Nikos Kakalis, Simon Kirchin, Joshua Knobe, Arto Laitinen, Sören Landkildehus, Gerald Lang, Neil Levy, Andreas Lind, Bertram Malle, Erasmus Mayr, John McDowell, Al Mele, Lije Millgram, Alan Monahan,

Marta Moreno, Carlos Moya, Luke Mulhall, Dan O' Brien, Lilian O'
Brien, David Oderberg, Francesco Orsi, Catherine Osborne, Charlie
Pelling, Charles Pigden, Christian Piller, Tom Pink, Bill Pollard, Josep
Lluis Prades, John Preston, Anthony Price, Michael Proudfoot, Stathis
Psillos, Chris Pulman, Andrew Reisner, Sabine Roeser, Valerio Salvi,
Elizabeth Sandis, Severin Schroeder, Nik Shackel, John Shand, Ali
Sharukhi, Maureen Sie, William Sin, Gianfranco Soldati, Ralph Stoecker,
Tom Stoneham, Fred Stoutland, Philip Stratton-Lake, Bart Streumer, Julia
Tanney, Nassim Taleb, Roger Teichmann (who taught me by example
that the correct response to many a philosophical claim is 'if you like'),
Kevin Timpe, Teemu Toppinen, Tom Tyler, Sam Vice, Robert Vinten, Ken
Westphal, Andrew Williams, André Wunder, and Anna C. Zielinska.

I have also been helped enormously by the questions of audiences at
talks and seminars given in Amersfoort, Amsterdam, Athens, Barcelona,
Bath, Belfast, Birmingham, Bled, Buffalo, Cape Town, Delft, Delmenhorst,
Dunedin, Durham, Edinburgh, Genoa, Grenoble, Girona, Helsinki,
Henley, Jyväskylä, Keele, Leeds, Lisbon, London, Lund, Manchester,
Murcia, Oxford, Potsdam, Reading, San Francisco, St. Andrews, Stirling,
York, and Valencia, as well as those of my fellow contributors at *Flickers
of Freedom* and my incredulous graduate students at Oxford Brookes
University.

For research environments and travel grants I remain grateful to
Oxford Brookes (who awarded me a sabbatical in Spring 2006 which
helped me to get things started), the LOGOS project 'Modal Aspects of
Materialist Realism' (HUM2007–61108, MCYT–Spanish Government),
the NOMOS Network for Applied Philosophy, the PERSP Network for
the Philosophy of Perspectival Thoughts and Facts, The Alexander S.
Onassis Public Benefit Foundation, and the wonderful Philosophy
Department at University of Reading (where I undertook my PhD).

Many thanks to Dan Bunyard for commissioning the book in January
2006 and Priyanka Gibbons who took over in mid-2007 and, knowing
more about human motivation than any theorist, successfully com-
bines much-appreciated patience with timely prodding. It has been a
great joy to work with both on various projects, including this one. At
Palgrave Macmillan I would also like to thank Melanie Blair for all her
help with pre-production, as well as two anonymous referees for their
helpful comments and suggestions.

This is the third time that Robert Vinten has compiled the index and
helped with proofreading and I have begun to dread the day when he

politely declines to do so again. Special thanks must also be given to Vidhya Jayaprakash and her team at Newgen Publishing and Data Services for going well beyond the call of duty in their meticulous work during various stages of production, including copy-editing. I am additionally grateful to Lynn Reznick at Offthemark, for her patient assistance in securing the rights to reprint ten of Mark Parisi's insightful cartoons, and to Florian Kugler at the Kunsthistorisches Museum in Vienna, who very helpfully arranged for permission to reproduce the cover image of Pieter Bruegel the Elder's painting of over 200 children engaged in play activities.

Assorted sections from the first two chapters draw from 'The Objects of Action Explanation', to be published in *Ratio*, Vol. XXV, No. 3, September (2012); a different selection of parts of Chapters 1 and 2 are forthcoming in French translation as 'L'explication de l'action: des types distincts', in (ed.) R. Clot-Goudard, *L'Explication de l'action: perspectives contemporaines, Recherches sur la philosophie et le langage*, n°29 (Vrin); a considerably earlier version of Chapter 3 appeared as 'The Explanation of Action in History' in *Essays in Philosophy*, Vol. 7, No. 2, Article 12, June (2006); parts of Chapter 4 have been adapted from 'Hume and the Debate on "Motivating Reasons"', in (ed.) Charles Pigden, *Hume on Motivation and Virtue* (Palgrave Macmillan, 2009), pp. 142–53; Chapter 6 shares material with 'Can Action Explanations Ever be Non-Factive?', forthcoming in (eds) B. Hooker, M. Little, and D. Backhurst, *Thinking about Reasons: Essays in Honour of Jonathan Dancy* (Oxford University Press); Chapter 7 reworks my essay 'Dretske on the Causation of Behavior', *Behavior and Philosophy*, Vol. 36 (2008), pp. 71–85 into the book's narrative; the second Appendix uses some of the same source material as 'A Just Medium: Empathy and Detachment in Historical Understanding', *Journal of the Philosophy of History*, Vol. 5, No. 2 (2011), pp. 179–200 and, to a lesser extent, 'Action, Reason, and the Passions', forthcoming in (eds) D. O' Brien & A. Bailey, *Continuum Companion to Hume*. Finally, small passages across the book have been adapted from my essays on 'Philosophy of Action' and 'Motivation' in (eds) A.C. Grayling, A. Pyle, and N. Goulder, *The Encyclopedia of British Philosophy* (Thoemmes Press, 2006). I would like to thank all related editors and anonymous referees for their assistance and, where appropriate, the publishers for permission to reuse material.

My wife Lizzie showed me how different contemporary philosophy of action would be if it were written in Latin, tolerated endless questions about English usage, and kept me company as we worked together for endless hours at our home desks. Finally, this book, like myself, ultimately owes its existence to my good parents, Anastasia and Alexandros. I dedicate it to them with deep gratitude for their continuous love, help, and support: ελπίζω να σας αρέσει!

Constantine Sandis
Oxford, September 2011

Analytical Table of Contents

Appendix I – The Ontology of Action   142

In which the metametaphysics of action is discussed with a particular focus on the work of Hornsby, Davidson, and Dancy.

Appendix II – Thought and Motive in Historiography   155

In which a re-enactment of the thought of Hume and Collingwood illustrates mutually compatible ways in which historical explanation may succeed.

Twenty Conflating Views to be Avoided

1. *The Conflating View of Behaviour* (CVB):
   A person's behaviour consists of the things she does: e.g. the movings of her body.

2. *The Conflating View of Action* (CVA):
   A person's actions consist of the things she does: e.g. her movings of her body.

3. *The Conflating View of Reasons* (CVR):
   The reasons for which we act are reasons *why* our actions occur.

4. *The Conflating View of Reasons for Action* (CVRA):
   The reasons for which we act are reasons *for which* our actions occur.

5. *The Conflating View of Things Done* (CVTD):
   What I am doing is *my doing* (of) it.

6. *The Conflating View of Doings* (CVD):
   My doing *x* is identical to the event (process, etc.) of my doing *x*.

7. *The Conflating View of Action Explanation* (CVAE):
   Whatever explains why we act explains why our actions occur.

8. *The Combined Conflation of CVR and CVAE*:
   The reasons for which we act explain why our actions occur.

9. *The Conflating View of Motivating Reasons* (CVMR):
   The reasons for which we act are identical to the things which motivate us to act (and vice versa).

10. *The Conflating View of Good Reasons* (CVGR):
    Good reasons for action are good reasons for being *motivated* to act (and vice versa).

11. *The Conflating View of Motivation* (CVM):
    A reason for being motivated to act is a reason for bringing it about that one is so motivated. [NB: this can be held with regard to both 'normative reasons' and 'motivating reasons'.]

12. *The Conflating View of Reasons Explanation* (CVRE):
The reasons for which we act can explain why we act.

13. *The Combined Conflation of CVA and CVRE*:
The reasons for which we act can explain why our actions occur.

14. *The Combined Conflation of CVM and CVR*:
Whatever motivated us to act is the reason why our action occurred.

15. *The Conflating View of Motivational Production* (CVMP):
What motivated an action most is identical to whatever produced it in a psychologically explanatory way to be further specified.

16. *The Conflating View of Nested Reasons* (CVNR):
A reason why A took x to be a reason to ϕ is a reason that explains why A subsequently ϕ-d.

17. *The Combined Conflation of CVNR and CVR*:
A reason why A took x to be a reason to ϕ is a reason *for which* A subsequently ϕ-d, i.e. nesting reasons are agential reasons.

18. *The Conflating View of What Is Done* (CVWD):
What I do when I x is my x-ing.

19. *The Conflating View of Triggering Structures* (CVTS):
Actions and/or events are causally triggered by their explanatory structures.

20. *The Conflating View of Triggering Reasons* (CVTR):
The reasons for which we act are the causal triggers of our actions.

That which is sought in an incorrect fashion is never obtained.

The I Ching

1
Objects and Objectives of Action Explanation

Being the book's opening chapter, in which we are introduced to a multitude of different explanatory aims and various related conceptions of behaviour. It is suggested that there is no such thing as a distinct enquiry of explaining action.

I KEEP six honest serving-men
(They taught me all I knew);
Their names are What and Why and When
And How and Where and Who.
I send them over land and sea,
I send them east and west;
But after they have worked for me,
I give them all a rest.

I let them rest from nine till five,
For I am busy then,
As well as breakfast, lunch, and tea,
For they are hungry men.
But different folk have different views;
I know a person small –
She keeps ten million serving-men,
Who get no rest at all!

She sends 'em abroad on her own affairs,
From the second she opens her eyes –
One million Hows, two million Wheres,
And seven million Whys!

Rudyard Kipling[1]

1.1   Action in the behavioural sciences

The term 'motivation' is most widely used to refer to either (a) the *things which motivate* us – often misleadingly termed our 'motives' or 'motivators' or (b) the state or process of *our being motivated* by (a). In post-Darwinian behavioural science, the topic of motivation arises as a search for (a) above, in direct response to the question 'why do animate agents act as they do?' Behavioural scientists including physiologists, sociologists, (motivational and evolutionary) psychologists, and psychiatrists typically construe this as a question about the causes of *behaviour*, characterised as something exhibited not only by humans but also by so-called 'lower' animals, as well as insects, plants, chemicals, fossils and other agents. The following quotation is paradigmatic of the ease with which such scientists typically choose to opt for the catch-all term 'behaviour':

> Although the words *behave* and *behavior* are often meant to refer to actions of living organisms, they are also commonly used to refer to changes and movements that nonliving objects undergo. This more inclusive meaning is consistent with the definition of *behaviour* provided by the *Oxford English Dictionary*: 'The manner in which a thing acts under specified conditions or circumstances, or in relation to other things.' So though we speak of the behavior of a dog or child, we also consider how one chemical behaves in the presence of another and how the stock market behaved yesterday ... I will use the unqualified term behavior and its derivatives to refer to either living or nonliving entities.[2]

Behaviour, so understood, is the *explanandum* or *explicandum* (that which is to be explained) common to the investigations of behavioural scientists whose task is to provide us with an explanation for it. Accordingly, behavioural theories compete to produce the most accurate *explanans* or *explicans* (that which does the explaining) of this behaviour, which they further take to be its cause or determinant.[3]

Proposed stimuli – to use the standard psychological term for any change or event which excites a nerve impulse giving rise to a physical reaction or response – may be either external (such as contact with a hot stove) or internal (such as a hunger pang). Thus, according to internal/ dispositional attribution theories of motivation – such as those first put forth by E. C. Tolman (1932), C. L. Hull (1943), J. Dollard and N. E. Miller (1950), and A. H. Maslow (1954) – our behaviour is primarily caused by mental attitudes (e.g. beliefs, desires and personal characteristics), drives (e.g. thirst or hunger, curiosity drive, manipulative drive), and needs (e.g. need for stimulation, need for control). By contrast, according to external/situational attribution theories of motivation – for example those of E. E. Jones and V. A. Harris (1967), L. Ross (1977), and D. T. Gilbert and E. E. Jones (1986) – it is primarily caused by non-mental items such as social norms, threats, or incentives (e.g. money, esteem and the rewards of success). At a glance, it seems obvious that both approaches may happily interact in everyday motivation: incentive factors can awaken drive states (which is why bakeries channel their fumes out onto the main street, while public houses do not) and food generally tastes better when we are hungry (hence the practice of delaying meals to build up a good appetite).

According to *mechanistic theories* of motivation – including variants of ethological theory, sociobiological theory, and drive theory – such stimuli are all that is needed to explain behaviour. For this reason, these theories are typically called stimulus-response (SR) theories. SR theories make no principled distinction between animate and inanimate behaviour or human and infrahuman agency. Causes of human and animal behaviour are thus said to only differ in complexity from those of the mere motion of inanimate objects. Some SR theories allow for psychological states to have a causal function, but only so long as the states in question are non-cognitive (e.g. desires). By contrast *cognitive theories* – including variants of Gestalt theory, field theory, balance theory, expectancy-value (reinforcement) theory, psychoanalytic theory, and attribution theory – have largely arisen in response to some of the abovementioned distinctions, insisting that at least some behaviour (viz. 'intentional action') is instigated not by pure stimulation but through some source of information.

Cognitivists about motivation maintain that external or internal events are encoded, categorised and transformed into 'cognitive states' such as the belief that I am hungry. Mental processes are thus thought to intervene between stimulus inputs and behavioural outputs, hence the label 'stimulus-cognition-response' or 'SCR' theory. The causes of behaviour, it is consequently thought, must include cognitive parts of the agent's psychology. Be that as it may, cognitive theories remain mechanistic at heart, they simply assign certain operations to cognitive functions.

Despite their diversities, behavioural scientists by and large agree that:

(1) The *explanandum* of their investigations is 'behaviour' and/or 'action'.[4]
(2) Their *explanans* of choice is to be further identified as the agent's *motivation* (in the first of the two senses outlined above).
(3) The explanation given must be a causal one.

Thus, for instance, D.G. Mook states that:

> Questions about motivation, then, are questions about the causes of specific actions. Why does this organism, this person or ant or chimpanzee, do this particular thing we see it do?[5]

Richard Gross likewise tells us that:

> The study of motivation is the study of the causes of behaviour and all the major theoretical approaches within behavioural science as a whole are concerned with identifying these causes.[6]

Examples of the causes in question range from character traits to 'brain sites which, when stimulated, motivate the animal to terminate stimulation'.[7] Indeed, the term 'motivate' is here used in a fashion which renders it indistinguishable from phrases such as 'cause one to be motivated'. Ever since Nietzsche, such searches for causal determinants have been advertised as searches for the *true* or *real* reasons behind our *actions*, to be contrasted with whatever 'reasons' we might falsely think we are acting on. Culprits have included participants in both sides of the age-old nature v. nurture debate,[8] as well as those who think of all behaviour as a combined *product* of the two.[9] Freudians famously also take themselves to be uncovering the *real* reasons for which we act.[10] Likewise, the advertising campaign for Steven Pinker's 2002 book *The Blank Slate* ran as follows:

> Love, Hate, Lust, Envy, Fear: Are you ready for the truth behind your behaviour?

Behavioural scientists, then, consider the results of their experimental work to be in *direct* competition with the kinds of explanations we provide for our actions in everyday life, and their language is continuous with natural language.[11] The following introductory words from Bernard Weiner's deservedly successful book *Motivational Psychology* are typical of textbooks on the subject:

> It should be anticipated that the answer of the trained motivational psychologist will be 'better' than that of the layperson... For example, when a layperson explains why an individual is drinking water, he or she may say that the person is thirsty. When the layperson accounts for why another individual is eating, he or she may infer

that the person is hungry...the motivational psychologist, however, attempts to comprise these very disparate observations within the same theoretical network or explanatory system. Perhaps it is postulated that behaviour is determined by the amount of deprivation and the number of rewarded experiences.[12]

Unlike the layperson, the behavioural scientist aims at providing an answer which neatly fits within general theories that are applicable across many domains of behaviour including initiation, sustainment, and direction. This general outlook is even shared by that small minority of modern-day behavioural scientists who deny that the mental can be reduced to the physical. On such views, human behaviour is necessitated by irreducibly psychological forces.[13] The aim of the behavioural scientist is to defend the most plausible unifying theory of behaviour by 'integrating mechanisms, development, adaptation, and historical contingency'.[14] The resulting account should ideally be capable of being summarised in a single sentence, such as the following:

> All behavior – even behavior that brings misery to people – aims at adaptation to that [physical] environment.[15]

But are such generalisations really plausible? What exactly is it that behavioural scientists take themselves to be explaining scientifically when they talk about 'behaviour'? Most of them take their search for the ultimate *explanantia* to be at one with that of philosophers interested in questions relating to human nature and action. Many introductions to motivational psychology, for example, will include sentences such as the following:

> Rationalists saw human beings as free to choose between different courses of action, and so, in a sense, the concept of motivation becomes unnecessary. We behave as we do because we have chosen to do so and it is our reason which determines our behaviour.[16]

In the next section I propose that the term 'behaviour' is multiply ambiguous to the point of rendering statements such as the one above vacuous. I begin by distinguishing between three possible understandings, each subsequently associated with a different set of explanatory aims in the hope of making the reader wary of unspecified uses of the term 'because'. We will then be in a better position to evaluate a much-abused distinction favoured by many scientists, namely that between proximate and ultimate causes of behaviour.

1.2   Different conceptions of behaviour

Behaviour can, of course, be motionless. G. H. von Wright gives the example of pressing one's hand against a door to keep it closed.[17] Other examples might include standing still, refusing to answer a question by keeping quiet, reciting a poem to oneself, or staring at something intensely. Accordingly, motionless behaviour may (but need not) involve one's refraining from or omitting to do something. In the same passage von Wright also notes that the term 'behaviour' has misleadingly been used to refer not only to macroscopic (molar) activity but also to microscopic (molecular) activity, such as the neural processes that constitute the underlying physiology of bodily movement.[18]

Behavioural scientists invariably use the term 'behaviour' in any of the above senses. It is no small wonder that Fred Schreier confesses to have 'found tremendous difficulty in formulation' when he began to write his book *Human Motivation*:

> It must have been much easier to overcome the confusion of languages after the Tower of Babel than to find a way to overcome the differences in the conceptions and terms of the various schools and to express them in a 'neutral' language.[19]

Even if we restrict ourselves to behaviour involving outward bodily movement, there seem to remain (at least) three different things which we may have in mind:

(a) The (mere) movement of the agent's body.
(b) The event (b1) or process (b2) of the agent moving her body.
(c) *What* the agent did (viz. move her body).

The precise individuation of (a–c) is, of course, a matter of much philosophical debate. What follows is a *prima facie* sketch of their interrelations:[20]

(a) is a causal process or event, further specifiable (under a certain description) as a *movement* of the agent's body, in the intransitive sense of the term, according to which it doesn't take an intentional object. In Jennifer Hornsby's terminology, the movement in question refers to the agent's body's moving, and *not* to the agent's moving of her body.[21] We would not normally identify such behaviour as action.

(b1) may also be thought of as an event, but not obviously identical to (a). (b1) may arguably be described as a movement in the transitive sense of the word – viz. the *agent's* moving (of) her body (intentionally or otherwise). Event (a) is the bodily movement in which (b1) (the event of bringing the first event about) *results*.[22] The events featured in (a) and (b1) may thus be thought to be logically related, but not identical: a movement-T event is the event of bringing about a movement-I event.[23] Many philosophers are happy to call b1-events (but not a-events) 'action', for the sorts of reasons outline by A. C. Ewing below:

> An action occurs in times, has a duration, however short, is a change, and is not universal or again a 'thing'. That being so I do not understand what is meant by denying that it is an event.[24]

A common question in action theory is whether *omissions* and *refrainings* count as actions, or even as things we do. Omissions and refrainings can have durations and may even (though need not) constitute changes. It is true that to refrain from doing or omit to do x is to *not* do it, but my omitting to do x may well be identical to my doing y and, conversely, my doing x may be identical to my not doing y. So whether or not a certain piece of behaviour is an act or an omission is a matter of description. One may, of course, omit to do something by being inactive but this remains compatible with intentionally doing something else (e.g. punishing someone by making them wait). In what follows, then, I shall predominantly use 'action' as shorthand for behaviour that could be described in either way.

Some prefer to view actions as (b2) *processes* of bringing a-events about, it being a moot point whether or not processes are aspects of events. Such processes are typically seen as being causal i.e. as processes of agents and/or their minds causing a-events.[25] On some Aristotelian views, however, actions are *non-causal* processes of people doing things.[26] While both processes and events occur, processes – causal or otherwise – cannot be said *to happen*. In fact processes seem to differ from events in certain ways: they do not *extend* in time or have essential temporal parts, though they may contain sub-processes which persist for part or all of their time.[27] Most crucially, we can be engaged in a process as it unfolds over a period of time during which it may be interrupted.[28] In this regard, processes are akin to substances, whereas events are more fact-like, hence the strong intuition that no particular event could have been otherwise than it was (without being a different event).[29] One may, for example, be in the process of baking a cake without ever succeeding in baking one (without there being a cake-baking event). Similarly, the action of tying one's shoelaces is most naturally conceived not as a series of (albeit brief) bodily movements, each followed by a tiny shoelace movement, but as a single process allowing no sharp distinction between the agent's own movements and those of the laces. This conception blocks the view (favoured by event-theorists) that the psychological explanation of action is not concerned with any occurrences beyond the movements of the agent.[30] Conceptual observations are here supplemented by phenomenological ones (try to imagine *teaching* someone how to tie their shoelaces without a shoe present). On such a conception, the non-causal bringing about of an a-event is constitutive of all action, be it non-basic or otherwise. If, like me, you are always doing things but rarely get anything done, the process view of action will appeal to you.

von Wright, by contrast, takes the event/process distinction to map onto that between acts and activities:

> We shall distinguish between *act* and *activity*. To close a window or to kill a person is to perform an act. To smoke or to run or to read is to be engaged in activity... As acts are related to *events*, so are activities related to *processes*. Events happen, processes go on. Acts effect the happening of events, activities keep processes going.[31]

For my part, however, I cannot see why one cannot be engaged in the process of killing a person (say through gradual poisoning), or of closing a window during heavy wind. Indeed, the process view adheres to the *Oxford English Dictionary*'s first listed definition of 'action' as 'the *process* or *condition* of acting or doing (in the widest sense)'. This prematurely takes the preposition 'of' to be marking an identity as opposed to some other kind of a relation. So treated, the preposition is thought to function as it does in the phrase 'the city of Paris' as opposed to, say, 'the King of France' or 'the hunchback of Notre Dame', 'the memory of being young' (alas), 'the sister of Stalin', 'the pick of destiny', 'the house of Lords' and perhaps also – more contentiously – 'the state of belief', 'the property of being red' and 'the continent of Europe'.[32] If processes are different to events then the *process of* raising my arm cannot be identical to the *event of* raising my arm. So on the (b2) understanding of action, the 'of' in 'the event *of* my acting' does not mark an identity.[33] On a (b1) understanding, by contrast, the event of my raising my arm *is* my raising my arm: an action (which may or may not be identical to the process of raising my arm, depending on whether the b1-theorist distinguishes processes from events). It is also possible to hold a hybrid or disjunctivist view. For example Alexander Mourelatos maintains that actions are occurrences which divide into (i) activities (whose topic-neutral counterparts are processes) and (ii) performances (whose topic-neutral counterparts are events).[34]

The *OED* distinguishes the process definition from that of action as 'A thing done, a deed. Not always distinguished from act, but usually viewed as occupying some time in doing, and in *plural* referred to habitual or ordinary deeds, the sum of which constitutes *conduct*'. This brings us to (c), namely *what* the agent did: her deed (as opposed to her doing of it). We rightly talk of *acts* of doing things, but the *things* we do are not always actions (consider thinking, for example).[35] To do something is not necessarily to perform an action. By contrast, every performance of an action is a doing of something. Things done are neither bodily movements-I nor bodily movements-T, the latter b eing events or processes of our bringing about movements-I. Things *done* are to be distinguished from both the things we bring about and the events or processes of our bringing them about. This leads von Wright to maintain that:

> The thing done is the result of the action; the thing brought about is the consequence of an action. Primarily, the things done and brought about are changes (events).[36]

His reasoning here is partly affected by the additional thought that the term 'bring about' normally indicates 'that we achieved this by doing something else, such as pressing a button and thus releasing a spring'.[37] There is much debate on whether or not one can bring about the result(s) of one's action and, if so, whether this is done causally.[38] Whatever the answer, however, von Wright is mistaken to identify the thing done with the result of the action. *What* I do when I raise my arm is just that (raise my arm), not the bodily movement or end-state that my action results in (my arm going up), though the latter is arguably logically connected to the former.[39] Both are to be distinguished from the event, state, or process of acting, in much the same way as *what* we believe is to be distinguished from the event, state, or process of believing it.[40] John Macmurray makes a related point:

> The term 'action' is involved in the same ambiguity that recent philosophy has found it essential to resolve in the case of terms like 'perception' or 'conception'. It may refer either to what is done or to the doing of it. It may mean either 'doing' or 'deed'. When we talk of 'an action' we are normally referring to what is done...The analysis of the idea of action does not deal with the concomitants of action,

but with action itself; and it yields only the distinction between the *doing* and the *deed*. It may be convenient to refer to these two aspects of action by the Latin words which distinguish them – *actio* and *actum*.[41]

Strictly speaking, 'actio' (like 'cogitatio', which Macmurray contrasts it with) is not a verbal noun but a feminine third declension noun substantive, formed from the same past participle (of the verb 'ago'), of which 'actum' (which Macmurray contrasts with 'eventum') is the neuter fourth declension version; Macmurray's translation most likely reflects the English idiom arising from the legal context of the term 'actio'. Grammatical quibbles aside, there is evident conceptual space for the sort of distinction he is making here and it is *at least* as natural to talk of actions as things we do, perform, undertake, execute or carry out as it is to talk of them as our *doings* of such things. Similar semantic distinctions have been championed by J. L. Austin and others.[42] *Pace* Macmurray, who takes his distinction to demonstrate that actions are never events which happen but either activities we perform (in the sense in which acting contrasts with thinking) or deeds we do,[43] I see no reason to deny that the term 'action' may legitimately be used to refer to either (i) *what* we do or (ii) the event and/or process and/or activity of our doing it. On the contrary, this arguably accounts for the practice of applying conflicting predicates to an act performed and the performance of the act in question.[44] For example:

- I do not object to *what you did* (e.g. hang a painting) but to *your doing it* (in the middle of the night, in such a noisy way, etc.).
- *What she did* was not in the least scary but *her doing it* gave me a real fright at the time.
- He may have *done what* the rules required of him, but *his doing it* was completely accidental.
- I *did the same thing* as everyone else and yet *my doing it* was deemed irregular.

The general pattern may also be applied to utterances and beliefs:

- *What she said* may have been very clever but *her saying it* (to her employer) was less so.
- The fact that *what he believed* (e.g. that he would win the lottery) turned out to be true does not make *his believing it* (given the available evidence) any less irrational.

- Pascal thinks that *believing* in God is rational even if *what* is thereby believed is neither rational nor true.[45]

It would seem, then, that the terms 'behaviour' and 'action' have no obvious single referent, even when we restrict ourselves to acts involving visible bodily movements.[46] Given the insensitivity of both terms to the distinctions laid out above, one cannot fix an *explanandum* by invoking them with no further comment. In the next section I argue that, while disambiguating between (a–c) above is thus a necessary requirement for specifying an *explanandum*, it is insufficient.

1.3   What, why, when, how, where, and who

One obvious complication is that a piece of behaviour in any of the above senses may correctly present itself to us in a multitude of different ways, rendering the explanation and evaluation of any given action is relative to its mode of presentation.[47] But even to identify an action under a *specific* description is not yet to identify *what it is about it* that is to be explained. After all, depending on our aims or objectives, we may ask different things about it, each of which gives rise to a different *explanandum*, in turn requiring a different *explanans*: *how* it was done, *why* the doing of it occurred at time *t1* rather than at time *t2*, why *x* was brought about instead of *y*, and so on. The point has been forcefully made by Peter Achinstein who argues more generally that, unless we specify what question it is that we are asking of any given phenomenon we will have failed to fix a specific *explanandum* or 'object of explanation'.[48] Even if we restrict ourselves to *events* of people acting, it won't do to simply maintain (as Jon Elster, among many others, does) that to explain an event 'is to give an account of why it happened', let alone 'by citing an *earlier event* as its cause' (Elster 2007: 9).

Achinstein adopts the pragmatic attitude that 'we must begin with the concept of an illocutionary act of explaining and characterise explanations, by reference to this, rather than conversely'.[49] When we want to explain why A φ-ed, neither A's φ-ing nor the statement 'she φ-ed' qualify as *explananda*, for to identify an action under a particular description is not yet to identify what it is about it that is to be explained. Depending on our interests, we may ask all sorts of different things about the occurrence of an action, each giving rise to a different *explanandum*: not only *why* or *how* he φ-ed but why or how he φ-ed in such and such a way, at a certain time rather than another, for this or that reason, given his character or motivational set, and so on. *Explanantia* are thereby best understood as statements of fact whose *explananda* are neither sentences nor phenomena but *reperienda* or 'discoverables' viz. the things we seek to find out – e.g. *why* the bridge exploded *when* it did or why the *bridge* exploded and *who*, if anyone, was responsible.

Here are three such *reperienda*, each in turn corresponding to one of three conceptions of behaviour (a–c) outlined in § 1.2 above:

(i) Why A's body moved
(ii) Why A's action of moving her body occurred
(iii) Why A moved her body

In (i) we are searching for the *cause* of the event that was the movement of A's body. What is sought in (ii), by contrast, is the *cause* of the (related) event *that is* A's *moving of her body* . Finally, to provide an explanation of (iii) is to explain neither (i) why A's body moved – after all it may have moved *because* she moved it – nor (ii) why an event of her moving her body occurred; for to explain why someone did something is not to explain why anything – including the event of her doing the thing in question – occurred. Nor is it, incidentally, to explain *the thing* she did. For an explanation of *what* she did is not itself an explanation of *why* she did what she did, though we may successfully explain why we do things by re-describing the things we do in such a way that our goal or intention becomes apparent.[50] Rather, it is to explain why A performed the action of moving her body. It is less obvious that we are here looking for a *cause*, and it may even be that she did what she did for *no reason* at all, which is not to say that the *event* of her doing so was uncaused; in certain contexts it may even be that she needs no reason to act as she does.

It is worth emphasising that (i–iii) would remain distinct *even* on the implausible assumption that conceptions (a–c) are ultimately reducible to three different ways of characterising one and the same phenomenon for – as we have just seen – there is a range of questions we may ask of any given phenomenon (even under a tightly specified description) and their name is legion. Yet behavioural scientists rarely, if ever, specify which of (i–iii) it is that they are actually seeking to explain. Is it something we do, the event of our doing it, or just our bodies' movements-I that they are interested in explaining? Is it an action, and if so in which sense? They often write as if all searches are reducible to a quest for (i). Yet, strictly speaking (i) is of *physiological* rather than psychological interest.

The track record of philosophers is marginally better. They generally tend to concern themselves with (ii), whose study is of far more interest to social and political scientists, historians, and economists than it is to the layperson, who is typically concerned with (iii). As laypeople, what we are normally interested in is why a person did something, or why they did it at a certain time, for a certain reason, instead of something else, and so on, and not why the event of their doing it occurred.[51] One of a handful of philosophical exceptions is Jennifer Hornsby who explicitly relates the distinction between (ii) and (iii) to philosophical confusion over action explanation, observing that to request an explanation for why A did *x* is *not* to ask why the event of her doing it occurred, though both might legitimately be conceived of as behavioural *explanantia*:

> What a non-philosopher means when she accepts that there are actions is that the phenomenon of action is exemplified: people do things (for reasons). But she does not mean (even if it can be made obvious) that there are events each one of which is a person's doing something. The word 'action' is ambiguous. Where it has a plural: in ordinary usage what it denotes, nearly always, are *the things people do*; in philosophical usage, what it denotes, very often, are events, each one of them *some person's doing something*. We may find ourselves with views which we can readily express in the language of action, and then, finding it obvious that there are actions, we (as philosophers) assume that we have views which we can readily express in the language of events. Explanation of action is a case in point. *We may move from knowing that we have an instance of 'action explanation' straight to thinking that we have an explanation of an action (event).*[52]

Given the range of ambiguities discussed so far, assuming that the *explanandum* of behavioural explanation is some easily identifiable thing called 'behaviour' or 'action' simply won't do.[53]

1.4 Of frogs and chickens

Behavioural scientists often appeal to some version of the much-debated distinction between *proximate* or *proximal* causes – typically understood as immediate/efficient triggers of any given process or event – and causes that are *ultimate* or *distal* – usually thought to explain occurrences by placing them within some greater (often teleologically understood) explanatory structure or mechanism, such as natural selection, behavioural conditioning, or repression.[54]

Proximate and ultimate causes more or less correspond to Aristotle's *efficient* and *final* causes, though what Aristotle called a *material* cause (what any given thing is made up of) and what he called a *formal* cause (to be equated with the functional arrangement of the material cause)[55] are often both also assimilated into the notion of a cause that is proximal. Aristotle took his four causes to each offer partial – and collectively a complete – explanation of the production of any given thing – viz. the process of its coming into existence (often an act or activity of some sort). As such, he conceives of them as all sharing the same *explanandum*.[56] Contemporary scientists involved in heated disputes over the individuation and classification of different types of causes almost unanimously follow the philosopher in thinking that proximate and ultimate causes are both causes of the same thing.[57] Not only are they off the mark in doing so, but their shared assumption gives rise to all sorts of trouble (including the aforementioned disputes).[58]

According to the refreshingly pluralistic biologist Steven Rose, we can distinguish between different types of explanation relating to behaviour, each relating to distinct purposes and answerable via different methods:

... five biologists were having a picnic by a pool, when they noticed a frog, sitting on the edge, suddenly jump into water. A discussion began: why did the frog jump? Says the first biologist, a physiologist, 'It's really quite straightforward. The frog jumps *because* the muscles in its legs contract; in turn these contract because of impulses in the motor nerves arriving at the muscles from the frog's brain; these impulses originate in the brain because previous impulses, arriving at the brain from the frog's retina, have signaled the presence of a predatory snake'... 'But this is a very limited explanation,' says the second, who is an ethologist...'. The physiologist has missed the point, and has told us how the frog jumped, but not why... The reason why is because it sees the snake and in order to avoid it. The contraction of the frog's muscles is but one aspect of a complex process, and must be understood in terms of goals of that process'... 'Neither the physiologist's nor the ethologist's explanations are adequate,' says a third biologist, who studies development... 'the only reason that the frog can jump at all is because during its development... its nerves, brain, and muscles have become "wired up" in such a way that such sequences of activity are inevitable... or at least, the most probable ...'... 'None of these three explanations is very satisfactory,' counters the fourth biologist, an evolutionist. 'The frog jumps because during its evolutionary history it was adaptive for its ancestors to do so at the sight of a snake ...'... The fifth biologist, a molecular biologist, smiles sweetly. '... The frog jumps because of the biochemical properties of its muscles...'... Biologists need all these five types of explanation – and probably others besides There is no one correct type; it all depends on our purposes in asking the question about the jumping frog in the first case.[59]

Rose is right to claim that the different sorts of explanations on offer in such cases (whether we are talking about frogs, chickens, or humans) are not necessarily in any competition with each, their relevance depending on our interests. But I reject the implication that each answer tells us why the frog jumped, as opposed to, say, *how* it did so, or offering an account of what made the jump possible. On his view, to focus 'on any subset of explanations is to provide only a partial story; to try to understand completely even the simplest of living processes requires that we work with all five types simultaneously'.[60] Rose sees no explanatory competition because he takes the approaches to complement each other, each revealing but a small part of the answer we are after. Accordingly, the correlation between interest and relevance is seen to be one of degree rather than kind.

By contrast, I shall be maintaining that the questions answered by each of Rose's five scientists are theoretically independent; the correct answer to any given one may be compatible with numerous accounts of the others. André Ariew recently expressed a similar view:

[u]ltimate and proximate refer to two different *explanations* that answer different sorts of questions. Proximate explanations answer causal questions of individuals and the ultimate explanations answer questions about the prevalence and maintenance of traits in a population...Proximate explanations are dynamical as they cite the causal properties during an individual's lifetime including development and physiological processes. Reference to proximate causes answer various questions including, 'How does something get built?' and 'How does something operate?'. Evolutionary explanations (which substitute Mayr's 'ultimate cause') are not dynamical. Rather they are statistical explanations that refer to ensemble-level events that track trends in populations rather than the vagaries of individual-level causal events. By averaging out individual-level differences, evolutionary explanations pick-out patterns in common to all evolutionary events. That is how natural selection, for example, successfully unifies disparate evolutionary phenomenon under one explanatory description. Evolutionary explanations answer questions pertaining to the diversity of life,

including 'Why is something prevalent?' and 'Why will something continue to persist?'[61]

Ariew's comment focuses on the distinction between ultimate and proximate causes, but it is unclear whether all questions about behaviour neatly fall into these categories, especially so if these are understood in terms of either dynamical or statistical explanations. Consider some of the answers jokingly attributed to various famous figures in the internet's response to that age-old question about motivation: 'why did the chicken cross the road?':[62]

Woody Allen: For food. And perhaps a beverage too.

G.E.M. Anscombe: What happened was an expression of the chicken's intention to cross the road.

Aristotle: To actualise its potential.

Julius Caesar: To come, to see, to conquer.

Albert Camus: It doesn't matter; the chicken's actions have no objective meaning.

Johnny Cash: Just to watch it get crossed.

David Chalmers: Whatever reason it gives us, its zombie-twin could offer it too.

Paul and Patricia Churchland: There was a neuro-chemical imbalance in its brain, possibly caused by poor chicken-feed, though it's nothing that a few injections can't cure.

Bill Clinton: To protect itself from the embarrassment of its own conduct.

Paul Coelho: The whole universe conspired so that the chicken could get what it wanted.

Noam Chomsky: It was manipulated by the media into erroneously thinking that it was freely choosing to cross the road.

Christopher Columbus: It thought that India was on the other side.

David Copperfield: I made the chicken disappear and then reappear on the other side.

Jonathan Dancy: Because it would be worth it to get to the other side, or so the chicken supposed.

Miles Davis: That chicken was one cool bird!

Charles Darwin: Chickens, over great periods of time, have been naturally selected in such a way that they are now genetically disposed to cross roads.

Donald Davidson: It wanted to get to the other side and believed that it could get there by crossing the road and this belief-desire pair, which constituted the chicken's primary reason for crossing the road, caused it to do so through some non-deviant route which is impossible to specify. At least that would be the case if chickens had beliefs, which they don't.

Richard Dawkins: It had selfish genes.

Daniel C. Dennett: We must take an intentional stance towards that chicken, even though its mind wasn't reverse-engineered.

Charles Dickens: It was a far, far better road that he crossed than he had ever crossed before.

Emily Dickinson: Because it could not stop for death.

Bob Dylan and Sam Shepard: It didn't know whether to duck or cross, so it crossed.

Epicurus: To experience a pleasurable sensation.

Albert Einstein: Whether the chicken crossed the road or the road moved beneath the chicken depends upon your frame of reference.

Louis Farrakhan: The road represents the black man; the chicken is the white man. The chicken crossed the black man in order to trample him and keep him down.

Jerry Fodor: It had an innate road-crossing module, complete with all the necessary concepts. But we settled all that in the 1960s, so why are people still quoting Wittgenstein?

Sigmund Freud: It subconsciously identified the road with its father, who it wanted to cross.

Robert Frost: To reach the sidewalk less travelled by.

Stephen Jay Gould: It is possible that there is a sociobiological explanation for it, but we have been deluged in recent years with sociobiological stories despite the fact that we have little direct evidence about the genetics of behaviour, and we do not know how to obtain it for the specific behaviours that figure most prominently in sociobiological speculation.

Grandpa: In my day, we didn't ask why the chicken crossed the road. Someone told us that the chicken had crossed the road, and that was good enough for us.

G.W.F. Hegel: It wasn't a mere crossing but a transition from 'subjective mind' to 'objective spirit', effected through a historical moment of self-recognition.

Ernest Hemingway: To die. In the rain.

Werner Heisenberg: The chicken is distributed probabilistically on all sides of the road until you observe it on the side of your course.

Hippocrates: Because of an excess of phlegm in its pancreas.

Thomas Hobbes: For self-preservation.

Jennifer Hornsby: We need to distinguish between what the chicken does (cross the road) and the event that is its acting viz. its crossing (of) the road. Which do you seek to explain?

David Hume: Out of custom and habit.

Rosalind Hursthouse: It was an arational action, so it is a mistake (typical of a certain kind of theorist) to search for the chicken's reason for doing it.

John Hyman: Because it knew it was the road to Larissa.

Henry James: It doesn't need a reason to cross the road, it needs one *not* to cross it.

William James: It tried to cross it and this inner volition caused its act of crossing.

Carl Jung: The confluence of events in the cultural gestalt necessitated that individual chickens cross roads at this historical juncture, thereby bringing such occurrences into synchronicitous being.

Immanuel Kant: The chicken – being an autonomous being – chose to cross the road of his own free will, thus rationally willing that the maxim 'it is ok to cross roads' be universalised.

Sören Kierkegaard: It made a leap of faith.

Captain James T. Kirk: To boldly go where no chicken has gone before.

Martin Luther King Jr: It had a dream.

Joshua Knobe: There's no point relying on our armchair intuitions, so a team of us asked a random sample of people and 83% of them said it was to get to the other side (though a slightly lower percentage only agreed that it was doing so intentionally when the chicken's purpose was portrayed as being unethical).

Christine Korsgaard: To constitute itself as a road-crosser.

L.A. Police Department: Give me ten minutes with the chicken and I'll find out.

Layperson: To get to the other side.

Timothy Leary: Because that's the only trip the establishment would let it take.

David Lewis: Because it was possible, and every possible world is real. What matters is whether any of the worlds in which the chicken crossed the road is *actual*, and if so, why?

Benjamin Libet: Because of its neurological readiness potential which occurred milliseconds before the chicken reported its experience of intending to cross the road.

The Log Lady: Behind all things are reasons. Reasons can even explain the absurd. Do we have the time to learn the reasons behind the chicken's behaviour? I think not. Some take the time. Are they called detectives? Watch and see what life teaches.

Machiavelli: The point is that the chicken crossed the road. Who cares why? The end of crossing the road justified whatever motive there was.

Nicolas Malebranche: Because God caused it to cross when it willed to.

Market Consultant: Deregulation of the chicken's side of the road was threatening its dominant market position.

Karl Marx: It was an historical inevitability.

Abraham Maslow: It had a hierarchy of needs.

John McDowell: The chicken has no world in view, so does not operate within the space of reasons.

John Stuart Mill: To become a chicken satisfied.

Moliere: Because there was in it a road-crossing power.

Thomas Nagel: It was altruistic and crossed despite not wanting to go to the other side.

Barry Nalebuff and Ian Ayres: Why not?

Isaac Newton: Chickens at rest tend to stay at rest. Chickens in motion tend to cross the road.

Friedrich Nietzsche: The so-called 'drive' to cross roads is but a sublimation of the chicken's will to power.

Richard M. Nixon: The chicken did not cross the road. I repeat, the chicken did *not* cross the road.

George Orwell: Because the government had fooled him into thinking that he was crossing the road of his own free will, when in fact he was only serving their corrupt interests.

Derek Parfit: Its reasons are unimportant, what matters is that it crossed the road.

Blaise Pascal: It figured that it had less to lose by crossing, so made a leap of reason.

Daniel H. Pink: It was driven by a higher purpose to learn, to create, and to better the world.

Plato: It was acting under the guise of the good.

Marcel Proust: It was looking for the paradise lost.

V.S. Ramachandran: Because its neurons mirrored the full consequences of its act and he subsequently desired them.

Thomas Reid: It caused itself to cross the road.

Jean Renoir: Every chicken has its reasons, that's the one and only horrifying thing in this world.

Paul Ricœur: In order to configure a narrative which mediates between the world of action and that of reception.

Bertrand Russell: Only another chicken can know, by analogy from its own behaviour.

Gilbert Ryle: Whatever its motive this was not a cause of its behaviour but a disposition to behave in a road-crossing way.

Jean-Paul Sartre: It was either transcending its facticity or acting in bad faith.

Colonel Sanders: I must have missed it.

Michael Schumacher: It was an instinctive manoeuvre. The chicken didn't even see the road until he had already started to cross.

Arthur Schopenhauer: It willed to cross something and represented the road as being crossable.

Jerry Seinfeld: Why does anyone cross a road? I mean, why doesn't anyone ever think to ask, 'What the heck was this chicken doing walking around all over the place anyway?'

William Shakespeare: But soft, what bird on yonder asphalt trots?

B.F. Skinner: Because the external influences which had pervaded its sensorium from birth had caused it to develop a tendency to cross roads.

Michael Smith: Whatever answer one gives, it must presuppose a Humean story if it is to count as a reason-giving explanation.

The Sphinx: You tell me.

Oliver Stone: The question we should be asking is not 'why did the chicken cross the road?' but 'who was crossing the road at the same time, whom have we overlooked in our haste to observe the chicken crossing?'

Galen Strawson: Its P-reasons fully determined its action (A), just in case the P-reasons explanation of A that cites R and R only is a true and full P-reasons explanation of A.

Willie Sutton: Because that's what the other side was across of.

Nassim Nicholas Taleb: The chicken was no ordinary chicken but a black swan – we couldn't have predicted that it would cross the road and yet concoct post hoc explanations to convince ourselves otherwise.

Ruchard Thaler and Cass Sunstein: We nudged it.

Henry David Thoreau: To survive in the face of hostile elements.

Johann Friedrich von Goethe: The eternal hen-principle made it do it.

Darth Vader: The other side was dark.

G.H. von Wright: Its crossing the road retrospectively caused a prior neural event which in turn caused the muscle contractions and bodily movements involved in crossing.

Ludwig Wittgenstein: Russell's view is intolerable. – We see the chicken's behaviour *as* purposive. – A chicken can cross a road to get to the other side, but can it cross a road to get to the other side by next Thursday?

Malcolm X: It was determined to get across that road by any means necessary.

Many of the above characters (any resemblance to real people is purely coincidental) take themselves to be answering the same question as the authors, but this assumption is deeply implausible. Some of the responses, for example, seem focused on outlining one of numerous conditions (biological, historical, metaphysical, physiological, psychological, situational, sociological, and so on) for the very possibility of its crossing the road, or (alternatively) our being able to explain it. Others attempt to explain *how* it crossed the road, whilst others still offer potentially interrelated narratives in terms of the subject's attitudes, beliefs, culture, desires, dispositions, environment, goals, habits, instincts, motives, needs, outlooks, purposes, reasons, tendencies, and so on. As my first philosophy tutor once wrote, in a different context, 'this may not be a conclusion to please the tidy-minded, but untidiness is unavoidable where it reflects the complexity of the phenomena involved'.[63]

The possible compatibility of these different narratives does not entail that *any* combination of legitimate answers could apply to the same piece of behaviour, but it is worth noting that, by and large, the explanations on offer are not incompatible with those of the layperson.[64] They might provide additional information that is of interest, but in so doing they are not offering a better explanation of the same thing, but explaining various related factors. As a result, we shall be better equipped to paint an overall picture of how humans and other animals operate, but this is not what we are typically after when we want to know why a specific creature crossed the road.

1.5   Various *explananda*, various *explanantia*

When James Thurber quipped that 'it is better to know some of the questions than all of the answers' he was most probably thinking of knowledge of which questions were most pertinent to any given situation, or perhaps most important to life. But his remark can also be interpreted in the light of G.E. Moore's shrewd warning against the tendency to 'attempt to answer questions, without first discovering precisely *what* the question is which you desire to answer'.[65] The theorist who claims to have the *real* explanation for why someone did something is at best emphasising a change of topic e.g. from a question about practical reasoning to ones about human nature or physiology. I will have much more to say about such deceptive explanatory shifts in Chapters 2 and 3. Not even Ariew's liberal understanding of the dual *explanantia* that mirror the proximate/ultimate distinction can capture the variety of *explananda* that might interest us in even the most simple chicken case, let alone when even asking particularised questions such as 'why did the chicken cross the road now rather than later?' or 'why did she vote conservative given her own views about their educational policies?'

It is human nature to focus on similarities rather than differences, to note what things have in common and recall coincidence at the expense of the random and chaotic. No doubt there are benefits to viewing the world in this way, but reaching the truth is not always one of them. The ability to notice differences tempers the urge to unify, assimilate, reduce, or otherwise swallow up the diversity of things to be explained. Theories are no good if one has to distort the phenomena in order to make them fit.

The next chapter builds upon the distinctions presented so far to formally introduce six basic conflations relating to behaviour and its explanation that are frequently made by theorists across various disciplines, before examining some of their most influential philosophical proponents. As the book proceeds further conflations will be revealed, reaching a total number of twenty (though I have no doubt that there are many more about). I hope to show that once these are abandoned numerous issues thought to be problematic will cease to trouble us. As a result, theorists who previously saw themselves in various oppositions will reach considerable agreement over a range of issues.

2
Conflation in Action

In which our brave protagonist accuses philosophers and behavioural scientists alike of conflating various things that should be kept distinct. Said conflations are shown to provoke confused thoughts regarding the relations between reasons and actions.

> Come, sir, arise, away! I'll teach you differences:
> away, away! if you will measure your lubber's
> length again, tarry: but away! go to; have you
> wisdom? so.

Kent (pushing Oswald out)[1]

2.1 Introducing various conflations

So far, I have argued that most theorists typically conflate three distinct conceptions of behaviour (a–c). That is to say, they write as if the term 'behaviour' simultaneously refers to at least two (if not all three) of these. Occasionally one might give explicit expression to such a conflating view. Typically, however, it – and all the other conflating views described in this chapter and throughout the book – are to be attributed to their holders by inference to the best explanation of why they explicitly hold various other views and/or are engaged in certain debates that seem to presuppose the conflation in question. Let us call the view which maintains that this is actually so the *Conflating View of Behaviour* (CVB):

> A person's behaviour consists of the things she does: e.g. the movings of her body.

A typical example of someone committing themselves to CVB can be found in the Weiner quotation from § 1.1. Here it is again:

> It should be anticipated that the answer of the trained motivational psychologist will be 'better' than that of the layperson ... For example, when a layperson explains why an individual is drinking water, he or she may say that the person is thirsty. When the layperson accounts for why another individual is eating, he or she may infer that the person is hungry ... the motivational psychologist, however, attempts to comprise these very disparate observations within the same theoretical network or explanatory system. Perhaps it is postulated that behaviour is determined by the amount of deprivation and the number of rewarded experiences.[2]

This suggests that both the behavioural scientist and the layperson are trying to explain why a person is doing something (drinking water at time *t*). The answer 'because he is thirsty' we are told, is at best, incomplete: it doesn't tell us as much as the answers a scientist could give us would. Weiner however calls the behaviour to be explained an 'action' and, more tellingly, sees this action as a 'physical event'.[3] But, as we shall see, the explanation of why someone did something is *not* the explanation of a physical event. Weiner may be right to think that the explanation of all physical events must involve appeal to general laws from which the particular properties of the event in question may be derived, but be that as it may, the point would not be of much immediate help to someone trying to explain why a person did what he did.

Philosophers also frequently talk of behaviour;[4] however they usually offer some account of what kind of behaviour would count as action (which is not to say that they never consequently revert to using the term 'behaviour' in an ambiguous fashion). Consequently, CVB is a relatively rare occurrence in philosophy. Be that as it may, we shall see in §§ 2.2–2.4 below that most philosophers writing about action and its explanation make a related conflation, which I shall call the *Conflating View of Action* (CVA):

> A person's actions consist of the things she does e.g. her movings of her body.

It is also possible to subscribe to specific sub-parts of CVA. For instance, we saw in § 1.2 that von Wright distinguishes actions from the things we do (which he calls the 'results' of action) before proceeding to add that '[p]rimarily, the things done and brought about are changes (events)'.

CVA is itself a sub-part of CVB, for it conflates questions (ii) and (iii) presented in § 1.3. According to CVA, the things we do are things that can occur (and can be located spatio-temporally). Once we believe *this* we will inevitably also believe the *Conflating View of Reasons* (CVR):

> The reasons for which we act are reasons *why* our actions occur.

Some even go as far as to claim that the reasons for which we act are reasons *for which* our actions occur. I call this the *Conflating View of Reasons for Action* (CVRA):

> The reasons for which we act are reasons *for which* our actions occur.

Many philosophers are implicitly committed to CVRA.[5] Consider, for example, the following passage from G. F. Schueler:

> The issue is whether reason explanations of actions are somehow reducible to, or explicable in terms of, explanations of the *same set of states or events* that use only the concepts available to physiology and neurophysiology. The suggestive reason for thinking that the answer is No here is that … the content of my belief … along with the content of my desire … plays an essential role in the reason explanation of why I am *running towards the bus stop.*[6]

The trouble is that Schueler's clues lead in two opposing directions. For running towards the stop is not a state or event but rather, as Schueler himself describes it two paragraphs later, 'what I am doing'.[7] CVA arises from mistaking what I am doing with my doing it and then conflating the two in such a way that it becomes trivially true (given the conflation) that my reasons for the one must be a reason (indeed *my* reason, one would think) for the other.

The mistake occurs easily: because, we call both the things we do and the events of our doing them 'actions' (see Chapter 1, § 1.2), in theorising we find ourselves conflating – as Zeno Vendler does in the passages below – the deed we do with our act of doing it:

> John broke the window. What he did, the breaking of the window, is clearly an event. Therefore, it seems, some actions at least are events.[8]

What is an action is the *raising* of the arm: this is done by John … the raising of the arm is not caused by John but done by him.[9]

Likewise, in a paper whose aim is to answer the question 'what explains an agent's actions?' Michael Smith repeatedly alternates between talk of action being 'an event' and action being 'what an agent does whenever he acts',[10] and Jonathan Dancy, who is Smith's target in this piece, identifies a 'moving of the body' with a 'thing done' when attempting to distinguish between the transitive and intransitive sense of 'bodily movement':

> [W]e distinguish in the now standard way between two senses of 'bodily movement', the first being what we might call a 'movedness' of the body, something suitably preceded by and caused by some neural disturbances, and the second being a moving of the body, conceived as something done by an agent.[11]

Dancy here conceives of 'moving of a body' as something done by the agent. But agents do not *do* bodily movements, in either of the two senses distinguished above; what they do is move their bodies (and, if they are in the mafia, those of other people as well). Unlike a thing done, a moving of a body is an event that can occur at a particular place and time. This is why, after all, it makes sense to talk of such things (but not of the things we do) as bodily movements.

Both CVR and CVRA involve confused notions of reasons and their relation to action. While we can give reasons which explain why an event (that was an action) occurred, it is deeply misleading to call such reasons 'reasons *for* action', for it makes no sense to talk of events having reasons *to* occur.[12] To put the point in a slightly different way: there are reasons *why* things occur, and these things are sometimes said to occur for reasons – e.g. the reason why the process of sweating occurs is to cool the body down, yet the process of sweating does not occur for a reason any more than the setting of the sun does. We may well imagine a situation in which we have reason to make ourselves sweat, but that would be a reason *for our doing* something (namely causing ourselves to sweat), and not a reason for our sweating to occur. We do, of course, offer teleological explanations of certain natural occurrences but to say, for example, that the body's reason for sweating is to keep its temperature at a certain level (to cool it) is just a disguised way of saying that sweating causes the body to cool. The reason here is not the cause but the *effect* of sweating.[13]

This, clearly, is not the kind of reason explanation philosophers are after when they treat reason explanations of action as explanations of occurrences of some kind. Thus, for example, Paul Pietroski writes:

> Booth wanted to kill Lincoln in retaliation for his treatment of the South during the civil war…This explanation reveals why Booth

acted as he did, by providing information that makes his reason for action apparent, even if we find the reason insufficient (and the action deplorable). Following Davidson (1963, 1967a, 1971) and many others, I hold that rationalizing explanations cite causes, and that actions are events.[14]

Rowland Stout similarly claims that there are 'things that happen because they should' and that we should count our intentional actions among them.[15] His argument for this view makes it clear that he subscribes to the CVRA, and that he does so in virtue of also accepting CVA. Stout begins his argument by telling us that he is going to argue for the view that:

> [T]here is a causal explanation of why I go for a walk in terms of the fact that going for a walk actually serves a purpose for me rather than in terms of its simply being represented as serving a purpose.[16]

And that:

> In the philosophy of action, this Aristotelian claim is located in a very strong externalism about *reasons* for action. According to this strong externalism, the reason for my going for a walk is the *fact* that walking is good for the health.[17]

Tellingly, although he begins by addressing the question of 'why I go for a walk', when it comes to citing *reasons for action*, Stout does not talk of 'my reasons for going for a walk' but about 'the reasons for my going for a walk', that is to say reasons for why my going for a walk occurred. Soon after, he writes:

> My claim is that actions are the immediate results of causal processes which are sensitive to actual (external) means-ends considerations. ... Like Davidson, I claim that an event constitutes an action in virtue of being explained in terms of a justification of it.[18]

In short Stout assumes that the reasons why we do things are reasons for which our actions occur. Given this assumption (which amounts to the CVRA) he takes his argument for the view that the reasons for which we do things are facts to be an argument for the altogether different view that:

> [I]ntentional actions are unique among natural phenomena in that they happen because they should ... there are ways of *evaluating* actions

as rational or irrational, as justified or unjustified; and it is because they are rational or justified, according to such an a way of evaluating things, that they happen.[19]

But to say that an action was justified is to say that I was justified in doing it, not that the event which constitutes my doing it is itself something that is justified. Nor can Stout be speaking merely figuratively when he says that actions are things that happen because they should, for it is a vital part of his account that 'teleological explanation is a species of causal explanation' and that 'an account of such explaining must make reference to causal determination'.[20]

There are, of course, people who think that 'everything happens for a reason'[21] or that, as Hegel thought, the course of history has been rational in its course.[22] But what they seem to mean by this is that things happen according to 'God's plan' (or in the case of animists that of the universe). On such hypotheses, to say that the dormant volcano exploded for a reason is not to say that what caused the volcano's eruption was its reason for exploding. Rather, it is to say that God had a reason for making a world in which this dormant volcano would erupt. Indeed, we might also note that – on the theistic hypothesis – events in the natural world would still only be 'acts of God' in a metaphorical sense, for, more literally, they would either be the *results* or the *consequences* of God's actions – depending on one's account of action individuation.[23]

A slightly more powerful objection might be that, talk of God aside, historians legitimately use phrases such as 'the reasons for the fall of the Roman Empire'. But in doing so they do not imply that the Empire had its own reasons for falling (the way a person might do if people could fall intentionally[24]), but only that we can point to reasons (which explain) why it fell. John Broome illustrates a similar distinction by giving 'the reason for the cow's death was BSE' as an example of what he calls a non-normative reason. *Mutatis mutandis*, it is also not the kind of reason that anyone can act for.[25] Our *own* 'agential reasons'[26] for acting, will of course be related to the reasons which explain why actions occur, an issue I shall return to in the book's last chapter

What about CVR itself? While it does not assume that events occur for reasons, it nonetheless equates the reasons for which we act with reasons why events occur. We saw above that to offer an explanation of why someone did something is not to offer an explanation of why the event of their doing it occurred (and vice versa). The reasons for which we acted in a certain way cannot be reasons for the occurrence of the event of our so acting. To think otherwise is to subscribe to CVA (and, by direct implication, also to CVB). Yet, as argued above, CVA fails to distinguish between actions understood as the things we do and actions understood as the events of our doing such things. To hold CVRA is to consequently be committed to the thought that our every-day reasons for action can be equally understood as both reasons for which we do things (actions) and reasons for which these doings of ours (actions) occur.[27]

In the remaining sections of the chapter I trace some of the conflating views listed so far back to David Ross, Elizabeth Anscombe, Donald Davidson, and Thomas Nagel. In so doing I shall offer further arguments against them and – in that process – also introduce some additional, related, conflations. I shall not be suggesting that Anscombe, Davidson, and Nagel were the *first* to think as they do.[28]

2.2   Doing what happens

In his 1930 book, *The Right and the Good*, Ross offered an objection to consequentialism on the grounds that any action can be re-described in such a fashion so as to include what previously – under a different description of the same action – counted as a consequence:

> Any act may be correctly described in an indefinite, and in principle infinite, number of ways... I have secured my friends' reception of the book. What I do is as truly describable in this way as it is by saying it is the packing and posting of a book (It is equally truly describable in many other ways; e.g. I have provided a few moments' employment for Post Office officials.)... The intrinsic rightness of a certain type of act, not depending on its consequences but on its own nature.[29]

This is a neat move,[30] but in making it Ross inadvertently switches from talk of *what* he does to that of the *event* of his doing it ('the packing and posting of a book'), thereby adopting CVA. The switch is not required for his argument to go through, although it does highlight the sadly neglected question of whether the types of act branded as right or wrong by any given moral theory are meant to be event types.[31]

Ross's talk of descriptions fell on the ears of Anscombe who, while not caring for the use Ross put it to (she essentially accuses him of providing a theory that 'swallows up' all the consequences of actions[32]), famously asserted that 'the same action can be intentional under one description and unintentional under another'.[33] More importantly, for my narrative, Anscombe also seems to have inherited the ease with which Ross switches from talk of what is intentionally *done* to talk of *events* that are intentional under some description, thereby committing herself to CVA:

> It is ... *something done* that is intentional ... The only *events* to consider are intentional actions themselves.[34]

There is little room for the possibility that this might be a mere slip on Anscombe's part. Referring to a previous oral discussion, she writes:

> I myself formerly ... came out with the formula: I *do* what *happens*. That is to say, when the description of what happens is the very thing I should say I was doing, then there is no distinction between my doing and the thing's happening. But everyone who heard this formula found it extremely paradoxical and obscure. And I think the reason is this: what happens must be given by observation; but I have argued that my knowledge of what I do is not by observation ... In the face of this how can I say: I *do* what *happens*? If there are two ways of knowing there must be two different things known.[35]

Anscombe's question makes sense, as does her eventual answer to it in the sections that follow. The answer need not concern us here because the real puzzle is that Anscombe should think that *this* is what people found paradoxical about her formulation. In assuming this, all attention is diverted to a delicate picture of non-observational knowledge, and away from the far more obvious worry of what it is to do something that happens in the first place. The answer, perhaps, lies not in the notion of events but in that of processes. In a footnote, Michael Thompson recently made the following comparative observation:

> It is interesting, though, that *every sentence Davidson analyzes there is in the simple past*; the theme of the paper is 'He did it,' not 'He's doing it.' ... I will not comment on the matter, except to remark on the almost eerie contrast we find, in respect of this aspect, between the illustrative propositions given in the first six essays of Davidson's work and those provided in Anscombe's *Intention*. Davidson's are typically in the third person and past; Anscombe's are in the first or second person of the present progressive.[36]

Thompson stops short of suggesting that Anscombe might be working with a *process* notion of action (see § 1.2). Yet, while it is true that she identifies actions with events on a number of occasions:
    Anscombe also makes the following remark, no doubt under the influence of Aristotle:

> A man can *be doing* something that he nevertheless does not *do*, if it is some process or enterprise which it takes time to complete and of which, therefore, if it is to cut short at any time, we may say that he *was doing* it, but did not *do* it.[37]

What I was *doing* need not be something that I *did*. Conversely, I might instantaneously do something without there being a process of my doing it, and it is also possible that an event can involve all sorts of processes without being identical to their total sum.[38] It is perhaps tempting to think of what I was doing as *my* doing: a process. This is now just one thought away from the conclusion that (if what I was doing was a process then) what I did must be an event: what was happen*ing* v. what happen*ed*. But whilst Anscombe is right that what I did – unlike what I was doing – is akin to an event in being fact-like, it is a mistake to identify my doing *x* something with either the process or the event of my doing it. *What* I am doing should not be conflated with my doing it, for we do not do our own doings any more than we cheer our own cheering, smile our smiling, dream our dreaming, fear our fearing, or suspect our suspecting. To think otherwise is to adopt the *Conflating View of Things Done* (CVTD):

> *What* I am doing is *my doing* (of) it.

The mistake is an easy one to slip into. Alan White, for example, equates 'what we "do"' with 'our bringing something about', and von Wright claims that 'getting drunk is an event'.[39] Jennifer Hornsby offers an excellent analysis of what goes wrong when we conceive of things in this way:

> The phrase 'do something' can mislead, because it can sound as if it reported both an event that is a *doing* and a separate event that is *something* done. But that cannot be how it behaves. If I raise my arm at some time, raise my arm is something I do then, and my doing something then is my raising my arm then. But what I do – raise my arm – is not a particular event that happens at a time: the only event mentioned here is my raising of my arm.[40]

Moreover – and here I part company with Hornsby – we saw in § 1.2 that it is, in any case, a mistake to think that my doing x is itself identical to the process of my doing x, for the 'of' in question is not that of identity (as in 'the city of Paris') but rather signifies a different kind of relation (as in 'the pick of destiny'). If this were not so, then the process of my doing x would be identical to the event of my doing x (the very identity which Anscombe rightly seeks to deny) and, indeed – even more absurdly – to the rumour, memory, or hope of my doing x. It is important, then, to avoid the *Conflating View of Doings* (CVD):

> My doing x is identical to the event (process, etc.) of my doing x.

Some things that happen (e.g. volcanic eruptions) have little or nothing to do with what we do, whilst others (e.g. pollution) are the consequences of what we do. In uttering 'I do what happens' Anscombe signals a deeper – arguably logical or conceptual – connection between the things we do and certain sorts of events (a theme I briefly turn to in § 7.5). Her attempt to express it, however, here misfires. In keeping with her acceptance of CVA, Anscombe also commits herself to the thought that reason for an action seems to be a reason for what is intentionally done, in turn equated with an event that happens, thereby embracing CVRA:

> phrases such as 'under a description'...sometimes occur in hypothetical contexts or in a generalized way, as in: 'A reason for an action is a reason for it under some description.' Here the description must be supposed – by whoever has the reason – to be one that will apply to the act if it is done.[41]

Anscombe is right to say that the event of my doing something can have numerous true descriptions, but she appears to ignore the simple fact that there can be one event of my doing several different things: if *in* buttering the toast I am also making a mess, then I both (a) butter the toast and (b) make a mess, even though the event of my doing (a) is identical to that of my doing (b). What is re-describable is not the things I do but the events of my doing them. What is (or fails to be) intentional, however, is neither the event of my doing something, nor what I *do* (butter the toast, make a mess, etc.) but, rather my *action* of doing it, in the sense in which actions are things we perform. The claim that any given event is intentional under some description is thus best interpreted as stating that it is an event of intentionally doing at least one thing (whilst no doubt also doing a number of other things with no related intention whatsoever).

There is a Rylean test we can perform here that may help with any dilemmas regarding individuation. Gilbert Ryle famously noted that if I buy a pair of gloves I do not buy three things: a left glove, a right glove *and* a pair of gloves. Rather the left and right gloves together form the pair. Similarly, if Oedipus kills the old man and (thereby) kills his father, he does not both strike the old man *and* kill his father. There is only one thing he is being accused of doing here,[42] and whether or not he does it intentionally is a matter of how we describe *it*; the things we do, like the events of our doing them, can also be re-described in various ways.

It is tempting to think that this answer has been generated by the fact that the event of Oedipus' killing the old man *is* that of his killing his father (in this respect events seem to differ from facts). But we have already seen that the identity between the toast-buttering and mess-making events did not entail that only one thing (with at least two descriptions) was done. After all, I could have buttered the same piece of toast without making a mess e.g. by buttering it more carefully; the buttering wouldn't have been the same, but one of the things done as a result of it would. By contrast, Oedipus could not have killed the same old man without killing his father (regardless of whether Kripke was right to place the sort of necessity in play here on quite so high a pedestal as he does[43]). Indeed, the mess resulted from the *manner* in which I buttered the toast, whereas the fact that the man who was killed was Oedipus's father had nothing to do with the manner in which he was killed. Did he kill him intentionally or otherwise? This question is best answered by distinguishing between *de re* and de *dicto* intention: Oedipus kills the old man intentionally in both a *de re* and a *de dicto* sense.[44] Since the old man *is* his father, Oedipus may also be said to have intentionally killed his father in the *de re* sense of 'intentional'.[45] In the *de dicto* sense, by contrast, he kills his father unintentionally. Neither sense is more legitimate than the other, though the *de re* sense is certainly the most popular in ordinary discourse.[46]

If we now apply Ryle's test to Anscombe's own example of poisoning the inhabitants by replenishing the water supply, operating the pump, etc., it becomes clear that we have been presented with a case of an event of her doing (at least) three distinct things, for she could have operated the pump without replenishing the water supply, though not (all else being equal) in the exact same manner in which she did.

In sum, there can be a class of things we do intentionally, but no class of events that are intentional. In claiming that 'I do what happens',

Anscombe presents intentional actions as 'things that occur', leaving reasons for action to play the role of explaining why certain things occurred, or occurred as they did. Her piecemeal inquiry has taken us far away from the original starting point of an everyday assertion of what one intends to *do*. All but gone is the notion of action as some-one's *making* something happen,[47] and consequently agency is at risk of disappearing with it. As Paul Ricœur puts it, 'it is the opposition between action and event that has opened the way for the absorption of the first term by the second'.[48] In the next section we shall see how Ricœur is right that – in eroding clear-cut dichotomies – Anscombe's nuanced conceptual impressionism has, paradoxically, paved the way for Davidson's hatchet-carved cubist presentation of an agentless semantics of action.[49]

2.3   Primary reasons for conflation

Davidson's ontologically minimalist theory of action is fuelled by the methodology of his teacher, W. V. Quine,[50] but it is Anscombe's vision that gives it direction. The exact details of Davidson's position on action explanation are a matter of serious debate,[51] but one need only glance at the jacket blurb for *Essays on Actions and Events* to see conflation in action:

> Certain *events* are identified and explained as actions when they are viewed as caused and *rationalized by reasons.*[52]

Actions, so presented, are events whose occurrence is to be explained by the reasons which rationalise our actions (CVR), that these events are themselves 'rationalized by reasons' (CVRA). Davidson further states that a primary reason for action[53] is a reason *for* acting that 'rationalizes an action' and that 'there is a certain irreducible – though somewhat anaemic sense in which every rationalization justifies':[54]

> Straight description of an intended result often explains an action better than stating that the result was intended or desired. 'It will sooth your nerves' explains why I pour you a shot as effectively as 'I want to do something to soothe your nerves', since the first in the context of explanation implies the second; but the first does better, because, if it is true, the facts will justify my choice of action. Because justifying and explaining an action so often go hand in hand, we fre-quently indicate the primary reason for an action by making a claim

which, if true, would also verify, vindicate, or support the relevant belief or attitude of the agent. 'I knew I ought to return it', 'The paper said it was going to snow', 'You stepped on *my* toes', all, in appropriate reason-giving contexts, perform this familiar dual function.

The justifying role of a reason, given this interpretation, depends on the explanatory role, but the converse does not hold. Your stepping on my toes neither explains nor justifies my stepping on your toes unless I believe you stepped on my toes, but the belief alone, true or false, explains my action.[55]

Action is here both rationalised and explained by our mentioning something which, if true, would justify the action. Davidson says that a belief alone will do. Given his general insistence that the explanation of action also requires a pro-attitude such as desire, this must be a slip, Davidson's thought being that in citing a belief alone we nonetheless imply that there also exists a relevant pro-attitude. It might also appear that Davidson holds that true beliefs are good or justifying reasons, but his consequent use of the term 'anaemic' suggests otherwise:

Corresponding to the belief and attitude of a primary reason for an action, we can always construct (with a little ingenuity) the premises of a syllogism from which it follows that the action has some (as Anscombe calls it) 'desirability characteristic'. Thus there is a certain irreducible – though somewhat anaemic – sense in which every rationalization justifies: from the agent's point of view there was, when he acted, something to be said for the action.[56]

Reasons which explain action, then, will at best provide us with subjective justification, whereas Davidson is elsewhere clear that he takes morality and normativity to generally be objective.[57] Either way, Davidson's 'rationalizing reasons' share certain properties with what Michael Smith and Philip Pettit refer to as 'rational springs':

[T]here is a distinction to be drawn among good reasons, a distinction between two different senses in which something may be described as a good reason. The distinction is important from our viewpoint, because it generates a distinction between two kinds of theory that may each be described as a theory of rationality. The one kind we cast as a background theory, the other as a foreground theory.

The first sense of reason is that of a rational spring. A set of beliefs and desires can be a spring for the formation of a new desire or the performance of an action…the spring may be rational; it may be a type of intentional profile that makes it rational for an agent to form the relevant sort of output: in this way, it constitutes a good reason – in the sense of being a rational spring…

The second sense of reason is that of a rational ground. When a set of beliefs is a rational spring for the formation of a new belief, then the common presumption among philosophers is that the contents of those beliefs are rational grounds for forming the new belief. Take the beliefs that if p then q, and that p. These beliefs are a rational spring for believing that *q*, at least if other things are equal…Where the beliefs are a rational spring for believing that *q* – the (alleged) facts that if *p* then *q*, and that *p* – will be a rational ground for forming that belief. They will constitute a good reason for the agent to form that belief in a different sense of good reason from that of a rational spring; indeed the difference is so great as to mark a difference in *category*, as we might say. Where the rational spring consists of an intentional profile – a belief-state type – the rational ground consists of an assumed state of the word 'intended' – the way things are intended to be.[58]

Rational springs have a psychological reality which renders them proper objects of investigation by the behavioural sciences. The reasons we act upon, by contrast, are considerations which act as rational grounds.[59] Aware of the difficulty, Davidson offers an account of how 'rationalizing reasons' are related to 'justificatory reasons' that is mirrored in Smith and Pettit's account of the relation between springs and grounds. The picture is by and large a persuasive one. Nevertheless, if a primary reason is to be a reason which explains why one's action occurred (and there is no doubt that this is how Davidson conceives of primary reasons), it cannot also be a consideration one acted upon, no matter how intricate the correspondence between grounds and springs. Davidson's notion of a primary reason thus involves the assumption that a primary reason for an action must be capable of being both a rational spring of an event of our acting and a reason *for which* we act. This constraint can only be met if one accepts CVR. Such an acceptance could explain why Davidson holds both of the following views:

(a) Primary reasons can be reasons why we act.

and

(b) Our primary reasons for acting explain why actions occur.

Jennifer Hornsby has expressed a similar worry:

> What sort of thing is the primary reason now supposed to be? It cannot be what an agent has when she has a reason; for you may have the same reason to do something as someone else, but we are surely not to suppose that your believing and desiring something causes someone else's action.[60]

If CVR were true, Hornsby's objection could not even be articulated, for the reasons for which we act would be one and the same with the reasons that explain why our actions occur. This influential conflation has yielded a number of unfortunate consequences, the most important of which are explored in some detail in chapters two and three. A corollary of Davidson's stance is the identification of the considerations we act upon with the things which explain the occurrence of our actions. This thought, shared by many of his opponents, is one of the two main targets of chapter four. Finally, CVR also underlies Davidson's quest for a logical form of action sentences which reveals that *all* action-talk can be translated into event-talk.[61]

2.4   The view from Nagel

In *The Possibility of Altruism* Nagel treats reasons for action as reasons to *promote* the occurrence of certain things:

> Since it is people who have reasons – to act or to refrain, to promote or prevent things – the general description of how reasons operate should show this...we can say that every reason is a predicate R such that for all persons p and events A, if R is true of A, then p has a *prima facie* reason to promote A.[62]

To promote an event is to *bring it about*. Consequently, Nagel's view might be thought to resemble Roderick Chisholm's account of action as 'someone's making something happen' and of a reason for action as 'a reason for someone to make something happen'.[63] However, Nagel seems to think that reasons may be *directly applied* to events (and related phenomena), which in turn themselves promote ends:

> 'Events' is of course too narrow a word to cover the scope of A. A can be an act, event, state of affairs, and perhaps other things as well. A reason can apply to a specific event, like my turning on the radio ten

seconds from now, or to a very general state of affairs, like someone's being in good health. In the latter case any number of specific events may promote the end.[64]

But the bringing about of an event is hardly identical to the event brought about. One may perhaps speak of the event (x) of promoting some further event (y), but we would then be entitled to ask about reasons for promoting event x. This is because, as we have already seen, what I do (in this case 'promote an event') cannot be identical to the event of my doing it. Nagel's earlier work reveals him to be motivated by a range of conflating views which he subscribes to:

> [E]verything I do or someone else does is part of a larger course of events that no one 'does', but that happens...My reason for doing it is the *whole* reason why it happened, and no further explanation is necessary or possible.[65]

Referring to this last passage, Hornsby explains what is wrong with this way of thinking:

> It seems that up to a point we can meet the demands that Nagel puts on action explanation, and that beyond that point, they are of a sort that it is not susceptible to. The pressure of these demands is supposed to be felt when the internal and the external perspectives come together. In Nagel they are brought together through an equation of his reason for doing something with the explanation of 'why' it happened. ('My reason for doing it is the whole reason why "it" happened'.) But really Nagel's reason for doing something is not an explanation of anything happening. (His reason does not explain anything, although the fact that he had it may explain why he did something.) Nor is the explanation why Nagel did something itself a reason for doing anything. (The explanation gives his reason)[66]

In the light of the conflations identified in § 2.1 , we begin to see that Nagel is here presenting us with a false dichotomy that is no more helpful than those offered by behavioural scientists in Chapter 1.

2.5   Applied pluralism

I have tried to make the case for a pluralistic understanding of the concepts of action and its explanation. I began by distinguishing between various different conceptions of behaviour and action, before exploring an accompanying variety of distinct things that 'action explanation' may plausibly amount to – viz. different objectives of action explanation. It was demonstrated that numerous influential philosophers and behavioural scientists are guilty of conflating them.

The rest of this book is chiefly concerned with damage that these and other, related conflations have done to the philosophy of action and its explanation. They have given rise to improper questions with no possible good answer, irresolvable disputes, and misguided approaches. My aim is not to give correct answers to the questions being asked, but to rethink the terms in which the debates are set, primarily by recalling the diversity of *explananda* which fall under the name 'action explanation'.[67] Having noted these pluralities we are now in a position to appreciate their role in dissolving numerous debates concerning the proper study of humankind (Chapter 3), how the reasons we act upon operate (Chapter 4), nested explanations of action (Chapter 5), the structure of reason-giving explanations (Chapter 6), and the relation between triggering and structuring causes (Chapter 7).

3
What Makes an Action Explanation Proper?

In which the theoretical lessons of the first chapter are applied with the aim of dissolving two longstanding debates. The view that the explanation of action either must be or cannot be deductive–nomological is subsequently rejected.

> Know then thyself, presume not God to scan
> The proper study of Mankind is Man.
> Placed on this isthmus of a middle state,
> A Being darkly wise, and rudely great:
> With too much knowledge for the Sceptic side,
> With too much weakness for the Stoic's pride,
> He hangs between; in doubt to act, or rest;
> In doubt to deem himself a God, or Beast;
> In doubt his mind or body to prefer;
> Born but to die, and reas'ning but to err;
> Alike in ignorance, his reason such,
> Whether he thinks too little, or too much;
> Chaos of Thought and Passion, all confus'd;
> Still by himself, abus'd or disabus'd;
> Created half to rise and half to fall;
> Great Lord of all things, yet a prey to all,
> Sole judge of truth, in endless error hurl'd;
> The glory, jest and riddle of the world.
>
> Alexander Pope[1]

Social science means inventing a certain brand of human we can understand.

Nassim Nicholas Taleb[2]

3.1   Explanatory shifts

Pope's chauvinistic exclamation that 'the proper study of Mankind is Man' is as much a dismissal of ethology as it is of theology. But his quip about *what* to study plausibly also reflects a view about *how* to best study it. We find ourselves torn between two inadequate views of human nature, the beastly and the divine, when in truth we are neither gods nor (mere) animals but inbetweeners. A method of human studies can only be proper if it takes this as a starting point.[3]

The ever-renewing debates about whether or not the study of human action should proceed on causalist grounds fall perilously close to denying this truism. On the former view humans are bodily creatures which operate deterministically, on the latter they rise above (or live beside) the laws of nature in godlike fashion. In this chapter I aim to demonstrate that there is no singularly possible or proper way to engage in such an enterprise – no more than there is some uniquely acceptable method of determining why the chicken crossed the road (which is not to say that there are no criteria for the correctness of any given answer). In both cases, it is a mistake to frame the question of appropriate methods of study in terms of an either/or.

It is instructive to compare recent controversies in moral psychology concerning action explanation, with debates over the nature of the social sciences in general, and historical explanation in particular.[4] Participants can be roughly divided into two camps with regard to explanation. The first, *causalist*, camp (also referred to as either covering-law theorists or naturalists[5]) include J. S. Mill (1843), C. G. Hempel (1942), P. Gardiner (1952), J. Passmore (1958), K. Popper (1959), E. Nagel (1960), M. Mandelbaum (1961), A.J. Ayer (1964), N. Jardine (2000), and J. Elster (2007). These folk maintain that historical explanation is a subset of scientific explanation and, consequently, relies upon causal laws – e.g. of socio-economy – from which we can deduce facts about the (probable or actual) occurrence of historical events. The foundation for this thought may be attributed to Mill who in his *System of Logic* outlines four empirical methods of any experimental inquiry: (i) the method of agreement, (ii) the method of difference, (iii) the method of residues, and (iv) the method of concomitant variations.[6] Mill sees the science of human behaviour as such an inductive inquiry, differing from natural science not in kind but only in degree, due to the complexity of its subject matter (which decreases the precision of prediction). Human behaviour thereby falls under the 'law of universal causation', Mill arguing that action is 'not one thing, but a series of two things: the state of mind called a volition followed by an effect'.[7] The effect in question is bodily movement. Mill believes that the cause of 'bodily action' is a physical one – viz. a cause in a sense 'no different from that in which physical phenomena are said to cause one another'. Consequently, we can experience the connection between the two and (with the help of an 'argument from analogy for other minds' that Bertrand Russell stole),[8] construct a science upon it:

> Our will causes our bodily actions in the same sense, and in no other, in which cold causes ice, or a spark causes an explosion of gunpowder. The volition, a state of our mind, is the antecedent; the motion of our limbs in conformity to the volition, is the consequent ... the connexion between them is a subject of experience.[9]

Given sufficient information we may employ psychological generalisations in the construction of a social science. Motivated by this vision, Hempel writes:

> Consider, for example, the statement that the Dust Bowl farmers migrate to California 'because' continual drought and sandstorms render their existence increasingly precarious, and because California seems to them to offer so much better living conditions. This explanation rests on some such universal hypothesis as that populations will tend to migrate to regions which offer better living conditions.[10]

Social science typically deals with collective (as opposed to individual) actions. Whatever one's account of the former, it would be peculiar if these differed from the latter with respect to the issue debated here. Indeed, the crucial distinction to register cuts across that between individual/collective actions: just as the question 'why did this piece of bread nourish me?' is distinct from that of 'why does bread nourish?', so questions about particular actions (individual or collective) should not be conflated with questions about general dispositions. In both cases, answers to the latter may inform answers to the former, but we need to be careful about the way in which they do this.[11]

The opposing, *anti-causalist* party includes B. Croce (1921), R. G. Collingwood (1946), P. H. Nowell-Smith (1956), W. Dray (1957 & 1963), P. Winch (1958), I. Berlin (1960), W. Dilthey (1961), A. Donagan (1962), G. H. von Wright (1971), R. Bittner (2001), B. Flyvbjerg (2001), P. Hutchinson et. al (2008), and G. D'Oro (2008). Anti-causalists argue that historical explanation does not involve any causal laws but, rather, the citing of reasons for which historical figures acted as they did; reasons which, according to this second camp, need not be reducible to causes. Dray, for instance, states that:

> The function of an explanation is to resolve puzzlement of some kind. When a historian sets out to explain a historical action, his problem is usually that he does not know what reason the agent had for doing it. To achieve understanding, what he seeks is information about what the agent believes to be the facts of his situation, including the likely results of taking various courses of action considered open to him, and what he wanted to accomplish ... For explanations of the kind just illustrated, I should argue, the establishment of a deductive logical connection between *explanans* and *explanandum*, based on the inclusion of suitable empirical laws in the former, is neither a necessary nor a sufficient condition of explaining.[12]

The second debate I have in mind is a debate in moral psychology (and philosophy of mind in general) about whether or not reason-giving explanations of our actions rely upon causal laws. Tellingly, we can refer to participants in this debate using labels borrowed from the aforementioned debate on historical explanation – *plus ça change* ... [13] First, there are those who think that *all* reason-giving explanation of our actions is a subset of scientific explanation and, consequently, relies upon causal laws. The *causalists* in this debate include C. J. Ducasse (1925), C. G. Hempel (1962), D. Davidson (1963 & 1976), A. I. Goldman (1970), T. Nagel (1970), P. Railton (1978), F. Dretske (1988b), A. Mele (1992), and B. Enç (2003). So, for example, Ducasse writes:

> Explanation essentially consists in the offering of a hypothesis of fact, standing to the fact to be explained as case of antecedent to case of consequent of some already known law of causation.[14]

Hempel similarly maintains that a statement reporting the occurrence of the event being explained may be deduced from a statement describing the cause of the event together with a generalisation backed by causal laws.[15] Following Hempel, Davidson also defends a somewhat weaker causalist model of reason-giving explanation of action, denying that there are any bridging laws linking psychological propositions to natural ones:

> I emphasized the role of *causality* in our understanding of action, urging that an appropriate belief and desire could explain, and be the reasons

for, an action only if they caused it...There is a weak sense in which laws may be said to be involved which is not in dispute. Hempel holds, and I agree, that if *A* causes *B*, there must be descriptions of *A* and *B* which show that A and B fall under a law. This is a weak thesis, because if this is the only sense in which laws must be invoked in reasons explanations, someone might explain an action by giving the agent's reasons while having no idea what the relevant law was. I have argued that a causal relation implies the existence of strict laws belonging to a closed system of laws and ways of describing events, and that there are no such laws governing the occurrence of events described in psychological terms; we seldom if ever know how to describe actions or their psychological causes in such a way as to allow them to fall under strict laws. It would follow that we can explain actions by reference to reasons without knowing laws that link them.

Hempel, if I am right, believes all explanation requires reference, oblique or direct, or relevant known empirical laws. In that case, in order to explain events we must describe them in a way that reveals how laws are applicable.

This sounds like a forthright conflict, but in fact I'm not sure it is. For on the one hand, I'm not certain what Hempel requires us to know of a relevant law; and on the other hand, I haven't denied that there may be laws far less than strict or deterministic that we must know or assume to be true when we explain actions.[16]

The final sentence is particularly crucial in demonstrating that it is the strictness of the relevant laws that Davidson calls into question, and not their importance, let alone existence.[17] By contrast, *anti-causalists* regarding action explanation maintain that it is a sufficient condition of a reason-giving explanation of action that the reason cited renders the action intelligible. Chief proponents of this view include A. R. Louch (1966), A. White (1967), D. G. Brown (1968), N. Malcolm (1968), G. H. von Wright (1971), A. Collins (1997), F. Stoutland (1998), J. Dancy (2000), G. F. Schueler (2003), Tanney (2009), and G. D'Oro (2011). Thus, for example, Bittner writes that:

Reason explanations...explain an action by reference to an earlier state or event, which is the reason...A reason makes us understand something done for that reason not because there is a law to the effect that, given the state or event that is the reason, an agent produces action of this sort, for there may be no such law. A reason makes us understand something done for a reason not because it informs us of the causal history of the action, since for all we know it may not do that. A reason makes us understand something done for that reason not because reason and action can be encoded in some story form, for perhaps they cannot: people's doing things for reasons need not come in preformed plots. It seems, then, that the explanatory force of reason explanations cannot be reduced to that of some other type of historical explanation. It seems that the explanatory force of reason explanations is just their own.[18]

We might do well to view the above debates (concerning historical explanation and reason-giving explanation) as part of an overarching question of whether or not social science (including history, anthropology, criminology, and economic and political theory) is a branch of natural science. It is to this larger question that I now turn.

3.2   The Conflating view of action explanation

Causalists hold that all explanation of action presupposes the existence of strict causal laws. Conversely, anti-causalists commit themselves to the view that action explanation is not causal in the relevant sense. Charles Taylor summarises this general division of outlooks as follows:

> It is often said that human behaviour...is in some way fundamentally different from the processes in nature which are studied by the natural sciences...Against this view stands the opinion of many others, in particular of many students of the sciences of human behaviour, that there is no difference in principle between the behaviour of animate organisms and any other processes in nature, that the former can be accounted for in the same way as the latter, by laws relating physical events...Now the issue between these two views is one of fundamental and perennial importance for what is often called philosophical anthropology, the study of the basic categories in which man and his behaviour is to be described and explained.[19]

If what I have been arguing so far is right, then attempts to resolve the debate by defending either side make the mistake of conflating the explanation of why an (event that was an) action occurred with the explanation of why one or more people performed a certain action. Let us call this the *Conflating View of Action Explanation* (CVAE):

> Whatever explains why we act explains why our actions occur.

Table 3.1 Causalism v. anti-causalism

	Claims counting for (+)	Claims counting against (–)
Causalism	T: The events of our doing things must be explained causally.	F: The explanation of why we act as we do must cite a cause.
Anti-Causalism	T: The explanation of why we act as we do need not (and typically cannot) cite a cause.	F: The events of our doing things cannot be explained causally.

There is no reason to think in explaining why someone did something we will have also explained why the action which was their doing (of) that thing occurred, though there will of course be combinatorial constraints on any pair of explanations.[20] Given that only the latter object of explanation concerns events or processes, it is advisable to hold that a key difference here is that while explanations of why our actions occur must rely upon causal laws, explanations of why we do the things we do cannot. In accepting CVAE, causalists and their opponents extend the scope of their subject matter much too widely for their theories to be able to say anything true about it. The causalist truth about the explanation of the occurrence of events renders anti-causalism false. Conversely, the anti-causalist truth about the explanation of why we do what we do refutes causalism. As illustrated in Table 3.1 below, the troubling framework of CVAE ensures that the positive aspect of each position (+) cannot be accepted without commitment to an unwanted theoretical consequence (–). The flip side of this point is that the negative aspect of each theory cannot be rejected without the positive feature disappearing with it. The constraint of CVAE is such, then, that the rejection of a false claim in one theory leads to an equally objectionable falsehood in the other.

Once we reject CVAE, we are free to accept both truths (T) without committing ourselves to either falsehood (F). As noted in Chapter 1, commitment to CVAE need not be explicit. One may, for example, explicitly accept or reject the view that actions are events, thereby refusing to formulate matters as I have done in the table above. But in so doing they will have implicitly committed themselves to some form of CVA. In the rest of this chapter I focus on the most popular arguments against both the causalist and the anti-causalist truths (T) captured in the table above, demonstrating that they are doomed to fail because of their commitment to one or more conflating views.

3.3   Explanation and intelligibility

Many causalists argue that any attempt to explain an action without specifying its cause will at best render it intelligible. The claim that there is more to explaining an action than rendering it intelligible is based on the idea that once an action has been rendered intelligible we will have understood why someone *might* do it, but not why they *actually* did it. The thought here is that the reasons any given agent might have for acting could easily render any number of possible actions *intelligible* (i.e. for any set of considerations which we might state, a number of equally intelligible courses of action may be available to her), but they could hardly *explain* them all. A proper or true explanation of any given action can only be achieved if the agent acted as she did *because* of the reason cited in the explanation. From an explanatory point of view, narratives in terms of reasons that an agent had but did not act upon rate no better than just-so stories.

In the case of events this 'because' can only be understood causally. It should therefore not surprise us if theorists committed to CVA and CVR take it as obvious that all reason-giving explanations of action must be similarly causal. As noted in § 1.1, in behavioural science the notion of causation has come to be inextricably tied to that of motivation. The distinction between the explanation and intelligibility of human behaviour is accordingly cashed out in terms of causal *influence*. Once under the grip of this picture, the temptation to extend it to historical explanation is irresistible. Passmore, for example, writes:

> [E]xplanation by reference to a 'principle of action' or a 'good reason' is not, by itself, explanation at all...For a reason may be a 'good reason' – in a sense of being a principle to which one could appeal in justification of one's action – without having in fact the slightest influence on us.[21]

Similarly, in a paper whose main target is Dray's contention that the popular method of explaining actions in terms of underlying reasons which agents act in the light of cannot be construed as conforming to the covering-law pattern, Hempel writes that:

> [T]o show that an action was the appropriate or rational thing to have done under the circumstances is not to explain why in fact it was done...[T]he presentation of an action as being appropriate to a given situation, as making sense, cannot, for purely logical reasons, serve to explain why in fact the action was taken.[22]

The distinction between intelligibility and explanation is a good one. Consider an example[23] a passer-by finds a wallet on the street and takes it with her to the nearest police station. Why did she do this? Well, she might have done it because (she thought) it is the right thing to do with lost property. But she might have also done it because she mistook the station in question for her nearest bank branch. In this case she did what she did in order to keep the lost property for herself. But then she couldn't also have done it because lost property should be returned to the people whose property it is! (What was done was still what the principle demanded, even if the agent was acting against the principle; so how could the principle explain what was done?) So now we have two considerations which render one and the same action intelligible, but they cannot both explain it. This leads us to believe that neither consideration can explain it, since citing either as a consideration she may have acted upon in no way indicates that she did act for that consideration (for she may have acted on the other one). The event of her taking the wallet to the bank is one whose occurrence is consistent with either story being true. Consequently it isn't clear how either consideration could ever explain why it occurred.

If by contrast we cite a fact about her psychology – e.g. that she believes that all lost property should be returned – we have ruled out the possibility of her action having occurred because she believed the police station was a safe deposit box and intended to keep the money for herself.[24] Indeed, it starts to look as if this fact can explain why the action occurred for, unlike the considerations mentioned above, this fact rules out any other explanation candidate which might compete with it. The consideration has now entered the explanation but only because we have added to it the fact that she believed it. The psychological (intentional) explanation, that is, allows us to see what facts she deliberated upon. These facts cannot alone explain why the action occurred. It is true that she could have had this belief and not acted upon it, but in such a case we will need some further explanation why this is so, whereas we don't need any further explanation of why – *given* that she had this belief – she acted in this way.

There are also cases where one consideration can render two contradictory actions intelligible. Keeping to the wallet example, another reason for which the passer-by might have returned it is that it was full of money (perhaps if it was empty she would have left it on the street). If the reason attribution is correct we will have understood why she did what she did, but will we have explained her action? The worry is that the thought that it was full of money is compatible with both her returning the wallet *and* her keeping it, depending on her personality and/or current motivational set.[25] Here we have one consideration which renders two opposing actions intelligible (her keeping it and her returning it). In what way then could it possibly explain why either action occurred? Something is missing. The fact that the wallet was full of money cannot alone explain why either action actually occurred, for it renders both of them intelligible. What seems to be missing in this case is information about whether she thought lost property should be returned – or perhaps information about whether she was in desperate need of money, etc.

Such information need not even be about the passer-by's psychology, but any fact that will show one course of events to be more likely than the other. This need not be a consideration she acted upon,[26] but it may be. Indeed, there may be cases in which one and the same fact can explain action in two distinct different ways: qua consideration and qua probability factor. For instance, an agent may act upon the consideration that she is in need, but the fact that she is in need may also serve to explain her action in ways that don't require her to be conscious of it.[27] To give a different example, the fact that the sun is out explains why so many people are walking in the park, eating ice-creams etc. by rendering their actions intelligible. Could it also explain why the event of their doing such things en masse occurred? Given certain background conditions it could, if only indirectly: the event occurred because these people went out to enjoy the sun. The fact that the sun is out, given certain assumptions about human beings, renders it statistically probable that there will be many people in the park today. But it would also be understandable why this was so and, to this extent, it does not obviously call for further explanation.[28]

We might distinguish explanation and prediction that relies on intelligibility from the following: an alien being may detect correlations between the symbol 'The End' appearing on a screen and people leaving the room. Having knowledge of the term's natural meaning (but not its non-natural meaning),[29] it may predict with relative accuracy that once 'The End' appears on the screen people are likely to leave the room, without having the faintest clue as to why they are leaving then. It might even falsely assume that they are leaving because this phrase appears on the screen, yet that would be wrong.

3.4   The Influence constraint

As expressed in the quotations above, the Passmore–Hempel constraint on explanation is neutral on whether or not the required influence must be understood in terms of mental springs of behaviour, as Davidson, Smith and Pettit suppose it to be.[30] The temptation to think that it must is a likely residue of the question-begging assumption that 'if it is not an accident that I choose to do one thing rather than another then presumably there is some causal explanation for my choice, and in that case we are led back to determinism'.[31] Galen Strawson (himself a causalist) argues persuasively that 'one does not have to accept the causal theory' in order to distinguish between, on the one hand, explanations that are true and full and, on the other, ways of rendering action intelligible that are deficient in one or more of these respects. All that is required is that the reasons in question 'play a crucial role in whatever process it is that finally determines the nature of the action'.[32] This sufficient condition clearly falls short of straight-out causation (if that were all causation amounted to we might wonder why so much ink has been spilled in the attempt to produce an account of it).

Thomas Nagel expresses a version of the influence constraint, in a passage whose first line I already questioned in § 2.4:

> Everything that I *do* or that anyone else *does* is part of a larger course of *events* that no one 'does', but that happens, with or without explanation…There is no room in an objective picture of the world for an explanation of action that is not causal…The alternative form of explanation doesn't really explain the action at all…When someone makes an autonomous choice such as whether to accept a job, and there are reasons on both sides of the issue, we are supposed to be able to explain why he did what he did by pointing to his reasons for accepting it. But we could equally have explained his refusing the job, if he had refused, by referring to the reasons on the other side – and he could have refused for those other reasons: that is the essential claim of autonomy. It applies even if one choice is significantly more reasonable than the other. Bad reasons are reasons too.[33]

Intentional explanation, if there is such a thing, can explain either choice in terms of the appropriate reasons, since either choice would be intelligible if it occurred. But for this very reason it cannot explain why this person accepted the job for the reasons in favour instead of refusing it for the reasons against. It cannot explain on grounds of intelligibility why one of two intelligible courses of action, both of which were possible, occurred. And even where it can account for this in terms of further reasons, there will be a point at which the explanation gives out. We say that someone's character and values are revealed by the choices they make in such circumstances, but if these are indeed independent conditions, they too must either have or lack an explanation.

If autonomy requires that the central element of choice be explained in a way that does not take us outside the point of view of the agent (leaving aside the explanation of what faces him with the choice), then intentional explanations must simply come to an end when all available reasons have been given, and nothing else can take over where they leave off. But this seems to mean that an autonomous intentional explanation cannot explain the very thing it is supposed to explain, namely why I did what I did rather than the alternative that was causally open to me. It says I did it for certain reasons, but does not explain why I didn't decide not to do it for other reasons. It may render the action subjectively intelligible, but it does not explain why this rather than another equally possible and comparably intelligible action was done. That seems to be something for which there is no explanation, either intentional or causal.[34]

There are (at the very least) five distinct objects of explanation which Nagel seems to be conflating here: (i) why I did something; (ii) why my action of doing it occurred; (iii) why I did something for reason x rather than omit to do it, for reason x or y; (iv) why I did something for reason x rather than some other alternative, for reason x or y; (v) why I did x rather than y, tout court. And yet surely one can explain the first (why I did something) without explaining the second, third, fourth, or fifth – or so I shall argue. [35]

Suppose that I stay home for the reason that there will be too many people that I don't know at the party I have been invited to. Remaining neutral, for the moment, as to whether or not the above statement provides an explanation of why I stayed home, what is certain is that it does not explain why I stayed at home instead of going to the cinema instead. For an explanation of *this* we might add that I was tired, do not like the cinema, that nothing I wished to see was playing, etc. Likewise, to explain why I did not go to the party *for the reason* that there were many people there that I didn't know, we must add a further reason – e.g. that I am shy and/or have barely enough time for my close friends and relatives (after all if I had a different character, or was in a different situation, I might have gone to the party precisely because there were many people there that I didn't know). This further reason need not (though it could) be an *agential reason* – viz. the agent's *own* reason for acting (see § 2.1). That is to say, it need not be a consideration that I acted upon, but only something which explains, perhaps causally, why the reason I did act upon had that kind of influence on me (and, depending on the example, perhaps also why some other reason didn't have a stronger pull towards some other direction).[36]

For any given situation, there are numerous objects of action explanation, and no reason to expect that they must all share the same *explanans* (or even the same *type* of *explanans*). What Nagel calls an 'intentional explanation' (an explanation in terms of what I have called 'agential reasons') will only suit certain kinds of objects of action explanation – but it would be a mistake to infer from the fact that it cannot explain them *all* that it cannot explain *any* of them. Yet in conflating (i–v), this is exactly what Nagel has done. In so doing, he appears to accept both of the following:

> CVAE: Whatever explains why we act explains why our actions occur.
> CVR: The reasons for which we act are reasons why our actions occur.

Focusing on occurrences for a moment, we might also add that it is one thing to explain why an event (say, an action) occurred, and quite another to explain why it occurred *rather than* some other event. In the first instance, it might be sufficient to show why the occurrence was *probable*; in the latter we would need to show that it was *more probable* than the competing alternative – and one can imagine a scenario in which what needs to be shown is that the occurrence was inevitable. In each case, however, our object of explanation will be different.[37] Under no circumstances, however, would the fact that one has not shown the occurrence of any given action (say that of my staying at home) to be inevitable suggest that one must have therefore failed to explain why anybody acted as they did (e.g. why I stayed at home instead of going to the party). Returning to the arguments offered by Passmore and Hempel above, we can now see that they falsely assume one cannot explain why an action was performed unless one has shown that it (i.e. its occurrence) was inevitable. But we have now seen that such requirements on explanation are at best misguided. Considerations which render actions intelligible typically lead to an understanding of why the agent *might have* acted as she did. But if we also happen to know that these considerations were indeed the ones the agent acted upon we will have also understood why she *actually* acted as she did. As Stephen Toulmin has noted in a different context:

> If you protest that I must have some explanation (still meaning a 'scientific' one), that is your mistake; for there are some situations in which the demand for a scientific explanation is out of place.[38]

Once we appreciate that such difficulties arise only because of the various aforementioned conflations, we come to see that there is no unbridgeable gap between rendering a person's action intelligible, and explaining why it was performed; though we might wish to say that, strictly speaking, what explains why A did *x* is not her reason for performing the action *tout court* but a statement which *specifies* her reason for performing the action. To the extent that the study of history (or for that matter anthropology, criminology, and economic and political theory) is interested in *such* questions, they cannot hope to offer scientific explanations. But, of course, history and social science are just as often interested in other objects of action explanation, including many which may call for radically different methodologies, some more scientific than others. The explanation of a particular trend or tendency, for example, or the occurrence of a historical event such as the collapse of a nation's stock market and the depression that ensued, may well be deductive–nomological.[39]

In his influential book *Theory of Action* Lawrence Davis writes:

> While the explanation of Sam's action aims at displaying the action's intelligibility…explanation of…a 'mere' event, aims at displaying its *inevitability*. Reasons-explanations and causal-explanations differ, then, in their aims and the battery of concepts that apply to them.[40]

There is much truth to this remark, but in order to get to it we must restrict the object of action explanation to 'why Sam did what he did' and not 'why Sam's action occurred' (Davis's use of the term 'mere' betrays the fact that he is conflating the two, by suggesting that reasons-explanations are also explanations of events). For while we may do things for agential reasons that render our actions intelligible, the events which are our actions (of doing these things) are neither things we do, nor things that occur *for* reasons. As for the purported difference between reasons-explanations and causal explanations, this difference is real only if we take reasons-explanations to be explanations which give our reasons for acting. Yet a reasons-explanation of action could equally reasonably be conceived of as an explanation in terms of non-agential reasons which explain why an action was performed, or even why an event that happens to be an action occurred. If our object of explanation is of the latter type, our enquiry is more likely to concern itself with questions of probability and inevitability, but if it is of the former sort, we will be first and foremost interested in psychological intelligibility. If all we are after is the reason for which the person acted, then we are looking to render her action intelligible by specifying the reason(s) she *actually* acted upon, assuming it is true that the person acted upon that reason.[41] This reason must be the one the agent actually acted upon, but a reason need not cause my action for it to be true that it operated as a reason.[42]

The distinction between rendering intelligible and explaining suggests that explanation of action, like any other kind of explanation, must be factive in the sense that the explanation offered must be true.[43] If *x* really was the reason upon which I acted then it will have made a crucial difference to my action. It is fine to call this difference causal, if one likes, but that does not render the explanation itself causal. All that is required to explain why someone did something by citing the reasons they acted upon is that we render the action intelligible by stating a truth, namely a truth about why the agent acted. This truth (that *x* was a reason for their action) need not be a cause of anything, though certain causal explanations may mention or assume it. We will have understood why a person actually acted by being pointed to the right (agential) reason. Such understanding can be reached without our knowing why the event of their acting occurred, let alone why it occurred rather than some other event. But one must not confuse the motivation of action with its production.[44] Certain causal laws must evidently hold in order for any given action to be performed, but they need not relate the *explanans* to the *explanandum* (which is not to say that they cannot).[45]

On the way to developing his anti-causalism von Wright maintains that:

> The primary test of the claim to universal validity for the subsumption theory of explanation is whether the covering law model also captures teleological explanations.[46]

If the chief claim of this chapter is right, then what von Wright calls the subsumption theory (namely the view that all explanation of action is deductive nomological) will pass the 'teleology test' when our object of explanation is 'why a certain action occurred', and fail it when it is 'why someone performed a certain action'.[47] The anti-causalist objection against being 'forced into a mistaken view of their subject matter as a result of their preoccupation with a method they take to be necessary to any respectable enquiry'[48] is therefore valid, but ironically so, for causalists are similarly pushed to view their subject matter through an anti-rationalist preoccupation with a method which the latter mistakenly take to be necessary to *any* enquiry regarding human affairs. D'Oro, for example, unpacks arguments for the methodological autonomy of historiography in the following way:

> [T]he distinction between the methodology of the natural sciences and historiography is, contrary to Mill and Hempel, a distinction of kind rather than merely in degree. The goal of human explanation is not to predict but to make sense and this goal is best served by a different form of explanation, one in which the link between the *explanans* and the *explanandum* is conceptual rather than empirical ... explanations in the sciences of the mind differ from explanation in the natural sciences not because the former focus on human behaviour rather than natural events (this is indeed a superficial difference) but because they are concerned with the behavior of human beings in so far as it counts as action or as an expression of rational thought. To explain human behavior as an action, rather than a bodily movement, entails rationalizing it ... Historiographic explanations are thus 'rational explanations' and they are different from explanation in natural science not because they study different things ... but because they study them in different ways. To explain rationally requires constructing a practical argument and to establish a logical fit between an agent's beliefs and motives and his actions ... since in rational explanations the connection between the *explanans* and the *explanandum* is logical, not empirical, such explanations are at the same time justifications for the action: they are thus normative explanations ... The goal of natural science is the prediction and mastery of nature ... The goal of the sciences of the mind is to understand, and understanding requires 'making sense'. We understand human behavior as an action not when we try to predict a bodily movement, but when we grasp the rationale for acting in a given way.[49]

The trouble is that there is no one thing called 'human explanation' with a distinctive goal. Both the layperson and the scientist may have either prediction or understanding as their goal, and there are various legitimate methods one may use in order to do either. As the above-mentioned alien example demonstrates, we may predict through the use of understanding but may also bypass it – e.g. by appeal to statistics about past regulations. The former sort of prediction requires explanatory powers and, conversely, genuine explanation increases the probability of correct prediction.[50] Both forms are empirical, but only the first requires the ability to pick out actions. D'Oro is doubt-lessly right to distinguish between action and bodily movement, but the distinction cuts across that between prediction and understand-ing: a justified prediction of how people will vote at the next election may, but need not, be a causalist one. The anti-causalist who wishes to distinguish 'normative' predictions from deductive–nomological ones must conceive of them as forward-looking rationalisations in a sense weak enough to allow for the prediction of action that is arational, irrational, and/or akratic.[51]

One way of demonstrating that it is likely that either people (be they individuals or collectives) will act one way rather than another is to show that a certain kind of action would be *characteristic* of them. [52] We can accordingly predict, for example, 'that large numbers of per-sons will follow the advice of their doctors' simply in virtue of our hav-ing observed with regularity 'the psychological relation of dependence of men upon their physicians'.[53] In such cases our *explanandum* is an event, including events of people acting against their own better judge-ment. To the extent that D'Oro and others are working with one strict notion of action, at odds with the pluralistic attitude of this book, the debate collapses into a terminological one – for we could remain in agreement that the *explananda* of different forms of 'action explanation' are distinct.

Neither the prediction nor the explanation of action *need* be a nor-mative one, then. In fact Dray himself, despite being one of the most prominent defenders of the view that *historical* explanation is not causal, allows for the possibility of covering-law explanations of action:

I am arguing on conceptual grounds that there is a meaning of 'explain' which is already current in history, as well as everyday affairs, which does not entail determinism. I should like to point out also that I am not arguing from the possibility of giving rational explanations to the truth of libertarianism. For I cannot see – as some like Professor Winch apparently believe – that the giving of a rational explanation excludes the giving of a covering-law explana-tion ... I cannot see that we need even agree with what appears to be Professor Donagan's view on this: that rational explanations would at any rate have *point* only so long as we cannot give law-covered explanations of the same things. The two sorts of explanation are better regarded as belonging to different logical and conceptual net-works, within which different kinds of puzzlement are expressed and resolved.[54]

Dray's point here comes close to what I have been arguing, but with one important difference. Unlike Dray, I deny that we here have two logically and conceptually different explanations of one and the same thing. It is precisely because we have two different *explanantia* that two 'different kinds of puzzlement are expressed and resolved'. We can, of course, explain the same thing in different ways, and understanding what a person saw in an action is one such way of doing so. But we cannot have two different worries regarding one and the same thing; for, as we saw in § 1.3, what one is puzzled about simply *is* what one is trying to explain.[55]

3.5   From explanation to motivation

I have been distinguishing between the following methods, related to the explanation and understanding of human action, none of which is any more or less proper than any other:

ia) Rendering the process or event of one's acting intelligible – viz. explaining why/how/when/where it *might have occurred*.
ib) Explaining why/how/when/where the process or event of one's action *actually occurred*.

iia) Rendering it intelligible why/how/when/where a person performed an action – viz. explaining why/how/when/where she *might have done* what she did.
iib) Explaining why/how/when/where a person performed an action – viz. explaining why she *actually did* what she did.

Although he wouldn't have phrased things in quite this way, the distinction between (i) and (ii) lies at the heart of Max Weber's insistence that, whilst the discovery of general laws enables the prediction and *explanation* ('Erklären') of human action, it does nothing to further our *understanding* ('Verstehen') of it.[56] To explain why (ib) an action occurred is *not* to understand why the person may have acted as they did (iia). Conversely, the most complete understanding of any given person's reasons (iia) will fall short of an explanation of why the event of their acting occurred (ib). Alas, Weber's technical terminology leaves little conceptual space for either (ia) or (iib), thereby betraying a commitment to CVA and CVRA.[57]

The difference between (a) rendering an action intelligible and (b) explaining it is not causation but truth. The truth of the *explanans* will invariably be related to that of the *explanandum*, but it would be begging the question against the anti-causalist to insist that the relation between the consideration one acts upon and one's action must be a causal one. The temptation to think that this must be so arises from the further assumption that the explanation of action must point to the agent's *motivation* for acting, understood as a feature of their psychology. Thus, for example, Bernard Williams writes, in an oft-cited passage:

> Now no external reason statement could *by itself* offer an explanation of anyone's action. Even if it were true (whatever that might turn out to mean) that there was a reason for Owen to join the army, that fact by itself would never explain anything that Owen did, not even his joining the army. The whole point of external reason statements is that they can be true independently of the agent's motivations. But nothing can explain an agent's (intentional) actions except something that motivates him so to act. So something else is needed besides the truth of the external reason statement to explain action, some psychological link; and that psychological link would seem to be belief.[58]

Note how Williams equates *what* Owen did with *his joining* the army, thereby indicating allegiance to CVA:

> A person's actions consist of the things she does – e.g. her movings of her body.

His further claim about explanation signals that he also accepts CVAE:

> Whatever explains why we act explains why our actions occur.

And given that he takes all this to tell us something important about *reasons*, he is thereby also committed to CVR:

> The reasons for which we act are reasons *why* our actions occur.

Williams' tacit acceptance of these conflating views is closely tied to his understanding of explanatory statements as ones concerning the agent's *motivation*: only that which moves or motivates is thought to be capable of explaining our actions. In the next chapter I challenge this assumption, exploring the relation between the operation of reasons and their explanatory power in the light of the various distinctions and conflations outlined above. In particular, I shall be arguing that the notion of a 'motivating reason' only serves to fuel the confused notion that, if a statement about external reasons cannot explain why anything occurred then it cannot explain why anybody did anything. Philosophy, psychology, and historiography would all be better off without it.[59]

4

The Operation of Reasons

In which an account of the dual operations of the reasons we act upon is advanced. Philosophical disputes over the nature of so-called motivating reasons, it is claimed, are forged out of a conflating view shared by all participants.

Asked what motivates us, one explanation says that we are motivated by our own psychological states and the other says that we are not. How can they both be right?

Jonathan Dancy[1]

It is a heuristic maxim that the truth lies not in one of the two disputed views but in some third possibility which has not yet been thought of, which we can only discover by rejecting something assumed as obvious by both disputants.

F. P. Ramsey[2]

4.1   The theory of motivation

In the preceding chapters I sought to demonstrate that the debates over the nature of 'reasons for action' is largely the result of the mistaken assumption that all parties to the debates use the term 'action' to pick out the same the object of explanation. Indeed, many philosophers, I argued, are guilty of conflating two different senses of the term 'action', making it almost impossible to understand just what a 'reason for action' is meant to be. It is therefore unsurprising that misunderstandings pervade the theory of action explanation. I concluded that given these misunderstandings it is inevitable that there should be disagreement over what is to count as a successful example of reason-giving action explanation. More positively, I suggested that once we clear ourselves of these confusions, we may find that there is little left to disagree about.

Having introduced several conflations made by theorists in numerous disciplines (Chapter 2) and demonstrated the perils of their application across the social and moral studies (Chapter 3), I now wish to introduce a further complication to the story. So far, I have been presenting the debates in question as debates concerning the nature of 'reasons for action'. We shall see that these debates are typically conceived as being concerned with theory of motivation. Those involved tend to agree that the question concerning the nature of 'reasons for action' belongs to the theory of motivation and, consequently, that what they are debating is the nature of what they frequently refer to as 'motivating reasons' for action.

I call this common understanding of the debate (as being a debate concerning the reasons which motivate us to act) the *Conflating View of Motivating Reasons* (CVMR):

> The reasons for which we act are identical to the things which motivate us to act (and vice versa).

In the theory of good reasons we find the analogous *Conflating View of Good Reasons* (CVGR):

> Good reasons for action are good reasons for being *motivated* to act.

Variations of it (relating to intention and belief) might arguably be thought to underlie both and Pascal's wager[3] and Kavka's toxin puzzle[4] A related view is what we might call the *Conflating view of Motivation* (CVM):

> A reason for being motivated to act is a reason for bringing it about that one is so motivated.

This comes in both 'good reason' and 'motivating reason' varieties. What is problematic about all such views, I shall maintain, is that it is not at all clear that we need always be motivated by the reasons for which we act, or that the reasons which motivate us to act are (on those occasions when we act accordingly) the reasons *for which* we acted. Indeed, I shall try to show that there are things we can say about reasons which motivate us that are simply not true with regard to the reasons for which we act (and vice versa).

Each side of the debate on 'reasons for action', I shall conclude, has latched on to a different sense of 'motivation'; roughly speaking, one side treats it as a technical term identical in meaning to 'reasons for which we act', while the other gives the meaning it typically has in our ordinary usage (as well as in the theory of motivational psychology) as: whatever reason (causally) moves us to act (regardless of whether or not we view this thing as a reason *for* acting). CVMR leads each side to believe they are talking about one and the same thing ('motivating reasons'), and so, unless this view is rejected, they are bound to disagree.

The theory of motivation (TOM) is geared to the provision of a satisfactory account of our being motivated in terms of that which motivates us.[5] Accordingly, it is not concerned with the normative question of what *ought* to motivate us to act, but only with what possibly *could* and/or actually *does*. Of the numerous debates within TOM this chapter focuses on just two, both concerning the nature of the things that motivate us to act. The first of these is between Humeanism and anti-Humeanism, the second between what has been called Psychologism and non-Psychologism. The definitions that follow are fairly standard:

Humeanism: The view that we are motivated by reasons that are constituted by our desires and beliefs and/or aliefs.[6]

Weak anti-Humeanism: The view that we are motivated by reasons that need only be constituted by beliefs or aliefs.[7]

Pure anti-Humeanism: The view that we are motivated by reasons that are always constituted purely by beliefs and/or aliefs.[8]

Psychologism: The view that we are motivated by reasons that are *psychologically* real, and therefore, of an entirely different ontological category to normative reasons – which are conceived of as truths, facts, states of affairs, or propositions.[9]

Anti-Psychologism: We are motivated by reasons that are *not psychologically* real but, rather, of the same ontological category as normative reasons.[10]

Throughout these disagreements all disputants share a common assumption, namely the view that the things that motivate us are (at times by definition) reasons for which we act. Through this conflation, TOM is thought to be a theory of motivating reasons for action. I call this error the *Conflating View of Motivating Reasons* (CVMR):

> The reasons for which we act are identical to the things which motivate us to act (and vice versa).

The conflation is easy to make, because we ordinarily talk of being motivated by both considerations we acted upon and those features of our psychology that moved us to do so. To give two famous twentieth-century examples:

> I can only tell you I was *motivated* by many factors. First, by a *desire* to protect myself from the embarrassment of my own conduct. I was also very concerned about protecting my family. The *fact* that these questions were being asked in a politically inspired lawsuit, which has since been dismissed, was a *consideration* too.[11]
>
> I did it though, because he lied. Because he took you for a ride. And because time was on his side. And because I...I want you.[12]

We typically feel no pressure to disambiguate between being motivated by (i) our beliefs and desires *themselves* or (ii) the fact that we had them, let alone between different senses of the terms 'belief' and 'desire'.[13] This is because the concept of motivation is broad enough to capture them all. It does not follow, however, that TOM is a theory *about* the reasons for which we act, and yet it is a corollary of CVMR that this is so. The mistake is to think that *all* talk of motivation is talk about agential reasons, and vice versa.

In what follows, I shall maintain that the debates within TOM depicted further above are *caused* by CVMR, which we have independent reasons for rejecting and, consequently dissolve once we abandon it. This alone should generate suspicion of CVMR, but I believe we have independent reasons for rejecting it. Indeed, one consequence of my argument shall be that the most plausible version of each of the five positions outlined above is one that has no use for the concept of a 'motivating reason'. More importantly, there will be great convergence across the revised views, their differences being chiefly ones of emphasis and interest. In demonstrating this I shall instead employ the theoretically lighter notion of an agential reason (see § 4.2).

All participants across both debates may agree that Robert Audi's following sketch of what acting for a reason *typically* involves is by and large correct:

> Consider an ordinary case in which a representative agent, S (Sue let us say), acts for a reason. In the course of mailing impersonal invitations to a conference, she puts John's aside. Her reason: to delay it until after she sends him a condolence letter (his mother has died). If this case is *typical* of action for a reason, we may say the following. (1) Her action is explainable by appeal to her reason; for example she put the invitation aside in order to delay it until after she sends condolences. (2) She believes something to the effect that her putting it aside will delay it. (3) If asked why she is putting it aside, she will tend to answer by appeal to her reason. (4) Her action is, in some way, a response to, and occurs because of, her reason. For instance, if she ceased to have the reason because she decided to send no condolences, then (assuming she had no other reason for the action) she would no longer put the invitation aside. (5) In putting the invitation aside, she has a sense of what her reason for doing this is and of her action as a response to the reason. She may, for example, be aware of wanting to delay the invitation and of her action as delaying it. (6) She knows or believes that she is putting it aside, and knows why. (7) The action is, *relative* to her reason for it and her belief that the action will delay the invitation, prima-facie rational. And (8) she controls whether she carries the action out and, to some degree, how, It is up to her, for example, that she flips the invitation aside with her hands rather than her pen. Generalisations of (1)–(8) do not apply to all actions for a reason; but they hold in paradigm cases, and an account of acting for a reason should both unify and refine them.[14]

In the light of this agreement we should understand the debates outlined above as ones concerned with providing a unifying account of the basic *nature* of the reasons we act upon. Take the above example, where Sue's reason for her action was to delay sending John an invitation until after she had sent him her condolences. It seems that, although this statement gives us Sue's reason for her action, and thereby provides an explanation of it, we can offer different analyses of what the reason consists of. As Audi writes:

> We sometimes refer to people's wants, beliefs, fears, and other states as reasons for which they act. S's wanting wine might be stated as her

reason for leaving just before dinner. Such states express reasons as described above and might be called *reason states*... Facts may also be cited as reasons: the fact that Tom has a fine record might be the reason for which S asks him to speak. But while many kinds of things are cited as reasons for which an agent acts, the context normally provides enough information for infinitival expression of the agent's reason.[15]

Audi further suggests that a number of things might sensibly be cited as reasons for action, so long as they express the correct *teleological* relation between the agent and her action, referring to teleological reasons as 'reasons proper'.[16] We might analyse this teleological relation as follows: if I do A *in order* to bring about *x*, then the consideration I acted upon is the purported fact that my doing A will bring about *x* (I may or may not have some prior reason for being motivated to bring about *x* in the first place). It is therefore a mistake to contrast teleological reasons with considerations we act upon, as Stewart Goetz does in the following passage:

> Assume that I am aware that a particular woman is ill and that I send for a doctor... it is not the woman's being ill that is my reason for sending for the doctor. Rather, my reason is the purpose that the woman be well, which is grounded in the content of a propositional attitude such as my desire that she be well (which represents a future, non-actual state of affairs).[17]

If I send for the doctor with the purpose of ensuring that the woman becomes well then I act upon the considerations that (a) she is unwell and that (b) sending for a doctor will help to make her better, in which case (a) and (b) jointly operate as considerations I act upon, conversational implicature allowing us to render an action intelligible by only citing one of them.

As Michael Smith points out, we can accept:

> that reasons are teleological without enquiring further into what it is about the nature of reasons that makes it possible for reasons explanations to be teleological explanations – that is, explanations that explain by making what they explain intelligible in terms of the pursuit of a goal.[18]

Accounts of the nature of reasons invariably attempt to provide an answer to this further question. In Chapter 3, I presented some justification for an *influence* constraint on reasons explanation, and compared two fundamentally different understandings of the role in question, and their impact on accounts of action explanation. Unsurprisingly, they also underlie debates relating to the nature of the reasons for which we act.

4.2   Agential reasons

In §§ 2.1 and 3.3 I distinguished between, on the one hand, *a* reason or even *the* reason for A's doing *x* and, on the other, A's *own* reason for doing *x*, referring to the latter as an agential reason. So understood, agential reasons are operative in the sense that they are considerations that we act upon, as opposed to parts of our psychology that motivate us. A subset of agential reasons form what John Skorupski describes as reasons that we act *from* in a self-determining sense, requiring the capacity to assess reasons as such.[19] We humans often respond to considerations without acting from them in this strong sense, and many animals do so, while completely lacking the self-determining capacity.[20] But, as Dancy points out, it must at least be possible to act upon a normative reason[21] or, in my terminology, to turn a pure normative reason into one that is also agential. *Inter alia,* then, an agential reason might also be a normative reason – viz. some fact or state of affairs that counts in favour of a particular course (or set of courses) of action.[22]

Does this mean that what Williams calls 'external reasons'[23] can be internalised and, if so, must some mysterious ontological transformation have occurred? Dancy argues that the philosophical distinction between 'motivating' and 'normative' reasons as it is standardly conceived (with the former as psychological states and the latter as facts or states of affairs)[24] is in danger of denying the truism that one can act for the very reasons that favour one's action. He accordingly adopts a version of the distinction which allows normative reasons to meet the explanatory constraint of being 'capable of contributing to the explanation of an action that is done for that reason',[25] and motivating reasons to meet the converse 'normative constraint' of being 'capable of being among the reasons in favour of so acting'.[26] In an earlier article, however, Dancy suggests that philosophers might be altogether better off without a theory of motivation [27] If so, then we should not talk of two distinct *kinds* of reasons, but of two overlapping sets of reasons that are motivationally and/or normatively *operative* upon us[28] (it being an open question whether the former set is but a subset of the latter). This seems to me to be a preferable way of proceeding. In fact I shall be arguing that the very concept of a 'motivating reason' embodies a number of conflations that give rise to a number of spurious debates in moral psychology, debates that become completely intractable once these new conflations are combined with those we have witnessed so far, as I shall demonstrate they frequently are.

The dual role of reasons for action – normative and operative – has been frequently exploited in marketing campaigns. To illustrate:

Ten reasons to try Twitter today
 (1) Be part of a growing community
 (2) Get the latest news, gossips and tips
 (3) Make new friends
 (4) Find love
 (5) Track your favourite celebs
 (6) Share ideas and experiences
 (7) Get help and advice
 (8) Save money on text messaging
 (9) Grab last minute bargains and exclusive discounts
(10) Have fun! [29]

1–10 above are intended to describe desirable states of affairs, rightly or wrongly portrayed here as end results of joining Twitter. If one is attracted to any one or more of these as a goal then the purported fact that joining Twitter will result in its (or their) fulfilment could operate as an agential reason for them. It is hoped that such purported facts operate as agential reasons in virtue of also operating as normative or, at the very least, enticing[30] reasons to try Twitter or even (much more optimistically) reasons to try it *today*. If it is at all implied that the reasons in question apply universally this is unimportant, for such implicatures are easily cancellable. Consider, for example, the following two adverts:

Why join BT – something for everyone

> People join us for many different reasons – it all depends on what they're looking for. For some, it's because they want a chance to shape the future, and drive forward a new era of change. For others, it's because of the way that we look after our people, and encourage them to get the best out of themselves. Or maybe, because they want a foundation of technical training and experience that will open doors throughout the industry. Or simply because they like helping people get the very best out of today's communications technology. Whatever your reasons, we'd like to add to them. Read on, and discover how.[31]

Ten reasons to learn German

(1) Business
(2) The global career
(3) Tourism and hospitality industry
(4) Science and research
(5) Communication
(6) Cultural understanding
(7) Travel
(8) Enjoyment of literature, music, art and philosophy
(9) Opportunities to study/work in Germany
(10) Opportunities for exchange[32]

Both employ the notion of agent-relative reasons. In the first case alongside the explicit introduction of our desires or wants. Crucially, it is not the desires themselves that are being offered as reasons but, rather, the fact that some people want x or y. We might give something like the following account of these considerations:

> The status of a *consideration* illustrates the general connexion between the notions of thinking and of reason. A consideration is something to be taken into account in one's thinking, and the recognition of it is, in the nature of thinking, a step forward. Yet at the same time a consideration is something which tends to show that reason is on one side or other of the question. A fact will constitute a consideration bearing on a question just in so far as it constitutes a reason for making up one's mind about the question in one way or another. There is no such thing as [a] relevant but neutral consideration; and the side it takes is, to that extent, the side that reason takes ... In that kind of thinking where the question is whether to do something, the process of thinking normally involves wanting to advance into possession of that which gives one reason to do or not to do the thing ... It appears that if we want to study, in one sense, the structure of deliberation, we can take as a basic unit of analysis the idea of a fact being a reason for or against doing something.[33]

Whilst neither campaign claims that any of the proposed considerations are normatively binding, they do not deny it either. One could, of course, adopt a normatively more forceful approach:

Ten good reasons to eat organic food

(1) Organic products meet stringent standards.
(2) Organic food tastes great!

(3) Organic production reduces health risks.
(4) Organic farms respect our water sources.
(5) Organic farmers build soil.
(6) Organic farmers work in harmony with nature.
(7) Organic producers are leaders in innovative research.
(8) Organic producers strive to preserve diversity.
(9) Organic farming helps keep rural communities healthy.
(10) Organic abundance – Foods and non-foods alike! [34]

Here we are explicitly told that the reasons are *good*. As with previous adverts, 1–10 purport to state facts in the hope that, if and when the reader accepts them as such she may transform them into agential reasons for action. This can only happen if the reader takes them to be (a) true and (b) relevant to her actions, but we must take care to distinguish such enabling conditions for something's being a reason with the reason itself. We should take care not to conflate the claim that we cannot only be moved to act *unless* we already have certain passions with the claim that the passions in question are always *part* of our motivation.[35] Plato's Socrates warns against the basic fallacy that such a conflation would involve:

τὸ γὰρ μὴ διελέσθαι οἷόν τ᾿ εἶναι ὅτι ἄλλο μέν τί ἐστι τὸ αἴτιον τῷ ὄντι, ἄλλο δὲ ἐκεῖνο ἄνευ οὗ τὸ αἴτιον οὐκ ἄν ποτ᾿ εἴη αἴτιον.[36]

Finally, it is possible to portray potential agential reasons as deontically binding ones, that is to say, as reasons that we have a duty to respond to in a certain way. Table 4.1 below illustrates this by presenting resons offered by two opposing campaigns regarding the 5 May 2011 UK referendum on alternative voting (AV).

Statements Y (1–8) and N (1–8) are clearly incompatible sets, to the extent that it simply cannot be the case that all sixteen statements offer sound normative reasons. It seems plausible, then, that there exists important sense in which one can act for the reason that *p* even if it is not the case that *p*.[37] In addition, a statement might be true without offering the reason it is meant to be offering; indeed, given certain background facts, it could even favour the exact opposite action. Finally, any reason on offer might be pro-tanto rather than absolute i.e. it could be outweighed by other factors favouring a different course of action.[38] Despite all this, one may take any one or more of the above statements them to (individually or collectively) favour a certain course of action. In acting in accordance with such beliefs we transform apparent normative reasons into agential ones i.e. make the reasons our own *and* act upon them.

Table 4.1   Reasons for and against AV

Why You Should Vote 'Yes' to AV	Why You Should Vote 'No' to AV
Y1. It is a fairer voting system.	N1. AV is not a fair system.
Y2. First Past the Post isn't working … just a few thousand people determine every election result.	N2. Voting shouldn't be this complicated.
Y3. Changing the system to AV will mean that the majority get their voices heard; it will shut the door on extremist parties like the BNP.	N3. AV is unpopular in other countries.
Y4. Under AV everyone's vote counts and every MP is required to get the backing of a majority of voters.	N4. The winner in any election should be whoever gets the most votes.
Y5. A reformed system would strengthen the mandate of our MPs.	N5. Under AV the votes of the least popular candidate can decide who wins the election.
Y6. It really is as easy as '1, 2, 3'! If people still want to vote with a single X they can.	N6. The only vote that would count under AV would be Nick Clegg's (AV would give the Lib Dems extra seats).
Y7. AV is a small change that makes a big difference.	N7. Switching to AV would cost £130 million on electronic vote counting machines and £26 million on explaining the new system to voters.
Y8. Without AV the interests of the Labour Party and the people it represents go unheard.[39]	N8. AV would be wrong for Britain and wrong for the Labour Party.[40]

None of this is to say that aspects of our psychology may not be operative in motivating us to act; indeed, motivating us to act upon some consideration or another. Indeed, it is possible to explain a person's action by stating which of their psychological features motivated them to act. Such motive explanations are related to – yet importantly distinct from – reasons explanations – viz. explanations that cite our agential reasons for action. We shall see in due course that all explanations in terms of agential reasons presuppose some narrative regarding the agent's psychology. Be that as it may, the psychological story in question enables the reasons explanation without actually featuring in it.

4.3   Grounds and springs

In all the above campaigns, the reasons offered are best understood as things believed or desired (*quod credo* etc.) rather than our believings, psychological attitudes, or character traits (*neum fidem* etc.).[41] Indeed, features of our psychology are ontologically the wrong sorts of things to qualify as agential reasons. Facts about our psychology are by and large also ruled out, not on ontological grounds but because we do not typically act upon on considerations *about* our beliefs and desires. There are, of course, exceptions e.g. the fact that Jack believes his mother is an alien may be a reason for him to seek psychological help.

Michael Smith stresses both these points, adding that no fact – including facts about our psychology – is capable of explaining action. According to Smith only real features of our psychology (what he calls our intentional profile) can do so. On this view, the crucial difference between normative reasons and the reasons which explain our action – what Smith calls 'motivating reasons' – is an ontological one:

> By contrast with normative reasons, then, which seem to be *truths* of the form 'It is desirable that I ϕ', motivating reasons would seem to be *psychological states*, states that play a certain explanatory role in producing action ... motivating reasons and normative reasons are of quite different *categories*. For whereas motivating reasons are psychological states, normative reasons are propositions of the form 'A's φ-ing is desirable or required.[42]

Smith accordingly insists that the considerations I have been describing as agential reasons only render actions intelligible, and do so for different reasons than those for which 'motivating reasons' explain our actions. Recall Smith and Pettit's suggestion that the term 'good reason' is ambiguous between 'good rational *spring*' and 'good rational *ground*' (§ 2.3). The term 'good' is here being used in a technical sense to indicate that we can still make normative judgements (in this case judgements about one's rationality) when presented with statements concerning the relation between a person's psychology and his actions, much as Davidson claims that primary reasons rationalise actions and that 'there is a certain irreducible – though somewhat anaemic sense in which every rationalization justifies'.[43] Good reasons in this sense are not normative for, unlike normative reasons, rational springs are psychologically real.

Smith suggests that we should understand the motivating/normative reason distinction in terms of the distinction between foreground and background theories of rationality.[44] On this account there are two ways in which we can render actions intelligible, corresponding to the background and foreground theories of rationality and Smith's two parallel notions of a reason for action. From what Smith calls the 'intentional perspective' (related to our motivational set or intentional profile) I may explain my action 'by citing the complex of psychological states that produce the action ... my *motivating reasons*'.[45] From the deliberative perspective, by contrast, I cite 'the considerations I actually take into account in deciding what to do before I do it ... these considerations constitute my *normative reasons*'.[46] These agential reasons are, on Smith's own view, certain facts I reflect on when I deliberate. Smith claims that statements citing these facts may render our actions intelligible, but do not explain them, thereby affiliating himself with the set of philosophers described as causalists in § 3.1:

> [I]t would seem to be part of our concept of what it is for an agent's reasons to have the potential to explain her behaviour that her having those reasons is a fact about her; that the goals that such reasons embody are *her* goals. By contrast with normative reasons, then, which seem to be *truths* of the form 'It is desirable that I φ', motivating reasons would seem to be *psychological states*, states that play a certain explanatory role in producing action.[47]

The last sentence also suggests that the reason why Smith thinks that psychological facts will not do is that he holds a *Conflating View of Motivational Production* (CVMP):

> What motivated an action most is identical to whatever produced it in a psychologically explanatory way to be further specified.[48]

It is one thing to be the strongest motivator of an action and quite another to produce it. Unless we are automata, the mere presence of motivation plays an insufficient explanatory role in the production of intentional action (it is whole beings and not parts of their minds or brains that perform actions).[49] In taking mental states or episodes to play a *sufficient* role in the production of all intentional action CVMP rules out the very possibility of being in control of motivated behaviour. Actions are variously enabled, facilitated, motivated, and constrained by features of our psychology, but not produced by them.[50] It is perhaps possible to distinguish, as Donald Davidson and Wilfrid Sellars both attempted to,[51] between *x* producing our actions (causally) and *x* causing us to act, claiming that only the former is true of motivational states. There is no parallel distinction, however, our being motivated to act and our action being motivated. Consequently, CVMP cannot allow for the crucial distinction between the production of action and its (mere) motivation. *Inter alia*, CVMP also rules out the possibility of their playing a motivational role, at least on the plausible assumption that facts cannot be said to produce action.[52]

Having a certain belief or desire, by contrast, is a more plausible candidate for playing a suitable role in the production of action. Smith accordingly claims that, from the intentional perspective, we explain action 'by citing the complex of psychological states that produce the action ... by citing my *motivating reasons*'[53] – i.e. by citing (actual) rational springs (which are a subset – not all rational springs will render action intelligible/explain in the relevant sense, but then how are they springs/motivating?). From the deliberative perspective, by contrast, we cite:

> the considerations I actually take into account in deciding what to do before I do it ... these considerations constitute my *normative reasons* for doing what I do, at least as those reasons appear to me.[54]

These potentially normative reasons for acting are, by Smith's own admission, certain facts/considerations I reflect on when I deliberate. But to confuse explanations that cite agential reasons with ones describing motivational sets is to endorse CVMR:

> The reasons for which we act are identical to the things which motivate us to act (and vice versa).

A special instance of CVMP is conflating goals that move us with goals we act upon. Teleological reasons, as we saw above, are not motives but considerations relating to them. These may (but need not) include facts *about* actual or potential motives and other psychological phenomena. If I do A in order to achieve *x* then my agential reason is not my desire for *x* but something that I believe about *x*, e.g. that it is desirable, that I can achieve by doing A, etc. From the perspective of CVMR, by contrast, a motivated action is simply any act performed for a reason, just as Nagel takes a motivated desire to be one that is held for reasons.[55] It is such conflations that lead people to claim that truly altruistic acts are those which we know won't make us happy and/or that all actions aim at our own happiness. Yet the truth about human nature is that only a socio-path would feel no contentment in helping others, and only a pervert would help others *in order* to feel content. Abandoning CVMR enables us to see that a motivated action need only be an action one is motivated to perform, regardless of the provision of any reasons, thus leaving room for the reality of what Rosalind Hursthouse calls 'arational actions'.[56]

CVMR is embodied in the standard distinction between normative and *motivating* reasons. Indeed, the very notion of a motivating reason presupposes the existence of properties belonging to both normative and operative aspects of our psychology. Replacing it with the term 'explanatory reasons'[57] won't help since, as we shall see in Chapter 6, reasons for action cannot themselves explain anything. Using the two concepts interchangeably only serves to make things worse, for a rea-son *why* need not share many of the most central characteristics typi-cally associated with motivating reasons, such as motivating and being a reason one acts upon. Being explanatory, then, is neither a necessary nor a sufficient condition for being motivating. It may even be that the explanatory power of a reason that explains *why* one acted rules out the very possibility of its also being a reason *for* one's action in any sense (normative, agential, *or* motivating).

What is right in Smith's account is the insistence that the reasons for which we act do not explain why our actions occur. But even when we combine this truth with the thought that all explanation of action presupposes a basic Humean story, it does not follow that the considera-tions upon which we act are not our reasons for action, and that they do not explain why we do the things we do. All that would follow is that the explanation presupposes the availability of a basic Humean story about our psychology, one not couched in terms of reasons. Hornsby expresses this thought in the following way:

> To a question about why someone did something, an expected answer usually is: 'She thought _____' or 'She wanted _____'.

Philosophers' official version of an answer is 'She thought _____
and she wanted _____'. The official version is appropriate, because
someone who intentionally did something had a reason for doing it,
and, having a reason, she must have believed something about what
would be conductive to the satisfaction of some desire she had.[58]

Whether or not such a Humean story must be presupposed depends
partly on how we disambiguate the notion of 'desire' for, as J. Raz has
observed, we ordinarily employ the term in two strikingly different
senses, each related to a different operation of the will:

> The will plays two related roles in human life. A good deal of confu-
> sion is caused by confusing them. First and foremost the will is the
> capacity for intentional action...This fact determines one sense of
> 'to want'. In this sense to say that I did something because I wanted
> to do it...it to mark the action as intentional...in this sense of
> 'want' (which I will call the 'thin' sense of 'desire' or 'want') coerced
> actions are actions we do because we want to...The Second role of
> the will is related but different. We are attached to different possi-
> bilities to different degrees, and our attachments can differ in qual-
> ity. Expression of degree or quality of attachment are expressions of
> the will...Sometimes we do what we do unwillingly...sometimes we
> are forced to act against our will...sometimes we do things which
> we very much do not want to do but recognize an obligation to
> do. In this sense, not every intentional action is done because we
> want to do it. To say that we want to do it is to designate a possible
> attitude to an intentional action, rather than (as in the first sense
> of want) to designate it as intentional...I will call the second [sense]
> 'thick'.[59]

It is trivially true that all intentional action requires desire in the first,
thin sense.[60] By contrast, it is not at all obvious that action so desired
also requires the presence of any desire in the latter, *thick* sense,[61] let
alone one for the action in question.[62] A similar suggestion has recently
been made by Skorupski, who distinguishes between 'aim-eliciting' and
'substantive' senses of desire, concluding that once we do so it 'becomes
clear that the Humean model of motivation cannot be defended empirically, either directly or by appeal to implicit definition'.[63] The most
plausible accounts of motivation (as opposed to motivating reasons)
consequently appear to be *weak* Humean ones.

4.4   Communication breakdown

Stephen Darwall has suggested that Smith takes the term 'motivating reason' to mean something like 'a state which plays a certain role in teleological explanations' of a person's action, whereas anti-psychologistic opponents such as Dancy take it to refer to what I have been calling an agential reason for action.[64] Consequently, much of the disagreement between them occurs (largely) as a result of a conceptual misunderstanding. This is confirmed by the following remark that Dancy makes about Smith, which completely ignores the latter's understanding of the distinction between explaining an action and merely rendering it intelligible:

> I presume that he has in mind the idea that to explain an action is to show how doing that action can have come to seem worthwhile to the agent. The action is explained once we can show that doing it made good sense in the lights of the agent.[65]

We might summarise the disparity in their conceptual schemes as follows:

Smith's Usage: what motivates us = df. a motivating reason = df. a rational spring which motivates = a/the reason why action occurs.

Dancy's Usage: what motivates us = df. our motivating reason = df. a reason we act *upon* = that which explains why we act as we do.[66]

These usages are not random but emerge from the tacit acceptance of different versions of CVA, CVR, CVRA, CVAE, CVMR, and CVMP – each party primarily focusing on contrasting relata of each view. The result is an intractable debate, begotten by distinct understandings of both the objects of action explanation and the operative constraints (explanatory, motivating, normative, etc.) on being a motivating reason.[67]

According to Smith's perspective, a motivating reason is a reason that explains why an action occurred by pointing to the relevant belief–desire pair in one's motivational set:

> It is constitutive of an agent's actions that, under some description, they are done for reasons. But since an action is motivated behaviour, these reasons must be motivating reasons the agent has for doing what he did…the Humeans' interest in the claim that motivating

states are constituted by belief–desire pairs is fuelled by their belief that an event's being suitably explained by such motivating states is constitutive of that event's being an action.[68]

Dancy's terminology, by contrast, marks out a state of being motivated as 'a state with normative content such as that of taking something to be a reason', his notion of a reason for action constrained by the following characterisation:

> ... motivation is a relation that can occur between an agent and a consideration, it is not also one that can occur between an agent and a psychological state.[69]
>
>   There are these two ways of using the notion of a reason for *action*, which address different questions. There is the question what were the considerations in the light of which, or despite which, he acted as he did... There is also the question whether there was good reason to act in that way... We can normally explain an agent's *doing what he did* by specifying the reasons in the light of which he acted... A reason for acting can be *the reason why* one acted.[70]

We have already seen that Smith inherits his terminology from Davidson, though origins, however, lie much further back in history.[71] Dancy, in turn, attributes his notion of a motivational state to J. Raz, though an earlier incarnation may be found in the work of W. D. Falk who, in taking the reasons which 'impel' us to act to be psychological states which could 'function as causes of actions' was one of the first to use the actual term 'motivating reason'.[72] Perhaps the motivational psychologist J. S. Brown said it best when he wrote:

> There is no question that the idea of motivation or some similar notion appears in almost every systematic account of behavior... the ubiquity of the concept of motivation, in one guise or another, is nevertheless surprising when we consider that its meaning is often scandalously vague... We thus find ourselves in the position of trying to deal with an allegedly vital factor in the face of violent disagreements as to its origins, its essential nature, and its particular roles as a behavior determinant. [73]

In a similar spirit, R. Jay Wallace plausibly maintains that philosophy would be altogether better off without the concept of a motivating reason.[74] Wallace claims that agential reasons cannot explain action, whereas statements about our psychological states can do so, albeit in non-agential ways. Dancy has responded to this claim by noting that although psychological facts can and do explain our actions they do not do so in virtue of being reasons *for* them, yet that is exactly what 'motivating reasons' are meant to be.[75] This seems right, but for all we have seen could just give us further reason to reject the very concept of a reason that is explanatory, motivating, *and* agential.[76] There is nothing contradictory in the notion of being motivated by one's beliefs and desires. Indeed, given that motivation is a *causal* notion, the burden of proof is on Dancy to explain how a thing believed (which may not even be the case) could possibly move us to do anything.[77]

Darwall and Wallace's criticisms both evoke something akin to CVMR as the root problem, but neither associate it with any further conflations such as CVA, CVR, or CVRA. Wallace makes a distinction that is structurally similar to the sort I introduced in § 2.1, but ultimately quite different:

> [T]there seem to be two distinct explanatory questions that can be posed about an action that has already been performed. In one kind of situation, the *explanandum* is a more or less complicated stretch of bodily movement, about which we ask *what* the agent was doing; an answer to this question will ascribe to the agent a goal or aim, an intention in action that the bodily movement can be seen as sub-serving. The secondary explanatory question we can ask, by contrast, takes the agent's immediate intention in action as given, and asks *why* the agent did that. This is the question to which motivating reasons in Dancy's sense provide the answer.[78]

Wallace identifies the things we do with bodily movements, asking two different questions about them: '*what* was the agent doing?' and '*why* was she doing it?' But there is no reason to suppose that questions such as 'why did Sam go to the Supermarket to get milk?' cannot receive an answer couched in psychological terms, and that such answers will specify *reasons* why.

4.5 Controversy dissolved

Both the psychologism/anti-psychologism and the Humean/anti-Humean debates arise largely out of shared allegiance to CVMR. Anti-psychologism takes its cue from two truisms: (i) that it is possible to act for a normative reason – viz. a reason that counts in favour of an action – and

(ii) that normative reasons are anti-psychologistic. It infers from these facts that what moves us to action cannot be a psychological state (or, for that matter, any other feature of our psychology). Psychologism, in turn, takes its cue from two different truisms: (i) that we are – at least sometimes – motivated by psychological states and (ii) that motivation is causal notion (which is not to say that it need treat action explanation as being causal).

Psychologism and anti-psychologism thus each appeal by pointing out how incredibly foolish it would be to not reject the other. Thus, if we reject non-psychologism we are faced with two horns of a dilemma: either we cannot ever act for good reasons or the good reasons we act for are (necessarily) psychological phenomena. Conversely, if we reject psychologism we are left with an account that claims that (it is necessarily true that) we are never motivated by either our beliefs or our desires, or indeed the two combined. As with the debates discussed in § 3.1, what counts in favour of the former view is exactly what counts against the latter, and vice versa. Table 4.2 illustrates how each position makes favourable points (+) which one cannot accept without thereby committing oneself to a claim counting against it (–). Accordingly, each theory must adopt a (–) to retain its (+), or sacrifice its (+) to avoid a (–).

This is problematic because it is natural to side with psychologism with regard to motivation and non-psychologism as far as normative reasons are concerned. The Theory of Motivation, having been drawn on the assumption that we are motivated by the reasons for which we

Table 4.2   Psychologism v. anti-psychologism

	Claims counting for (+)	Claims counting against (–)
Psychologism	T: We are (at least sometimes) motivated by our psychological states.	F: Good reasons (we act for) are not psychologically real.
Anti-Psychologism	T: Good reasons (we act for) are not psychologically real.	F: We are (at least sometimes) motivated by our psychological states.

Table 4.3   Humeanism v. anti-Humeanism

	Claims counting for (+)	Claims counting against (–)
Humeanism	T: We are (at least sometimes) partly motivated by desires.	F: Desires are not parts of reasons we act for.
Anti-Humeanism	T: Desires are not parts of the reasons we act for.	F: We are (at least sometimes) partly motivated by desires.

act, has no theoretical space for such a position. In rejecting CVMR and related conflating views, by contrast, we are free to side with psychologists on motivation, and non-psychologists on reasons for action. Table 4.3 captures a similar situation with regard to the Humeanism/anti-Humeanism debate.

To paraphrase House M. D: they are both right, in the sense that they have convinced me that they are both wrong. We should be weak Humeans about motivation and anti-Humeans about the reasons for which we act, thus rejecting the very notion of a motivating reason.[79] None of this entails that we cannot be moved by our beliefs alone. We are frequently motivated by our beliefs and/or desires, but to say we act upon them is not to say that the considerations upon which we act (our reasons) are features of our psychology.[80] All concerned may thus agree that statements about y believing that *p* can explain why I did *x*, but do not do so by citing my agential reason.

It might be thought that the most plausible versions of the positions listed in § 4.1 converge, for, once stripped of their conflations, there is relatively little disagreement left. But this would be a misguided way of putting things, since in effect we would not be left with any theories at all. In the next chapter I turn to scientific theories of motivation said to be in competition with the layperson's understanding of agential reasons. I shall maintain CVM leads to exaggerated claims concerning the 'real' reasons that lurk behind our actions. These in turn give rise to a new set of conflations.

5
Nested Explanations

In which the author examines the relation between everyday reasons for acting and the various factors and forces which underlie them. A revised understanding of the true discoveries of experimental psychology is proposed.

The real foundations of their inquiry do not strike people at all.

Unless *that* fact has at some time struck them.

And this means:

we fail to be struck by what, once seen, is most striking and most powerful.

Ludwig Wittgenstein[1]

The trouble with progress
is that it always looks much greater than it really is.

Johan Nestroy[2]

5.1   Explanatory paths

Suppose that you are welcomed into a friend's home only to find, as you enter her living-room, a mutual acquaintance frantically stamping on your friend's coat. Unless you are a mind reader or have had a particularly strange upbringing, you will probably ask yourself the question 'why on earth is this person doing this to my friend's coat?' Different sorts of facts may serve to answer this question, in a plethora of interrelated ways (see Knobe and Malle 2002). Many will explicitly point to your acquaintance's psychology (e.g. through marked beliefs), others only implicitly (e.g. through unmarked beliefs), and a few might

82

completely bypass it. Here is a list, by no means exhaustive, of available modes of explanation (some will differ only linguistically, others by appealing to different sorts of factor):

(i)   Further specifying (be it explicitly or implicitly) what kind of action it was: whether or not it was intentional, voluntary, consciously performed, a mere reflex, etc. e.g. 'she didn't know what she was doing', 'she thought it was a carpet', , 'her older brother forced her to do it', 'she meant to avoid it but slipped' (categorial explanation).

(ii) Revealing her motive e.g. 'she did it out of jealousy' or out of spite, fear, lust, greed, envy, etc. that renders the action intelligible (motive explanation).

(iii) Re-describing what she did (thereby pointing to an intention, aim, goal, desire etc.) e.g. 'she was flattening it', 'she was testing the material', etc. (descriptive explanation).

(iv) Explicitly pointing to an intention, aim, goal etc. e.g. 'she was seeking attention', 'she wanted to dry her new shoes', and so on (teleological explanation).

(v)   Revealing facts about the agent's past experience (including upbringing) which she may or may not be conscious of e.g. 'she had a difficult upbringing', 'she went to school x' (where, as it is well known, they don't teach you manners), 'when she was a child her favourite coat caught fire', 'she was raised by coat-stampers', etc (biographical explanation).

(vi) Pointing to facts about the agent's culture (or background beliefs) e.g. 'where she comes from stepping on a coat is thought to bring good luck' , 'it is traditional to step on a person's coat before they leave on a long journey', and so on (cultural explanation).

(vii) Offering contextual information about the situation in which the action was performed e.g. 'the coat was on fire', 'it was a bet', 'they are rehearsing a play', 'everyone had agreed it was a hideous coat', etc. (situational or contextual explanation)

(viii) Appealing to character traits of the agent e.g. 'because she is cruel' or clumsy, insolent, superstitious, weak-willed, etc (trait explanation).

(ix) Appealing to the agent's psychological state e.g. 'because she was drunk' or on drugs, under hypnosis, annoyed, worried, nervous etc. (mental-state explanation).

(x)   Pointing to facts about the agent's *beliefs and desires* e.g. 'because she believed it was a carpet and wanted to dry her feet', 'she believed it would bring good fortune and wanted to wish the owner luck', 'she wanted to humiliate the owner and thought this was the most efficient way of doing so', etc (Humean explanation).

(xi) Providing information relating to the individual agent's medical condition e.g. 'she suffers from paltomania','she was born with an aggressive disorder', 'she forgot to take her Quaaludes' etc. (medical explanation).

(xii) Pointing to some general fact about human nature, e.g. 'most of us are born with aggressive tendencies', 'and so on (nativist explanation).

(xiii) Pointing to the considerations in the light of which she acted (things the agent believed). These may or may not be good reasons but – at least typically (and, according to Plato, always) – the agent will have taken them to be *good reasons* for acting (reasons which favoured the action) e.g. 'because, as she believed, it was a carpet', 'your friend asked her to', 'the coat was on fire', and so on (reasoning explanation).

Not all of the above will be available in each case, but nor is it ever the case that only one of the above methods is the correct one. Which of the above methods we choose may depend on what we are trying to explain, on whose action it is (our own or someone else's), and on what information is already available to us. None of the reasons offered are any more or less *real* than any of the others.[3] Are any more *basic*? (i–xii) cite reasons *why* she stepped on the coat but do not explicitly mention agential reasons. These can only be given by xiii. Compare xiii with x: *What* she believes (that it is a carpet) may be her reason for stepping on it, but her believing this (or the fact that she believes it) is not a reason for doing much, except perhaps for seeing an optician.

5.2 Nests for all reasons

If I explain the stamping of my friend's coat by stating that in her home country it is traditional to step on a person's coat before they leave on a long journey, I am implying that my friend is going on a long journey. Within the context in which her action occurs, stating this latter fact cannot alone explain why our acquaintance was stamping on her coat. By contrast, in her home country there might be no need to mention the tradition at all, because it is already common knowledge. In fact the action may be so familiar as not to require an explanation at all, unless one is seeking to know why she is acting in accordance with the tradition in question (for that would be a correct redescription of the act in question). Whilst the appropriate explanation changes in each case, the agent's reason for acting need not do so. In some contexts we best explain action by citing an agential reason, in others we explain it by stating some further fact which nests this reason into a wider explanatory context, be it cultural, biological, autobiographical, or whatever. Once we have given an explanation in terms of a person's agential reasons, there will always be, as Dancy puts it, 'a possible further question how it was that the agent was the sort of person to be influenced by such features'.[4]

Reason-nesting statements serve to render an action intelligible but do not typically do so in virtue of citing agential reasons. Rather, they most frequently explain why the agent took said reason to count in favour of her action. An agential reason can, however, be nested in another one. Teleological reasons, for example, tend to nest within each other: I did *a* in order to do *b* and I wanted to do *b* because of *c*, etc. But note how each new agential reason offered is for some further action, or some related belief or desire. They are not all agential reasons for one and the same action. In cases where we act upon more than one agential reason, it is possible for one agential reason to nest itself within another agential reason for the same action. Just as the protagonist in the Dylan lyric at the start of the previous chapter had several agential reasons for taking the child's flute, so I might order a pizza Fiorentina not only because I am hungry, but also because I like the taste of pizza, I am a vegetarian, I need some protein, and I want it. These factors may collectively function as my agential reasons for what I do, but that does not prevent some of them from nesting within others. The fact that I am a vegetarian explains why I ordered the Fiorentina pizza rather than, say, a pepperoni one. But it may, in certain circumstances, also explain why I was hungry, needed protein, and so on.

Basic empirical facts about human nature make possible all sorts of nesting relations. The taste of food becomes more pleasant to people when they are hungry, and so we might be tempted to skip lunch in order to better enjoy a feast, though we might equally ruin our dinner by snacking beforehand,[5] against our better judgement.[6] Similarly, incentive factors can awaken drive states, for example the aroma from the pizza oven might stimulate my hunger. In such a situation my smelling the aroma from the bakery may motivate me to order a pizza Fiorentina, but it is not my agential reason for doing so. Similarly, what motivates one to buy a bottle of Sprite (the advert portraying happy Sprite drinkers having an energetic time on the beach) may not be my reason for choosing to buy it over some other drink. My agential reason for choosing it might be the thought that it will taste nice,[7] the advert being the cause of my having this thought. It is such examples, and not abstract theories, which should dictate how we ought to conceive the relation between our agential reasons and the facts within which explanations in terms of them might nest.

By definition, only those facts that are considerations I act upon qualify as agential reasons. One common indication of a fact's not being an agential reason is that the agent was not aware of it and consequently could not act in the light of it. It would be wrong to make this a necessary condition, for we may be aware of all sorts of explanatorily relevant facts without acting upon them (e.g. that we were educated at a certain school etc). It might also be premature to think of the indicator in question as being a sufficient condition for failing to qualify as an agential reason as this would simply beg the question against various theories such as Freud's. Be that as it may, the burden of proof is on Freud and others to show how something that I am not conscious of could count as an agential reason. Various features of our psychology, including repressed wishes, desires, beliefs etc., may of course *motivate* us to act one way or another, but we already saw in the previous chapter that CVMR is in error to equate anything that motivates us with an agential reason. In addition, facts about ourselves that we are not conscious of (e.g. relating to our childhood, some past traumatic event, our current motivational set, or whatever), like all other facts that we are not aware of (including all sorts of trivia), may explain why we thought something was the case (in spite of all the contrary evidence) and/or why we took – or indeed *mis*took – it to favour a particular course of action.

To insist that the facts in terms of which agential reasons are nested *must* be capable of explaining the action in question is to hold the *Conflating View of Nested Reasons* (CVNR):

> A reason why A took *x* to be a reason to φ is a reason that explains why A subsequently φ-d.

I am not claiming that facts within which agential reasons nest may never serve to explain said action, but only that it is not always the case that they do so. In the sections that follow I demonstrate that various psychologists, philosophers, and cognitive scientists assume otherwise. Many of them further mistake the reasons that explanations in terms of agential reasons are nested within for those agential reasons themselves, thereby embracing the *Combined Conflation of CVNR and CVR*:

> A reason why A took *x* to be a reason to ϕ is a reason *for which* A subsequently ϕ-d i.e. nesting reasons are agential reasons.

The conflations are dangerous because they quickly lead to the view that, in uncovering nesting reasons of all sorts, theorists reveal *real* or *true* explanations of our actions – ones that are in direct competition with the layperson's explanation that are consequently dismissed as naive or otherwise flawed. In the case of the combined conflation we are often told that the discovery in question reveals the agent's *real reason*, one which may be radically different – perhaps even geometrically opposed to – what he foolishly believes his agential reason to be. In what follows I shall chiefly focus on psychoanalytic theory and some recent work on implicit associations, but the general line of argument may is applicable to a host of theories conducting their business under the broad banner of human nature studies, including many of those presented in Chapter 1. As we saw there, the study of human nature is indeed highly relevant to the explanation of action, but not in as direct a fashion as it is taken to be.

5.3   Reasons in the abyss

Motivational forces often lie outside our realms of knowledge, beyond our immediate control and often beyond any control at all.[8] There will not always (or even frequently) be a traumatic experience underlying our everyday actions, but the further we step back into trying to explain the beliefs, desires, values, and general character traits which underlie our actions, the more likely it becomes that rational explanations will give way to explanations which involve our cultural background, upbringing, education, or human nature. Reasons sooner or later have to come to an end, though it would be absurd to take this to show that all thought and action is irrational.[9]

Factors we are not conscious of (be they psychological, biographical, or whatever) need not reside in one's 'subconscious', nor need they be negative.[10] An explanation of why A took *x* to be a reason for performing a certain action, for example, may refer to factors as diverse as her upbringing, a past trauma, her family's medical history, or a disposition innate in most human beings or animals at large. Such explanations may in turn be further nested within neuroscientific facts that 'explain why a person is more prone than normal to inhabit certain mental states – e.g. depression, which makes A more liable to act for a certain kind of reason than someone with a different neuroscientific make-up'.[11]

Consider the following example (hopefully not too close to home for any of you): Professor X's essay grading is easily affected by his emotional mood, yet X is under the delusion that he is doing so *purely* on grounds of actual merit – a certain essay is seen as being stylish and well-researched, another as lacking structure and/or failing to provide decent arguments etc. The merit of any given piece (whatever it might actually be) cannot itself depend on his beliefs and/or underlying moods. Rather the beliefs are, however deficiently, tracking a merit that is external to them – such is their direction of fit (we need not get fixated here on any particular theory of value). Let us further suppose that our academic acknowledges that his beliefs may be false or inaccurate, while taking himself to be a reasonably good and impartial judge, by no means affected much by anything as banal as an emotional mood. In sum, he takes himself to be guided by *what* he believes the merit of any given essay is and has the second-order belief that his first-order beliefs are (at the very least) reliably based on stable criteria which he is sufficiently sensitive to.

Assuming the personal mood attribution above, we can safely say that at any given time his emotional moods (in turn invariably caused by factor *x* or *y*) *made him* perceive certain essays in a certain way, thus causing him to believe that the considerations of merit which he is principally guided by dictate that he ought to give them the grades that he does. This is clearly a case of self-deception, for Professor X does not perceive the underlying cause of his thoughts regarding the academic merit of any given essay, let alone the ultimate cause(s) of these – causally intermediate – moods. A similar tale could be told via situational attributions of the sort described by Milgram (1963), Isen and Levin (1972 & 1975), Doris (1998 & 2002), and Haidt (2001), or indeed a mix of psychological and situational attributions.

Such explanations work at a sub-rational level. By this I don't mean that personal or situational factors do not operate rationally (though this will frequently be true in varying degrees), but that related explanations of what moves us to see and act as we do cannot be given purely in terms of reasons *for which* we do so. Professor X's moods are not the 'true' or 'real' reasons for which he thinks and acts as he does, any more than finding a penny in a phonebooth is someone's 'real reason' for helping a passer-by with directions. The Professor's reason for thinking and acting as he does are things he believes to be true of the essays. Personal and situational attributions give us a causal, non-rational explanations of *why* we take ourselves to have certain reasons for acting. The mood theory, for example, explains why Professor X took certain (seeming or actual) considerations to be reasons for grading the essay as he did e.g. why he perceived that reference to Freud's introductory lectures as being lazy, when in a different mood he may have found it imaginative. His agential reasons, by contrast, are not his moods themselves but the considerations which – given his moods – he came to focus *on* and be moved *by*. We can thus distinguish between the following:

(1) The moods which explain (a) why X had certain non-evaluative beliefs about the essays, (b) why he took the things he believed as reasons for giving a particular set of (value-based) grades to the essays, and (c) why he weighed his reasons as he did (thus giving rise to further evaluations).
(2) X's reasons for believing what he believes about the essays.
(3) X's reasons for grading the essays as he does, namely *what* he believes the related values of the essays are.

We could doubtlessly give a considerably more complicated picture, one that includes numerous additional sources and channels of motivation, in turn giving rise to new objects of explanation. These would all relate to those listed above in explanatorily informative ways, but could not serve to reduce them. Underlying experiences, drives, and motives are no more (or less) real than the considerations we act upon. Our agential reasons are typically just those considerations that we take to be our reasons.[12] By contrast, we may be completely in the dark with regard to the motivation behind our perception of the world. So much is obviously right in Freud.

Consider this standard example from one of Freud's own lectures, concerning *new* patients of his:

> [I]t constantly happens that a person whom I have brought in from the waiting-room omits to shut the door behind him and almost always he leaves *both* doors open ... this carelessness on the part of

the patient only occurs when he has been alone in the waiting-room, and has therefore left an empty room behind him; it never happens if other people, strangers to him, have been waiting with him ... the patient's omission is neither accidentally nor senselessly determined ... he had formed a picture of a crowd of people seeking for help ... He now comes into an empty, and moreover extremely modestly furnished waiting-room, and is shocked. He has to make the doctor pay for the superfluous respect which he had intended to offer him: so – he omits to shut the door between the waiting-room and the consulting-room. What he means to say to the doctor by his conduct is: 'Ah, so there's no one here and no one's likely to come while I'm here' .... The analysis of this small symptomatic action tells you nothing that you did not know before: the thesis that it was not a matter of chance but had a motive, a sense, and an intention, that it had a place in an assignable mental context and that it provided information, by a small indication, of a more important mental process. But, more than anything else, it tells you that the process thus indicated was unknown to the consciousness of the person who carried out the action, since none of the persons who left the two doors open would have been able to admit that by this omission he wanted to give evidence of his contempt.[13]

Notice how Freud characterises the unconscious factor here in terms of meaning and intention. On his picture of the mind, unconscious phenomena operate identically to conscious phenomena, but without our knowledge. Does it really make sense to talk of unconscious motives and goals as opposed to motivations? In the 1950s, some of the volumes in the 'neo-Wittgensteinian current of small red books' questioned the general conceptual framework of psychoanalytic theory.[14] Davidson describes their pervading worry as follows:

> It seems then, that there are two irreconcilable tendencies in Freud's methodology. On the one hand he wanted to extend the range of phenomena subject to reason explanations, and on the other to treat these same phenomena as forces and states are treated in the natural sciences. But in the natural sciences, reasons and propositional attitudes are out of place, and blind causality rules.[15]

Leaving aside Davidson's mischaracterisation of Freud's method,[16] this remark successfully captures the worry at hand – viz. that blind causality seems to leave no room for the rational aspect of psychology. This is not because there is anything contentious about the notion of a psychological cause functioning in a non-rational manner(it is not remotely controversial to maintain that reason-governed behaviour is affected by psychological factors we are not conscious of). The denial that all of our reasoning is done consciously is similarly plausible. What *is* problematic, however, is the further suggestion that we may act upon intentions or considerations that are not readily available to our consciousness. Such claims form part of a more general set of views about contrasting the explanations of lay-people with the so-called 'real' reasons for action discovered by science.[17] I gave some examples of these views in § 1.1 before proceeding, in Chapter 2, to argue that they were committed to CVR. I now turn to versions of the view that are additionally committed to CVMR and CVNR.

5.4   Purported confabulations

A Freudian acquaintance once tried to convince me me that the *real reason* for philanthropy and animal-rights activism is guilt. Such assumptions are prevalent among those who those who postulate pervasive unconscious drives that permeate everyday behaviour, from Nietzsche and Freud to public manipulators, air dealers, and social critics such as E. Bernays (Freud's nephew) and V. Packard.[18] On the view defended in this chapter, by contrast, any truth in the guilt narrative can be easily (and informatively) reconciled with the reasons explanations people ordinarily give for their philanthropy and activism and, indeed, their everyday behaviour.

Consider the following passage by Bernays:

> A man buying a car may think he wants it for the purposes of locomotion, whereas the fact may be that he would really prefer not to be burdened with it, and would rather walk for the sake of his health. He may really want it because it is a symbol of social position, an evidence of his success in business, or a means of pleasing his wife. This general principle, that men are very largely actuated by motives which they conceal from themselves, is as true of mass as of individual psychology. It is evident that the successful propagandist must understand the true motives and not be content to accept the reasons which men give for what they do ... what are the true reasons the purchaser is planning to spend his money on a new car instead of a new piano? Because he has decided that he wants the commodity called locomotion more than he wants the commodity called music? Not altogether. He buys a car, because it is at that moment the group custom to buy cars.[19]

That Bernays embraces CVMR is evident from his juxtaposition of true *motives* with *agential reasons*. In addition, his identification of the question 'why did he buy a car?' with that of 'why did he buy a car rather than a piano?' suggests a commitment to CVR equivalent to that attributed to Nagel in § 3.4. Of course, the motives that Bernays points to are not at all irrelevant to understanding and predicting action. On the contrary, they may well be real reasons and, as already argued in § 3.3, substantial enough to contribute to a social science of action.[20] Bernays is right to agree with 'the psychologists of the school of Freud who have pointed out that many of man's thoughts and actions are compensatory substitutes for desires which he has been obliged to suppress'.[21] The reasons in question, however, are not usually in competition with those offered by the layperson. Rather, they typically serve to explain why people have the agential reasons that they do. The failure to realise this is an acceptance of CVNR, in Bernays' case combined with a number of other conflating views with detrimental effects for his overall psychological theory.

Similarly, the new edition of Packard's *The Hidden Persuaders* wears CVMP on its cover in claiming to reveal 'what makes us buy, believe – and even vote – the way we do'. Here are two paradigmatic examples of the kind of evidence that Packard takes to be conclusive:

> Psychologists at the McCann-Erickson advertising agency asked a sampling of people why they didn't buy one client's product – kippered herring. The main reason people gave under the direct questioning was that they just didn't like the taste of kippers. More persistent probing however uncovered the fact that 40 percent of the people who said they didn't like the taste of kippers had never in their lives tasted kippers!
>
> The Color Research Institute...was testing to see if a woman is influenced more than she realizes, in her opinion of a product, by the package. It gave housewives three different boxes filled with detergent and requested that they try them all out for a few weeks and then report which was the best for delicate clothing. The wives were given the impression that they had been given three different types of detergent. Actually, only the boxes were different; the detergents inside were identical... In their reports the housewives stated that the detergent in the brilliant yellow box was too strong; it even allegedly ruined the clothes in some cases. As for the detergent in the predominantly blue box, the wives complained in many cases that it left their clothes dirty looking. The third box, which contained what the institute felt was an ideal balance of colors in the package design,

overwhelmingly received favorable responses. The women used such words as 'fine' and 'wonderful' in describing the effect the detergent in that box had on their clothes.[22]

What do these experiments reveal, other than the implicit biases of the very people conducting them?[23] It seems to me that the most interesting thing they show is just how deeply our agential reasons may be nested within psychological facts that we have no awareness of whatsoever, and may even distance ourselves from in good faith, without any explicit hypocrisy. The subjects may to a significant degree be strangers to themselves, but does it follow that they are ignorant of their agential reasons?

In the first example people who have never tasted kippers claim that their reason for not purchasing them is that they do not like their taste. Packard assumes that since they do not know – and it may indeed be false – that they do not like the taste of kippers then the alleged fact that they do not like their taste cannot be their reason. But this reasoning is fallacious. Packard might well be right that falsehoods cannot explain why people actually act as they do,[24] but having rejected CVR we now see that there is no reason to take this to show that a person can only act for the reason that p if they know (or at the very least if it is at least the case) that p. I may act for the reason that p even if it is completely irrational for me to believe that p, so long as I do believe it. Packard may have uncovered why the subjects of the first experiment believed that they did not like the taste of kippers (though he does not tell us), but whatever the explanation it could not possibly show that what they took to be their bad taste was not a consideration that they acted upon.

The second example may be deconstructed in a similar way. The subjects are indeed wrong to think that each of the detergents they try has a distinct set of effects, and we are offered a very plausible inference to the best explanation of why they *perceive* their effects as being distinct when they are not. It might consequently be true that there is a psychologically interesting sense in which they would choose to purchase the detergent in the third type of box because of the packaging, but this explanatory reason is not in competition with their agential one and the fact remains that they would choose his box because they think it contains a better detergent, this supposed fact being a consideration that they act upon – viz. their agential reason.

The sorts of studies documented by Packard would later be revived by Nisbett and Wilson:

... passersby were invited to evaluate items of clothing – four different nightgowns in one study (378 subjects) and four identical pairs of nylon stockings in the other (52 subjects). Subjects were asked to say which article of clothing was the best quality and, when they announced a choice, were asked why they had chosen the article they had. There was a pronounced left-to-right effect, such that the rightmost object in the array was heavily chosen. For the stockings, the effect was quite large, with the right-most stockings being preferred over the left-most by a factor of almost four to one. When asked about the reasons for their choices, no subject ever mentioned spontaneously the position of the article in the array. And, when asked directly about a possible effect of the position of the article, virtually all subjects denied it, usually with a worried glance at the interviewer suggesting that they felt either that they had misunderstood the question or were dealing with a madman.[25]

Nisbett and Wilson famously undertook to show that we are largely ignorant of the 'cognitive processes underlying our choices, evaluations, judgments, and behavior',[26] concluding that 'one has no more certain knowledge of the working of one's own mind than would an outsider with intimate knowledge of one's history and of the stimuli present at the time the cognitive process occurred'.[27] Nisbett and Wilson argue that the *real* reason for this ignorance is not simply that we have 'no direct access to higher order mental processes'[28] but, rather, that our mental reports are 'based on a *priori*, implicit causal theories, or judgements about the extent to which a particular stimulus is a plausible cause of a given response'.[29] They conclude:

> ... subjects may have been making simple representativeness judgments when asked to introspect about their cognitive processes. Worry and concern seem to be representative, plausible reasons for insomnia while thoughts about the physiological effects of pills do not. Seeing weight tied to a string seems representative of the reasons for solving a problem that requires tying a weight to a cord, while simply seeing the cord put into motion does not. The plight of a victim and one's own ability to help him seem representative of reasons for intervening, while the sheer number of other people present does not. The familiarity of a detergent and one's experience with it seems representative of reasons for its coming to mind in a free association task, while word pairs memorized in a verbal learning experiment does not. The knit, sheerness, and weave of nylon stockings seem representative of reasons for liking them, while their position on a table does not.[30]

One problem with Nisbett and Wilson's analysis is its deep commitment to such basic conflations as CVB, thereby preventing them from distinguishing between causes of bodily behaviour and reasons for action. This failure is ironic because their own argument unintentionally suggests that laypeople might be making just such a distinction. But if so they would be right to do so: the position of a pair of stockings on a table is rarely, if ever, a reason for preferring them. It could, however, explain why we come to think of them as better knit etc. – even though they are not. What we are fabricating in such a case is not a tale about our agential reasons (those were real as they struck us) but a tale about the quality of the stockings. It is not the subjects who are misled by theory, but the researchers analysing the data. The subjects are quite right to intuitively distinguish between what I have been calling agential reasons, and the cognitive (or indeed conative) nests that underlie them. If those in charge of the experiments explicitly asked them questions about the latter and not 'about reasons for their choices' they may have received very different answers.[31] This not to say that we are aware of all the associations we make, but only that it was common knowledge that we are influenced by all sorts of factors we are not aware of long before empirical science revealed the existence of specific factors that had previously been unsuspected. It is not laypeople who 'cannot correctly identify the stimuli that produced their response',[32] but theorists who cannot correctly specify what they are asking their subjects to explain. It is perhaps poetic justice that these theories do not work for the reasons we are given.

As noted in § 5.1 above, there will be as many reasons *why* a person acted as they did as there are explanatory paths – all equally real. So there is no single fact we can point to as *the* reason why somebody acted as they did, though naturally the number of false accounts available will always exceed that of true ones. It is perhaps more informative to speak of a person's real or true reason *for* their action, namely whatever consideration they *actually* acted upon (assuming there was only one). We saw in § 2.1 that, in everyday parlance, the term 'reason for' is sometimes used to refer to the reasons *why* x happened and that it is consequently important to distinguish between *a* reason/*the* reason for A's doing *x* and A's reason for doing *x*.[33] We may now consider, in the light of this, the following pairs of propositions:

(i)   *The* reason for her choosing product A was the colour of the packaging.
(ii) *Her* reason for choosing product A was the colour of the packaging.
   (a) The reason for the cow's death was BSE.
   (b) The *cow's* reason for dying was BSE.

Nisbett and Wilson conflate (i) with (ii), supposing that, since an agent's reason for choosing *x* could indeed be the reason why she chose it, when it is not so it cannot be the *real* reason for her action but some imaginary one which she has rationalised into existence.[34] Notice, however, that the difference between (i) and (ii) is identical to that between (a) and (b). Yet (b) makes no sense under ordinary circumstances. Similarly, (ii) makes little sense in the sorts of situations described in the experiments above, though one may well consciously choose to buy a product because they like the packaging.[35] It as fallacious, then, to infer (ii) from (i) as it is to infer (b) from (a).[36]

Unlike propositions of the form shared by (i) and (a), propositions such as (ii) and (b) are about agential reasons. A person may hide their real agential reason from others, and we may even come to deceive ourselves about the real reasons behind our past actions not long after we have performed them but, at the moment of action, it is our motives, needs, drives, and associations that we are most commonly ignorant of – not the considerations we act upon. This is not to suggest that we are infallible about our agential reasons at the time of action; this could only be the case if we always acted *from* reasons.[37] Ultimately, criteria for determining what our reasons were are behavioural, but the behaviour in question will include what we tell others and ourselves. These criteria are defeasible , for it is undoubtedly possible to deceive ourselves (as well as others) through rationalisation.[38] Indeed, in § 5.5 I shall be arguing that, to the extent that we buy into certain scientific theories, we risk misidentifying agential reasons, in both our own case and that of others.

off the mark.com   by Mark Parisi

I MADE CHERRY SOUP, CHERRY SALAD, CHERRY-ROASTED CHICKEN AND CHERRY COBBLER IN CHERRY SAUCE...

THE REAL REASON GEORGE WASHINGTON CHOPPED DOWN THAT CHERRY TREE

Consider, for example, a case of doing a small favour for your boss. It is not too hard to convince oneself that one was acting out of kindness or loyalty when in actuality one was equally (if not more) motivated by cowardliness or some other kind of fear. In such a case is one also confused about one's *teleological* reasons – viz. that subset of one's action-guiding aims, desires, goals, intentions, or desires that one acts in the light of? Of course, the intention to perform a kindness for one's boss is very different from the wish to receive a large Christmas bonus or a heavy promotion, and it may well be that we humans can at times and perhaps even systematically fail to realise that we are moved by the latter prospect more than the former goal. That is not up for dispute. What I am questioning, however, is whether in such a case we can, without our realising it, be acting upon the *consideration* that we have the latter goal rather than the former intention. If not, then our ignorance does not relate to the reality of agential reasons but to the existence of some psychological feature.

We saw in § 4.3 that the conflation of motivational facts with facts about teleological reasons is but a special form of CVMR. You may think that you performed a certain action just to make your boss happy when, in actual fact, you were equally motivated by the prospect of your own future well-being. But it would not follow from this that you were acting upon the unconscious thought this would be a good means to achieve this end, let alone that you were consequently wrong to think that you did it because she asked you to, in order to make her happy, and so on. It would take a truly divided personality to be mistaken about such things. Indeed, it is not even clear that a being that is consistently confused about such things would even qualify as a person.

The term 'real reason' is thus being used mischievously by those who claim that the discovery of nesting and/or motivating reasons trumps any beliefs we have about our agential reasons, as if the relation between them were that of actual truth v. mere appearance. In actual fact the term serves to indicate a shift of discourse, from issues pertaining to practical reasoning to the question of background psychology. Our beliefs and desires do indeed 'secretly' move us to act, but they do not do so *qua* reasons for action; we no more act in their darkness than we do in their light. The trouble with Freud is that, for all his claims about the ego not being a master in its own house,[39] he remains an ardent rationalist through and through.

Critics are wrong to dismiss the entirety of Freud as an elaborate hoax.[40] To understand human beings it is not enough to be told their agential reasons. We need to know what motivates us (both as individuals and as members of a species), in particular what moves us to see the world as each of us does, taking what we see to be a reason for acting (or omitting to act) in one way or another. There is much of great value that psychology and cognitive science can teach us here. But what these theories do not do is reveal to us our true agential reasons. These rarely need uncovering, though we may of course quickly come to misremember, or altogether forget, past agential reasons. We may discover surprising psychological truths about why and how this could happen, but the explanations in question would not reveal agential reasons *for* misremembering or forgetting. As Jacques Bouveresse has observed, 'what psychoanalysis teaches us about ourselves may not be primarily, or uniquely, what it thinks'.[41]

5.5   Implicit bias and aliefs

Recent empirical studies have yielded new fascinating insights into implicit associations[42] that affect our daily actions in ways that we are unaware of, and which can only be controlled indirectly through calculated efforts over long stretches of time even once we do become aware of them.

Brave readers may wish to take one of the implicit association tests devised by *Project Implicit*, a collaborative research effort between researchers at Harvard University, the University of Virginia, and University of Washington: https://implicit.harvard.edu/implicit/demo/ selectatest.html.

The research leaves little doubt that implicit associations lead to a range of prejudices or biases that affect our daily interaction with people.[43] Inter alia, they also affect decision-making behaviour relating to education, elections, information, invitations, job hiring, and the workplace, thereby raising concerns in an area of ethics that has come to be known as epistemic injustice, following Miranda Fricker's groundbreaking book of the same name.[44] But despite these developments in scientific testing and ethical awareness, much of the recent literature on implicit associations retains the problematic conflations of its ancestors. Consider, for example, the following remarks on implicit bias by Jolls and Sunstein:

> Theories of implicit bias contrast with the 'naive' psychological conception of social behavior, which views human actors as being guided solely by their explicit beliefs and their conscious intentions to act. A belief is explicit if it is consciously endorsed. An intention

to act is conscious if the actor is aware of taking an action for a particular reason ... In contrast, the science of implicit cognition suggests that actors do not always have conscious, intentional control over the processes of social perception, impression formation, and judgment that motivate their actions.[45]

In a footnote, they add that:

'Naive psychology' refers to laypersons' intuitions about determinants and consequences of human thought and behavior, especially their own. Modern treatments were largely inspired by Fritz Heider's book, *The Psychology of Interpersonal Relations* (1958), which initiated systematic investigation of how laypersons' intuitions differ from scientific understanding.[46]

What is naive, however, is the assumption that our implicit biases *guide* our actions in any way that is in tension with the lay person's reports on her agential reasons and intentions. The difficulty with implicit associations is that they could not possibly work like this; if, *per impossibile*, they did, they would be far easier to detect and control. To have an implicit bias for or against x is to be disposed to view its features in a more positive or negative light than you otherwise would, but it is the features as you see them that guide your actions and intentions. Let me try and illustrate with an example.

   Consider George, who gives a job to Jack instead of Susan because it seems to him that, while they are equally skilled and experienced in all other respects, Jack is a faster typist. George's being perfectly aware that this was his agential reason for giving Jack the job is compatible with his being unaware that (i) Susan is an equally fast typist, if not faster, and/or better skilled and/or experienced in other respects, and (ii) that his false belief is driven by an implicit bias against women. The claim that George gave the job to Jack rather than Susan, not because Jack is the better typist but because George has an implicit gender bias, is strictly speaking true – but highly misleading. It is true because (a) it is false that Jack is a better typist than Susan and (b) George really does have a gender bias which affected his behaviour. But it is misleading insofar as it implies that George was not motivated by the thought that Jack is a better typist, and did not act upon the relevant agential reason. The two explanatory narratives are perfectly compatible, with neither being more real or true than the other (though the narrative in terms of agential reasons may be nested within the implicit bias one, to form former a deeper motivational picture which of the two is more helpful will depend on a number of things, such as how well we know Jack, whether we are primarily interested in background drives or conscious deliberation, and so on.

To try a slightly different example, the psychologist Paul Bloom may well be right to claim that we have a penchant for hidden essences, but could his experimental research really explain – as the subtitle of his most recent book puts it – 'why we like what we like'?[47] The notion is as exaggerated as the thought that any one or more theories could explain 'why we do what we do'. We did not need to await Bloom's research to 'discover' why so many of us prefer expensive cereal to unbranded economy versions – it's because it tastes better to us; and we can even name the ways in which it does so: fresher, crunchier, healthier, sweeter, etc. What experimental psychology can reveal is the placebo mechanism through which expensive cereal tastes this way to us, whilst cheaper packaged (but otherwise identical) cereal doesn't. These facts nest explanations in terms of our reasons for liking or doing things, they do not replace them. It is not as if two types of product both taste identical to us yet we mysteriously prefer one to the other. Rather, our judgement about how they taste is impaired by certain psychological factors whose ultimate basis may prove to be biological, even in scenarios where cultural differences remain highly relevant. If Bloom cannot explain why we like what we like, he certainly can't explain why we want what we want, let alone why we consequently try to do or get it. We want what we want because it appears to us to have certain features that we consciously value. An innate penchant for hidden essences can only explain why we find (or mistakenly think that we will find) certain things attractive.[48] Indeed, Bloom's research may explain why he himself carves his explanations out so neatly.

Tamar Gendler has recently introduced the notion of 'alief' in order to explain behaviour resulting from various arational associations, be they innate or situational, implicit or explicit. She characterises aliefs as follows:

> A paradigmatic alief is a mental state with associatively linked content that is representational, affective and behavioral, and that is activated – consciously or nonconsciously – by features of the subject's internal or ambient environment. Aliefs may be either occurrent or dispositional.[49]
>
> An alief is, to a reasonable approximation, an innate or habitual propensity to respond to an apparent stimulus in a particular way.[50]

Leaving aside the question of whether something may be both a mental *state* and a behavioural *propensity*, I wish to focus on Gendler's account of the role aliefs are thought to play with regard to the explanation of action. Gendler claims that aliefs provide:

> ...an alternative that falls somewhere in between a classic reason-based explanation (of the sort offered by belief/desire accounts) and a simple physical-cause explanation (of the sort offered by accounts that appeal to physical or chemical descriptions).[51]

This alternative, she believes, is required to explain an array of behaviours that otherwise remain stubbornly opaque. Alief, on her view, is what explains:

> ...the tendency of the avowed anti-racist to respond differentially to Blacks and Caucasians – even as she reiterates her commitment to their equality...What explains the tendency of a person who has set her watch five minutes fast to rush, even when she is explicitly aware of the fact that the time is not what the watch indicates it to be? What explains her reluctance to eat fudge shaped to look like dog feces, to drink lemonade served in a sterilized bedpan, to throw darts at a picture of a loved one – even when she explicitly acknowledges that the behaviors are harmless?[52]

Is such behaviour really so difficult to understand without postulating states of alief? To answer this question, I believe, *pace* Gendler, that we need to separate behaviour influenced by explicit associations from that influenced by implicit ones. Consider her example of being reluctant to eat a piece of fudge whose shape is unappealing to us, whilst recognising that the shape does not in any way affect its taste or nutritional properties (such as they are). In the case in which we are aware of our association, *what* is alieved (that the fudge is dirty, or whatever) has the same explanatory function as the belief *that* I make this association. Indeed, the action is not obviously rational, since it may be perfectly justified to refuse to eat the fudge on the very grounds that one associates it with faeces. We may even find someone who lacks such inhibitions peculiar, to the point that their lack of preference regarding the shape of anything they eat is in greater need of explanation ('he must be *really* hungry', etc.).

In the case of implicit associations, no such explanation is available. But there is no reason to suppose that this is because aliefs have some mysterious function that lies between that of being an agential reason for and a cause of our behaviour. A far simpler explanation would be that the associations we are unaware of explain why we misperceived things in such a way that we took some (real or alleged) feature of the situation to be a reason for behaving in a certain way, in circumstances where we would not have done so had we not made the association in question. So understood, implicit associations act as straightforward causes; however, what they directly cause is not our behaviour but the way we see the world. This in turn affects our behaviour in a range of familiar ways. It is true, then, that cognitive scientists discover motivational factors that lend themselves to previously unavailable explanations of behaviour, but the explanations in question are nested ones and not in competition with those of the layperson. *A forteriori*, we should also reject Gendler's conclusions that verbal reports 'tell against' the view that actions activated by aliefs are intentional.[53]

To say that A alieves that *x* is *p*, then, is but a misleading way of saying that she (implicitly or explicitly) associates *x* with *p*. So understood, Gendler is right to claim that actions are 'generated by' aliefs[54] which 'typically activate behavioral proclivities',[55] and that aliefs make people more likely to act one way rather than another. The question of 'alief-motivated behavior',[56] by contrast, is considerably more complex. From a legal point of view, for instance, it is of vital importance that one does not conflate implicit association with unconscious motivation. Consider the question of whether discrimination based on implicit bias was racially *motivated*. It may be equally misleading to say that people are *guided* by implicit aliefs, though not their explicit ones. The liability for acts guided by explicit aliefs is considerably greater than that activated by implicit ones.

The tunnel vision of CVNR continues to cause theorists to misunderstand the way their own theories function. One cannot help suspecting that psychological theories frequently lack relatively basic psychological insight. In misinterpreting their own discoveries, those that produce them either fail to reveal or undersell the true and often fascinating insights of their views. Their exaggerations, when perceived as such, can also deflect attention from important truisms through a wholesale rejection of the views in question. This would be a mistake, for the application of a flawed theory may nonetheless be fruitful.[57] In fact the history of science is replete with muddled or mistaken theories that nonetheless produced results in a non-accidental way which would forever change the daily life of humans, such as Newton's laws.[58] But misguided theories can only work up to a point, for there will always be a context in which the error of the theory will have drastic effects on our applications of it.

In this chapter I have said much about how explanations in terms of our agential reasons *don't* work. The next chapter explores how they *do* work. Agential explanations consist of *statements* revealing that a person acted for this or that reason, complete with all the relevant implications concerning their psychology (thereby presupposing a sufficiently Humean truth). I shall argue that it is a mistake, however, to place any kind of explanatory constraint on the reasons for which we act. The notion of a reason that cannot explain actions may seem paradoxical, but the impression is misleading: we explain actions by citing the reasons for which an agent acted. This account, I maintain, is preferable to the current disjunctive and non-factive alternatives on offer.

6
The Structure of Agential Explanation

In which the author engages with the work of his teacher in a tribute intended to show that all reason-giving explanations are factive. A controversial consequence of this conclusion is that the reasons for which we do things do not themselves explain why we do them.

When I try to put my finger on just why truth is so important to us, what comes to mind most readily is a thought that may perhaps seem unpromisingly banal but that is, nevertheless, unquestionably pertinent. It is the thought that truth often possesses very considerable practical utility.

Harry G. Frankfurt[1]

6.1 Factive reality

We have seen how philosophers disagree about both the ontology of agential reasons and whether or not explanations in terms of them are causal. They almost unanimously assume, however, that agential reasons are alone capable of explaining *why* we act. After all, we are reminded, we can be said to act *because* of them. Thus, for example, Kieran Setiya writes:

> [T]aking something as one's reason, in acting on it, is taking it as an *explanatory* reason, taking it to be a reason that explains one's action (Setiya 2007: 23).

In this chapter I question this assumption, concluding that it is not agential reasons themselves that explain why we act but statements about them. The distinction might seem academic, but it has genuine theoretical consequences that count to its advantage. In particular, it allows us to reject disjunctivist accounts of acting for reasons that are unpersuasive without recourse to the counter-intuitive view that action explanation need not be factive.

The trouble is that things are not always as they appear to be to the agent. If agential reasons are considerations we act upon, then these things (irrespective of whether we categorise them as beliefs, things believed, belief contents, propositions, purported facts, possible states of affairs, etc.) may, on any given occasion, turn out to be false/not be the case. While falsehoods may render an action intelligible by explaining why it *might* have been performed, they cannot possibly explain why it was *actually* performed (let alone why the event of A's performing it occurred). The thought that agential reasons are commonly thought to be capable of explaining action is thus vulnerable to an objection from the possibility of false beliefs.

Dancy bites the bullet and accepts that in those cases where *what* the agent believes is false, her actions may be explained by the falsehood in question – viz. the reason she acted upon.[2] In Dancy's own terminology, action explanations which cite agential reasons are *non-factive*, in the sense that what the agent believes (AR) can explain her action (A) even if it (AR) is false. If this sort of non-factivism holds true then we cannot infer both A and AR from a correct explanation of the form 'the reason why it is the case that *A* is AR'.[3]

It is more natural, however, to think that only *truths* are capable of genuinely explaining anything, of making it *truly* understood, as the title to Christopher Peacocke's book-length defence of realism about meaning would have it.[4] We do, of course, use the term 'explanation' in ways which do not imply that the explanation given is true, and accordingly speak of people offering 'poor explanations' or explaining things incorrectly.[5] However, such explanations are generally thought to be putative, not genuine: they do not *actually* explain anything but merely purport to. A poor explanation of action will at best correctly point to why someone *might* have done something, without offering any true information about why they *actually* did so (as noted in Chapter 2, one can thereby render action intelligible without genuinely explaining it).

Dancy's treatment of the non-factivity of agential explanations as exceptional makes it clear that he is not concerned with mere intelligibility, but with the genuine explanation of actual behaviour. His claim that AR can explain A even if AR is false thus stands in provocative contrast to many people's intuitions.

If falsehoods were capable of providing such real (one is tempted to say *true*[6]) explanations we would care a lot less about the truth of our beliefs than we actually do. The debate between creationists and evolutionists, for instance, would be inconsequential if we were happy to grant genuine explanatory power to falsehoods. This thought should not be confused with an argument from the *metaphysical obscurity* of 'how invoking a putative fact that does not obtain can do explanatory work'.[7] My complaint, rather, is that it is a basic *truism* that to have a genuine explanation of anything the *explanandum* must in some sense, however loose, result *because* of the *explanans* and this can only happen if the latter is actually the case.[8] James Lenman puts the problem as follows:

> The biggest headache for anti-psychologists such as Dancy however is furnished by cases where the agent's belief is *false*. The fact of Angus' being fired is naturally adduced to explain his punching his boss in cases where he has indeed been fired. But in cases where Angus punches his boss, believing mistakenly that he has been fired, it seems quite wrong to say he so acts because he has been fired. In such a case we surely must retreat to a psychologised explanation if we are to have a credible motivating reason explanation at all.[9]

I agree with Dancy's opponents that we should resist non-factivism. Having now abandoned the dubious notion of a motivating reason,[10] however, we have no reason to take Lenman's to be a decisive objection against non-psychologism about *agential* reasons.[11] Both Dancy and his critics are mistaken to suppose that his accounts of non-factive explanation and the reasons for which we act must stand or fall together. The possibility of rejecting (a) non-factivism whilst holding on to (b) non-psychologism about agential reasons becomes apparent once we realise that (a) results from a *conjunction* of three assumptions that incorporate (b) without being reducible to it:

  (i) Agential reasons are considerations external to the mind (non-psychologism).
 (ii) What we consider to be the case may be false (cognitivism).
(iii) Agential reasons are capable of explaining action (agentialism).

I believe we should hold on to (i) and (ii) but reject (iii). Indeed, the problem of false belief may itself be taken to confirm that (iii) is false, though I think that we also have independent grounds against this premise. None of this is to say that agential reasons may not *feature* in action explanations (regardless of the truth of our beliefs), but only that their role is not that of *explanantia*. Much of this chapter is geared at developing the above line of reasoning.

Dancy explains that all he 'was doing in maintaining that reasons-explanation is not factive' was to deny the first premise of an 'apparently sound argument' that 'has a false conclusion',[12] conceding that this approach might lead one, as Aristotle warned, to say 'things that nobody would say unless defending a theory'.[13] While he admits that 'it is odd to suppose that on occasion a nothing (something that is not the case) can explain a something (an action that was done)', Dancy concludes that 'we can live with this oddity. Or rather that it is not as odd as people make out'.[14] I am not so sure about this. But in the penultimate section I make the additional suggestion that, either way, it is unhelpful to suppose that (i) and (ii) entail that it makes sense to predicate truth or falsehoods to agential reasons. Rejecting this hidden premise allows one to resist the conclusion that action explanation is non-factive while holding on to all three of the premises listed above.

6.2   As Dancy believes

Wayne Davis recommends an approach that is similar in spirit to that which I have been pursuing:

> We need to distinguish the claim that actions can be explained by reference to reasons from the claim that the reasons are what explain the actions. The former is true, the latter false. The statement that my reason for saving was that my son will need money for college does explain why I saved. But it does not follow, and is not true, that my reason explains my action. For my reason was that my son will need money for college. That something will be true in the future cannot explain the fact that I did something in the past. Moreover, my action would have the same explanation even if I were wrong in thinking that my son will be going to college.[15]

Dancy has responded by stating that while Davis 'appeals to a nice distinction between saying that actions can be explained by reference to reasons and saying that the reasons are what explain the action',[16] this is of no help to him. The trouble, as Dancy sees it, is that statements of the form 'her reason for A-ing was AR' cannot *in their entirety* be the *explanans* (of her A-ing), for they contain the *explanandum* – viz. 'her A-ing' as a part. He writes:

> After all, 'his reason for ϕ-ing was that p' is equivalent to 'he ϕ-ed for the reason that p', which contains his ϕ-ing as a part. If so, it appears that the *explanans* must be the reason for which he ϕ-ed and that alone.[17]

Dancy takes it as obvious that the *explanandum* is the action itself – viz. his φ-ing – yet it is as contentious to presuppose that the *explananda* in question are actions as it is to assert that their *explanantia* are agential reasons. In claiming that the statement 'he φ-ed for the reason that *p*' already contains the *explanandum* Dancy in fact begs the question against some plausible accounts of the relata of explanations. Hempel and Oppenheim, for example, famously argued that we would do best to conceive all *explananda* and *explanantia* as sentences and classes of sentences, respectively.[18] Alternatively, one could follow Peter Achinstein's 'ordered pair' and 'no product' propositional views, which I sympathised with in § 1.3, and according to which 'we must begin with the concept of an illocutionary act of explaining and characterise explanations, by reference to this, rather than conversely'.[19] To recall, on such a view *explanantia* are best understood as statements of fact whose *explananda* are neither sentences nor phenomena but rather *reperienda* or 'discoverables' – viz. the things we seek to find out (*why* the bridge exploded when it did, as opposed to the actual explosion of the bridge or a sentence describing it).[20]

Achinstein's approach serves to highlight the proximity between *explanandum* and *explanans*, for in wishing to explain why the bridge exploded as and when it did we are after the *reason* it did so. This reason, which we seek to discover, *informs us* of the very thing we want to explain. The reason cannot be specified independently of any understanding of the thing to be explained – and vice versa,[21] which is not to say that either forms a part of the other. *Explanantia* are not contained in statements of the form 'he φ-ed for the reason that *p*' as these are statements *about* what the agent's reason for acting was. As such, they explicitly state what the agent's reason was. But they are not statements *of* the reason nor, per impossibile, *of* the action. This would explain why any implicatures relating to the truth of the agent's belief may be easily cancelled without loss of meaning.

Dancy's non-factive view, in contrast, is that in sentences such as 'his reason for doing it was that, as he believed, *p*', the phrase 'he believed' should be taken appositionally:

> [T]he point of this rephrasing of things is that it removes any suggestion that the explainer is committed to its being the case that *p*. This helps with my second difficulty, which is how 'that p' can explain anything when it is not the case that *p*. A familiar form of argument threatens. Where the agent's belief is false, his reason must be that he believed that *p*. But he will not be acting for a different reason just because he is in the right on the matter. So even when he is right, his reason must still be that he believes that *p*, not just that *p*. I try to undercut this argument

(whose conclusion was already shown to be false by the crumbly cliff example) by denying that explanation in terms of reasons is factive, i.e. that the *explanans* in such cases must itself be the case. First, it is not required for the purposes of the sort of light that reasons-explanations cast on action that things should be as the agent supposed. Second, it seems perfectly possible to continue at least some forms of reasons-explanation with a denial of the contained clause, thus: his reason for doing it was that *p*, a matter about which he was sadly mistaken.[22]

He claims further that the explanatory statement 'his reason for doing it was that it would increase his pension' is not factive, because we can add that 'he was quite wrong' to think that it would do so, without this affecting the explanation in any way:

> If reasons-explanations were themselves factive, as causal explanations are supposed to be, such a continuation would lead to incoherence or contradiction. But no such result emerges. The point of all this is, of course, that if reasons-explanations are not factive there is no need to turn to 'that he believed that *p*' as the agent's reason wherever it is not the case that *p*. Of course it is odd to suppose that on occasion a nothing (something that is not the case) can explain a something (an action that was done). But I maintain that we can live with this oddity. Or rather that it is not as odd as people make out.[23]

But what we infer from the abovementioned explanatory statement is not 'that *p*' but that he supposed that *p*.[24] Dancy claims that the whole statement can be true even if what he calls a 'contained part' might not be. But the phrase 'that it would increase…' is not a part of what is being *stated*, let alone 'the thing that does the explaining'.[25] After all, we are entitled to cancel any implicature that this is actually being stated with no explanatory loss. In Brandomian terms, we have made no discursive commitment to its truth. For we strictly imply only that the agent took things to be a certain way and acted accordingly. This is central to our explanation of the action. Since the statement is not itself an agential reason, we must conclude that, strictly speaking, agential reasons do not explain action.

We are now in a position to resist the thought that 'a thing believed that is not the case can still explain action'[26] without abandoning non-psychologism. What explains the action in such cases, as in the more fortunate ones, is the whole statement. We explain actions by *citing* one or more agential reasons, thereby implying strictly that (a) the agent took *p* and/or *q* to count in favour of her action and (b) acted accordingly. But the explanation is not done by the reason cited. What is stated (implicitly or otherwise) is not the thing that the agent believed but, rather, the purported fact that the person acted upon that belief. If *this* turns out to be false then the statement would fail to provide us with a genuine explanation. Even cases where we wrongly agree with the agent's belief at the time of acting and therefore (successfully) explain their action with a simple 'they did it because *p*', what does the explaining is not the falsehood 'that *p*' but the implied truth that they acted upon the belief that it was. The explanation is only non-factive in the sense that a falsehood can feature in an explanatory statement that is true. The reason cited does not itself even contribute to the explanation. Just as the statement 'this was her cat' can, if true, explain why the animal followed her without the cat being an *explanans*, so the statement 'this was her reason' is capable of explaining why the agent acted as she did.

6.3   Enabling to imply

In a more recent article, Dancy defines 'non-factive' explanations as ones whose correctness does not require 'that what is offered as an *explanans* in fact be the case'.[27] But the *explanans* on offer is not identical to the agential reason, just a statement *about* it. The explanation does not require things to be as the agent took them to be because what the agent took to be the case (regardless of whether she was right or wrong to do so) does not explain her action. Dancy is right to say that 'the fact that he is wrong about whether *p* should not persuade us that his reason was something else, something that he was not wrong about',[28] but this is compatible with the *explanans* not being an agential reason, but a fact about one. Consider his own example of a 'perfectly correct explanation':

(a) His reason for doing it was that it would increase his pension.[29]

If all it took to make an explanation non-factive is the *attribution* of potentially false beliefs, then the above explanation would certainly fit the bill. But (a) itself may well be a *true* statement about his reason. Consequently, it cannot be said to explain, by a falsehood, the very property which Dancy identifies as the mark of non-factive explanations.[30] On such a conception the above explanation would count as factive, for if the statement were false – viz. if it is not true that he acted for the reason that it would increase his pension – it could hardly explain any action. Conversely, if the statement is true, it could explain an action of whether things were actually as we are told the agent took them to be.

It is perhaps possible to distinguish between an explanation and an *explanans* – the latter being only a *part* of the former, namely the part that does the explaining. Dancy seems to suggest as much in writing that 'the whole can be true as an *explanation*, though the contained part, the thing doing the explaining, is not'.[31] I have already questioned the extent to which reasons cited may even count as *explanatory parts* of statements. To this we might add the worry that if only part of an explanation does the explaining, it is unclear what function the rest of it has.

There is an obvious objection to my line of argument so far, namely that when asked to explain our actions we tend to simply state the considerations we (take ourselves to have) acted upon. Similarly, when we explain the acts of others we frequently do so by directly stating their reasons, as follows:

(b) He did it because it would increase his pension.

Are these not instances of explaining an action by stating the reason itself and not through some further statement about what one's reasons are? Not if (b) is elliptical for statement (a) further above, as John Hyman supposes:

> [T]he canonical form of a sentence stating or giving a reason for doing or believing something is 'A F-ed because p' or B believes that q because p.[32]

Dancy (2011) acknowledges the 'factive pressure of the word "because"' but denies that this factive way of giving a reasons-explanation exhausts the possibilities, warning us that 'the selection of one rather than another way of giving a reasons-explanation as canonical' is 'arbitrary and tendentious'. But the fact that no one form is canonical does not entitle us to simply ignore the form given above, for it is not a question of *favouring* the factive form over the teleological (or vice-versa). Rather, all reasons statements must be translatable (without change of meaning) to any of the standard forms of explanation, on pain of failing to qualify as explanatory.

Explanatory statements which cite agential reasons, then, conventionally imply that the agent did indeed act upon the reason cited. This in turn implies (also strictly) that the agent had the relevant beliefs, all of which supports the view that agential explanation consists of statements *citing* our reasons (or facts related to such statements).

These statements form no part of our agential *reasons,* but are made implicitly whenever agential reasons are cited. To mention the consideration one acted upon, in response to a request for an explanation of one's action, is to strictly imply that it was the case; by contrast, to say that one acted for this or that reason, involves no more than a *conversational* implicature about what was the case, and conversational implicatures, it is commonly acknowledged, are easily cancellable without loss in meaning. The statement that this was his reason for doing it is altogether different from the statement that it would increase his pension and the truth of either one is independent of the truth of the other. Only the truth of the former is required for either statement (a) or (b) to explain his action.

I follow Dancy in allowing 'that someone's acting intentionally is always explained partly by her believing something, or that her believing as she does is always at least relevant to the explanation'. I also follow him in denying that we can infer from this that 'the agent's so believing was any part of the reason she had for acting as she did'.[33] Facts about the agent play a crucial explanatory role in statements which cite agential reasons, without being identical to either the statements or the reasons cited. Dancy argues further that the *phrase* 'A's reason for ϕ-ing is that p' is not factive because 'A can act for the reason that p even where A is mistaken about whether p'.[34] But this is only true if non-factivity amounts to no more than the truth of the explanatory statement *as-a-whole* being independent from whether or not it is the case that p.

It is worth undertaking some further Gricean litmus tests by way of comparison. Consider the following statement:

(c) I missed the lecture because I overslept, but this was not a consideration I acted upon.

In the above scenario the explanation is non-contentiously factive: if it is false that I overslept then the attempted explanation is not a genuine one. In stating that I missed the lecture because I overslept, I am implying that my sleeping is a reason that is explanatorily relevant. This implication is strict, it being far from clear what it would mean to state:

(d) I missed the lecture because I overslept, but my oversleeping was not a reason why I missed the lecture.

The reason in question is not an agential one, because it is not a consideration I acted upon. Thus it can be perfectly true that:

(e) I missed the lecture because I overslept, although I had no idea that I had done so.

By contrast we would need to tell a seriously complicated story in order for the following to make sense:

(f) I took an umbrella because it was raining, although I had no idea that it was raining.

This is because 'it was raining', in umbrella-taking contexts, typically functions as an *agential* reason. *Eo ipso*, the following statements also make little sense outside of extraordinary explanatory contexts:

(g) I took an umbrella because it was raining, but this was not my reason for taking one.

(h) I took an umbrella because it was raining, but I did not believe that it was raining.

In so far as I am citing the consideration I acted upon, to cite it is to strictly imply that (i) I acted upon this consideration and therefore (ii) took it to be the case. Such examples stand in stark contrast to Dancy's illustrations of non-factive explanations, which have the following form:

(i) My reason for taking the umbrella was that (as I thought) it was raining, but it was not raining.

I have already conceded to Dancy that it can be true that my reason for acting is 'that *p*, even if it is not the case that *p*. Thus we may say:

(j) She took the umbrella because it was raining, or so she supposed.

Statements such as (i) and (j) are factive, for in what they assert is not to be identified with what the agent in question believed at the time of action (which may be false when the statement itself is true, and vice versa). They are statements about agential reasons and, *inter alia*, agential beliefs. To simply say (in looser language) that she took the umbrella because it was raining would only *conversationally* imply that she took it for the reason that it was raining even though it *conventionally* implies that (a) she believed it was raining and (b) acted accordingly. The truth of the statement is dependent on the truth of both (a) and (b), but not of (c) her supposition that it was raining.[35]

For similar reasons (here echoing Moore's Paradox), statements such as the following two make little sense:

(k) The (purported) rain motivated her to take an umbrella, but she did not take one for the reason that it was raining.

(l) Her reason for taking an umbrella was that it was raining, but she
did not believe that it was raining.

Michael Smith has appealed to related counterfactuals with the aim of
demonstrating that 'while an explanation in terms of a fact presupposes
the availability of a Humean explanation, the reverse is not true'.[36] This
may well be so, but we already saw in Chapter 4 that it is an empty
victory to infer that agential reasons are psychological states. Once we
abandon the notion that agential reasons are capable of explaining
action, the debate between Dancy and Smith evaporates, for neither
side would any longer be entitled to place an explanatory constraint
on the notion of an agential reason. Yet it is such constraints that lead
to both Dancy's claim that falsehoods can explain action and Smith's
suggestion that agential reasons are more closely associated with psychological states than Dancy supposes.[37]

   Smith's observations cannot alone persuade Dancy that psychological facts (including facts about our perceptions of where our reasons lie)
form even *part* of action explanations in terms of agential reasons. This
is because of his neat distinction between reasons and those conditions
which *enable* certain considerations to count as reasons – viz. things
without which reasons could not themselves do the explaining they do.
In his own words:

> There is a difference between a consideration that is a proper part of
> an explanation, and a consideration that is required for the explana-
> tion to go through, but which is not itself a part of that explanation.
> I call the latter 'enabling conditions'.[38]

With this distinction in place, it emerges that what is required for an
explanation to make sense cannot be part of the explanation itself. In
the case in point, facts about the agent's psychology etc. need to be in
place in order for the consideration(s) they acted upon to explain why
they acted as they did, but these facts do not themselves form part of
the explanation being provided (the one in terms of agential reasons):

> The suggestion is therefore that the believing, conceived tradition-
> ally as a psychological state, is an enabling condition for an explana-
> tion which explains the action in terms of the reasons for (that is in
> favor of – the good reasons for) doing it. This condition is required
> for that explanation to go through. That is, in the absence of the
> believing, what in fact explains the action would not then explain

it, either because the action would not then have been done at all, or because, if it had, it would have been done for another reason and so have been explained in another way. But the believing does not contribute directly to the explanation.[39]

While the distinction between enablers and reasons is a solid one, it is unclear that an analogous distinction is available between enablers and explanatory statements. This is because, as we have already seen, what is stated when one offers an explanation in terms of agential reasons is not the consideration that the agent acted upon (which, as Dancy concedes, the explainer need not commit herself to), but *that* she acted upon such a consideration. This implicature is not merely an enabling condition of the statement being explanatory, but the core of the very statement itself. That it forms no part of the agent's reason lends further support to the view that agential reasons do not themselves explain action.

I agree with Dancy that we can 'explain action by laying out the considerations in the light of which an agent acted, without committing ourselves to things being as the agent conceived them to be'.[40] The 'laying out', however, crucially involves numerous implicatures which the explanation is reliant upon. And whilst implicatures about what the agent believes are cancellable, statements that cite agential reasons conventionally imply that the agent acted upon certain beliefs. This is no mere enabling condition, but a core part of the explanation that cites agential reasons. Cancel it and you have no such explanation at all.

To say that agential reasons do not explain action is not to say that we cannot explain action by citing such reasons. To understand why A acted as she did, merely understanding that *p* is not sufficient: one must understand *that* she acted upon the reason that *p*. This brings us to the vexed question of the very nature of agential reasons. In the next section I argue that Dancy's insistence that action explanation need not be factive is ultimately founded on the misguided idea that locutions of the form 'that *p*' refer to certain entities, specifically ones that can in certain contexts be termed 'reasons'.

6.4   Ontological concerns[41]

Wayne Davis has objected that the suggestion that motivating reasons are things that explain actions is undermined by the fact that motivating reasons are intentional objects. Davis argues that to think of reasons as explanatory is to treat instances of the locution 'that *p*' as referential – viz.

as 'occupying the position of a quantificational variable', when in truth such locutions are 'no more referential' than 'to ϕ':

> Motivating reasons are intentional objects. Instances of 'A's reason for ϕ-ing was that p' may be true, and we can explain their truth conditions. But it is misguided to ask 'What sort of thing is the referent of "that p"' therein. It does not have a referent.... We get the same sort of false antimony if we wonder how someone thinking of the perfect husband can be thinking of anything, given that what she is thinking of does not exist.[42]

Dancy responded as follows:

> Davis... appeals... to his view that in 'his reason for ϕ-ing was that p' the 'that p' is not referential. I allow this, taking it to mean that it need not be the case. But I still want to say that something that is the case can explain an action, by standing as the reason for which it was done.[43]

In a more recent publication Dancy expands on this view, suggesting that '"that p" also names an "intentional object" – viz. the sort of thing picked out by the expression "what we believe"' and could thereby qualify as a motivating reason.[44] Yet this is exactly what Davis is denying. His point is not simply that 'that p' is not referential in the sense of 'need not be the case' (as in the misleading analogy with the perfect husband). Davis's point is that when one states that x did A for the reason that p, the that-clause no more refers to something that is not the case than to something that is. One should not mistake this for the nominalist suggestion that (strictly speaking) there are no things believed, for the claim is not about the non-actuality of referents but about the actuality of non-referrers. This is not to suggest that questions such as 'what am I thinking?' have no true answer or to deny sense to phrases such as 'I am referring to the belief that p', but merely to point out that the accusative here is a possible feature of people's psychology and not some mysterious entity 'that p' which may be variously described as a belief, a consideration one acts upon, a fact, a reason, etc.

'That p' is not the name of some object, actual or otherwise, about which it is possible to have various so-called attitudes or states e.g. of accepting, assuming, believing, concluding, considering, disbelieving, doubting, dreaming, expecting, fearing, forgetting, holding, hoping, imagining, judging, knowing, perceiving, predicting, reasoning, regretting, rejecting, supposing, suspecting, taking it to be the case, thinking, wishing, and so on. Nor is it a possible object we could be related to through processes or events such as those of acting upon one's thought, announcing, asserting, claiming, declaring, denying, explaining, exclaiming, implying, indicating, informing one, maintaining, pointing out, praying, pretending, prophesising, proposing, proving, repeating, revealing, requesting, saying, signalling, stating, suggesting, uttering, warning, or writing. If it were, there would be one thing (a *type*, if you like) called 'that *p*' which X suggests, Y predicts, and Z suspects. And yet it would not follow from the fact that X suggested that *p*, Y predicted that *p*, and Z suspected that *p* that Z suspected the *thing* that X suggested and Y predicted but, rather, that he suspected that things would be as X suggested and Y predicted.

Likewise, if A says something silly e.g.that fatty foods are healthier than fruit,it does not follow (indeed it makes no sense to think) that what is silly is *that*fatty foods are healthier than fruit. Nor can we reduce the silliness of what A said to its being silly of A to say it, for in certain contexts it may be very clever of A to say such a silly thing (perhaps her boss has made it his life's motto). To give a final example,suppose that A accepts that it will rain, B hopes that it will rain, C acts upon the consideration that it will rain. It would be a mistake to conclude from all this that A accepts *what* B hopes, namely the same consideration that C acts upon. For the meaning of 'that *p*' *qua* thing believed is different to that of 'that *p*' *qua* consideration *qua* fact, or indeed *qua* reason (cf. Hyman 2011). As Alan White has put it, what is said is not an object to which one does something called 'saying'; and what is translated, filled or interrupted is not an object to which one does something called 'translating', 'filling', or 'interrupting'.[45]

Despite certain parallels in their conclusions, White's argument should be distinguished from. Quine and Prior's proposal (later also taken up by Davidson) that we should parse sentences of the form 'Arthur said that it was raining' as 'Arthur said that/it was raining' rather than 'Arthur said/that it was raining'.[46] Anthony Kenny comes closer to White in responding to Prior with the added suggestion that expressions of the form 'it was raining' are not names either.[47] Philosophers have alternatively been tempted to introduce the technical term 'proposition' as an umbrella term for that which X *believes*, Y *hopes*, and Z suspects – signifying something like 'what is conveyed by a sentence'.[48] This has the absurd consequence, however, that if I am afraid that Russell will come back to haunt me then *what* I fear is (but) a proposition, indeed the very same one that my enemies *hope* (whatever it might mean to hope a proposition). Similarly, I may tamper with the *record* of my statement, but it makes no more sense to talk of my thereby destroying the statement or proposition 'that *p*' than it does to talk of destroying 'that *p*'.[49] What was recorded was the statement conveyed by the sentence used to record it, but this does not entail that what was conveyed stands or falls with the record (though Stalin may have come close to believing something like this). Mutatis mutandis, if I act for the reason 'that *p*' and you exclaim 'that *p*' but then quickly take it back, you do not take back my reason. Nor do you take back your 'token' exclamation, which is why there is no mileage in appealing to the type/token distinction for the purposes of demonstrating that 'that *p*' is a referring term.

White distinguishes between two different senses of the term 'belief': the belie*ving* and the thing belie*ved*, the former being something a person can be said to have and the latter something they believe – viz. that *p*.[50] If what I have been suggesting is right, we should be distinguishing not between two but between *three* different things: the belie*ving*, the belie*f*, and the thing belie*ved*. More importantly for our purposes, it would seem that 'that *p*' cannot be identified with the *reason* that *p* any more than it can with the *reasoning* that *p*. We may, of course, elucidate the concept of an agential reason by reminding ourselves that they are considerations which we may wrongly take to (a) be the case and (b) count in favour of an action, but should not infer from this that agential reasons are themselves sometimes identical to facts, truths, or states of affairs.[51]

It is helpful to look at Latin grammar here,[52] since it highlights the clear distinction between the use of the word 'that' as a verbal clause (as in 'vereor *ut*') and as a noun clause (as in 'vereor *quod*'). This is also true of ancient and modern Greek (e.g. 'πιστεύω πως' or 'πιστεύω ότι' v. 'πιστεύω αυτό', in the modern) and French ('je pense *que*' v. '*ce* que je pense'); the second construction in each pair is demonstrative in the sense that we could say 'I believe *precisely* that', whereas the first is not. By contrast, the English language does not explicitly discriminate between a conjunction in a verbal clause and a relative pronoun, thus making it all too easy to conflate the two through amphiboly. These and other translation exercises confirm that it is a mistake to think that clauses of the form 'that *p*' are typically nominal as opposed to verbal. *A fortiori*, such clauses do not necessarily pick out referents (be they existing or hypothetical), let alone ones that are reasons. In philosophy it has become commonplace to think of them as demonstratives. It is, for example, the assumed starting point of Davidson's highly influential paper 'On Saying That'.[53] But it is telling that the examples focused on are of locutions such as 'that *p*' as opposed to 'whether *p*'[54] or 'to ɸ'.

Even if it were true that agential reasons can explain our action, it would not follow that our actions are sometimes explained by falsehoods. The mischaracterisation of reasons as being true or false is not aided here by the supposition that the clause in phrases such as 'my reason is that p' is a demonstrative one. No matter what the explanatory power of agential reasons, then, no genuine explanation in terms of agential reasons can be non-factive in the sense in which the *explanans* is 'something that may or may not be the case'.[55] A corollary of this outcome is that we must reject Dancy's argument against causalist interpretations of explanations that cite agential reasons, for it relies on the thought that the former are factive but the latter are not.[56] Ironically, philosophers on different sides of the reasons/causes dispute are united in their assumption that agential reasons are alone capable of explaining *why* we act.[57] Until this common assumption is abandoned, all progress in the theory of action explanation will be compromised.

6.5   Disjunctivist moves

Perhaps the most obvious compromise is that of adopting a disjunctivist perspective according to which agential reasons explain action when they are 'true', but not when they are 'false'. Dancy himself has offered general reasons why there need not be any common ingredients between veridical and illusory cases of any given phenomenon,[58] and asserts that, while his own view is that statements of the form 'A's reason for ϕ-ing is that p' do not entail that p, a disjunctive account is worth considering in order to accommodate the doubts of those who disagree with him.[59] One such account has recently been put forth by Maria Alvarez, according to whom our actions are to be explained by *what* we believe in veridical cases and by facts about our believing what we believe when our beliefs are false:

> Dancy thinks that expressions such as 'Her reason for failing him was that, as he supposed, he had cheated, (although he hadn't)' are not strictly speaking contradictory, and he thinks that this suggests that this form of words provides an explanation of her action that is not factive. I think that Dancy is right in saying that such statements allow us to explain the relevant action but wrong in saying that such explanations are not factive. For the *explanans* here is 'she supposed that he had cheated (although he hadn't)'.[60]

Alvarez rightly points out that, in the above sort of case, the *explanans* is the statement *that* she was acting under a certain supposition; a simple statement *of* the presupposition itself will not do if the implicature that she was acting upon the supposition in question is cancelled. Whilst concurring with her opinion that 'it is possible to embrace a non-psychological conception of motivating reasons and yet to reject the view that a true explanation can ever have a false *explanans*',[61] I reject the conclusion she draws from it:

> Dancy's suggestion can be right only for veridical cases; in error cases it must be the agent's believing what he believed that explains his action, since what he believed, being false, cannot be what explains the action. In any case, the believing that 'contributes' to the explanation is a fact, and not a psychological state, even though it is a fact concerning a psychological state.[62]

I have tried to show that we should be wary of the intuition that *what* one believes can ever explain one's action *on its own*; for, in offering an explanation in terms of the considerations upon which an agent acted, we implicitly state that she acted upon such considerations (an implicature which cannot be cancelled without explanatory loss). In fact, 'that *p*' is not the name of any object at all, let alone one that may be further identifiable as a reason. *Mutatis mutandis*, the truth or falsehood of any assertion to the effect that some person acted for the reason that *p* is completely independent from the question of whether or not it was actually the case that *p*.

As things stand, it seems *prima facie* possible that (a) the events of our acting are causally determined by the beliefs and desires which motivate us to act and that (b) these causes are to be distinguished from our agential reasons. In the next and final chapter I explore whether (a) and (b) are indeed compatible by investigating the relations between various kinds of things which we might count as an action explanation. Whilst we have seen how one might go about devising a taxonomy of such things, we should nevertheless expect the answer to any question regarding one form of action explanation to limit the range of answers available to parallel questions regarding another form of explanation. In so doing, I shall be examining Fred Dretske's account of action explanation, which seems to me to be the most promising way of developing a positive account, though my own answer shall be a negative one.

7
Spheres of Explanation

Being the book's final chapter, in which Dretske's distinction between triggering and structuring causes is critically explored. The limits of compossibilities between different spheres of explanation are glimpsed at and a sketch for further research is drawn.

I hear a knock on the door, rise and walk to the door, seize the handle, turn it, and push or pull the door open … What was the reason then? The knock? My hearing the knock? The question: Why did you open the door? could be answered equally well: 'There was a knock on the door' or 'I heard a knock on the door' or 'Somebody was knocking' … But how can *hearing* a knock or a sound, a 'mere' perception or sensation, be a *reason* for doing something?

G. H. von Wright[1]

7.1 Triggers and structures

Much of this book has focused on the theoretical perils of various conflations relating to actions, reasons, and explanation. I have tried to demonstrate that once we separate different notions of each of these things, previously intractable debates dissolve and the truths emphasised by competing views converge to form a coherent picture of how different questions we might ask about action and its explanation relate to each other. So far, I have been emphasising the distinction between different sorts of questions that are often conflated. In this last chapter I investigate what kind of constraints we need to place on some of their relations. In particular, some explanations of why the events of our acting occur will not be compossible with certain explanations in terms of agential reasons.

121

I propose to examine this and other distinctions by looking at Dretske's sophisticated proposal for how causal explanations, in terms of the agent's beliefs and desires, might run parallel to both reason-giving explanations and neuroscientific ones. One of the chief attractions of this proposal, for my purposes, is that Dretske is a non-psychologist with regard to agential reasons. Another is that he distinguishes what we do from the bodily movements involved in our doing it, as well as between two different ways of explaining behaviour. Despite these virtues, however, I shall be arguing that Dretske's account ultimately renders our reasons for action epiphenomenal and must consequently be modified or rejected. I conclude with a brief sketch of what an alternative account of the causation of action might look like, one that leaves space for people to act in the light of agential reasons.

The notion of behaviour, for Dretske, signifies something that creatures *do* as opposed to what *merely happens* to their bodies as a result of some external force:

> [We should not] confuse movements which are brought about by internal events with their being brought about by these events. The former is an event, a movement, something that happens…the second, I shall argue, is a piece of behavior, possibly an action, something the rat *does*.[2]

So understood, behaviour is a causal process and not the result or effect of such a thing. Dretske remains neutral on whether all behaviour, so understood, would count as action, let alone action that is voluntary and intentional (a point I return to further below). Action, for Dretske, is any causal process that may be explained by citing the behaving animal's reasons for undergoing it.[3] His account accordingly identifies behaviour with the causal process of a bodily movement's being caused by an internal event. It thus lies somewhere in between that of von Wright (who identifies action with the process of an agent bringing about a bodily movement) and that of Davidson (who takes actions to consist of the subset of bodily movements that are intentional under some description).[4]

Dretske uses the term 'cause' in two different (though related) senses, distinguishing between what he calls '*triggering* causes' and what he calls '*structuring* causes':

> In looking for the cause of a process, we are sometimes looking for the triggering event: what caused the event C *which* caused the M. At other times we are looking for the events that *shaped* or *structured* the

process: what caused C *to* cause M rather than something else. The first type of cause, the triggering cause, causes the process to occur *now*. The second type of cause, the structuring cause, is responsible for its being *this process*, one having M as its product, that occurs now. The difference…is familiar enough in explanatory contexts. There is a clear difference between explaining why, on the one hand, Clyde stood up *then*, and explaining, on the other hand, why what he did then was stand up (why he *stood up* then). He stood up *then* because that was when the queen entered, or when he saw the queen enter the room. He *stood up* then as a gesture of respect. The difference between citing the triggering cause of a process (the cause of the C which causes M) and what I have been calling its structuring cause (the cause of C's causing M) reflects this difference.[5]

While Dretske does not enter ontological or metaphysical debates about the nature of causes and causal relations, one can infer from his general account that he takes triggering – viz. mechanical or automatic – causes of behaviour to be mental states, events, or processes and structuring causes to be the 'representational contents' of the aforementioned states – viz. things we believe, desire, fear, suspect.[6] Both triggering and structuring causes are taken by Dretske to be capable of explaining something about an event or an occurrence. The opening line of the above quotation suggests that we have one object of explanation (one *explanandum*) to which we can attribute two (different kinds of) causes. But the second half of the passage suggests that there are *two* objects of explanation here: why he stood up *then*, and why he *stood up* then. Dretske there explicitly states that there are two things to be explained, this time identifying one as an *event* (which is caused by the triggering cause) and the other as the background conditions in which the triggering cause causes the event in question (conditions which are caused by the structuring cause).[7]

As Dretske suggests, so long as we are clear about what we are doing it is harmless to refer to both as the cause of one and the same thing. Indeed, this way of putting things may sometimes be preferable, for there are (at least) two different kinds of things we might ask about *any* one given process or event, and – depending on what we are asking (i.e. what we are trying to explain), we will sometimes be looking for a triggering cause, and at other times for a structuring cause of the event in question. However we must not lose sight of the fact that for any given event we have (at least) two different *explananda*. In Dretske's example quoted above these were why an event occurred *now* (we might have also asked why it occurred at this location, or at this speed) and why *that* event – as opposed to some other one – occurred at all. On his view, the former requires a triggering cause as its *explanans*, and the latter a structuring cause:

> A *structuring* cause...helps explain, not why D or M is occurring now, but why, now, D is causing M (rather than something else). Failure to appreciate the difference between bodily movements (or external changes) and the behavior having those movements and changes as a product – hence, failure to appreciate the difference between a triggering and a structuring cause of behavior – is, I suspect, partly responsible for the mistaken idea that whatever triggers the behavior, whatever causes the beliefs (B) and desires (D) that (by causing M) constitute the behavior, must be the ultimate (causal) explanation of that behaviour.[8]

The idea here seems to be that the difference between triggering and structuring causes of behaviour relies on a distinction between behaviour and its products or results. This implies that there are two occurrences to be explained. This in turn requires two different causal *explanantia*:

> The difference helps to explain why one can know what caused each event constituting a process without knowing what caused the process. One can know what caused C (some triggering stimulus S), know what caused M (namely C), and still wonder about the cause of C's causing M. In this case, already knowing the triggering cause, one is clearly looking for the structuring cause of the process – what brought about those conditions *in which* C causes M (rather than something else).[9]

An earlier passage from the same book supports this reading:

> Think of one animal's catching sight of another animal and running away. The approach of the second animal (let this be the stimulus S) causes certain events (C) to occur in the first animal's central nervous system: it *sees* S. Together with relevant motivational factors, these perceptual events in the animal bring about certain movements M: the animal *runs*. To oversimplify enormously, S causes C, and C in turn causes M. This much might be inferred from casual observation – the animal ran *when*, and presumably *because*, it saw the intruder. But why did the sight of the intruder (C) cause flight (M)? Why did the animal run away? The intruder, after all, was not a predator. It was in no way dangerous. It was, in fact, a familiar neighbor. So why did C cause M? This question is a question about the structuring, not the triggering, cause of the process C→M.[10]

Dretske here distinguishes between the triggering cause of event M and the structuring cause of process C→M. But what of the structuring cause of M and the triggering cause of C→M? We have not been told anything about these things. This is because Dretske's distinction between two different sorts of causal *explanantia* is really a disguised distinction between two different *explananda*, each of which has a different explanatory cause. It makes no sense to say of each of these *explananda* that they have both a structuring and a triggering cause. Rather, what we want is a causal explanation (provided by C) of why the (mere bodily) movements M (running) occurred and a separate causal explanation for why C→M (the entire process of C causing M) occurred. What we are looking for here are not two different causes of one and the same event (e.g., in the sense that we might ask two different things about it), but rather two different causes, each of which explains the occurrence of a different event (or process).

Consider this further example of Dretske's:

> The bell rings (S), and this produces a certain auditory experience (C) in the dog. The dog *hears* the bell ring. These sensory events, *as a result of conditioning*, caused saliva to be excreted (M) in the dog's mouth. What, then, causes the dog to salivate? Well, in one sense, the ringing bell causes the dog to salivate. At least the bell, by causing the dog to have a certain auditory experience, triggers a process that results in saliva's being secreted into the dog's mouth. Yes, but that doesn't tell us why the dog is doing what it is doing – only why it is doing it *now*. What we want to know is why the dog is salivating. Why isn't it, say, jumping? Other (differently trained) dogs jump when they hear the bell. Some (not trained at all) don't do much of anything. So what causes the dog to salivate? This clearly, is a request, not for the triggering cause of the dog's behaviour, but for the structuring cause. It is a request for the cause of one thing's causing another, the cause of the auditory experience causing salivary glands to secrete. And once again, it seems, the answer to this question lies in the past, in what learning theorists describe as the *contingencies* (correlations between the ringing bell and the arrival of food) to which the dog was exposed during training. If salivation is thought of as something the dog *does* (not simply as a glandular event occurring *to* the dog or *in* the dog) – if, in other words, it is thought of as *behavior* – then the causal explanation for it resides, not in the stimulus that elicits the behavior, but in facts about the dog's past experience.[11]

For Dretske's purposes, classical (Pavlovian) conditioning plays the same functional role as operant (Skinnerian) conditioning, genetic determination, upbringing, duress, or any other cause that structures emitted behaviour (be it intentional or otherwise[12]). In the above case we are informed that the event of the dog's salivating has both a triggering cause (the ringing of the bell) and a structuring cause (that the dog was exposed to correlations between the bell's ringing and the arrival of food), but that the causal explanation of the dog's *act* of salivating is typically provided by the structuring cause alone. The fact that the dog was exposed to certain correlations does not explain (causally or otherwise) why saliva was excreted from the dog's mouth but, rather, why the ringing of the bell caused him to salivate. That is to say, it does not explain why M occurred, but why the C→M process – which Dretske identifies with the dog's behaviour – occurred. By the same token, the ringing of the bell cannot (alone) explain why the dog salivated. For that we need both the triggering and the structuring cause: the dog salivated because the bell rang and he had already been subjected to the aforementioned training. Both these facts form parts of one and the same causal explanation of why the dog salivated. Only the second fact, however, provides a full causal explanation of a different *explanandum*, namely that of why the dog salivated *when the bell rang*. Dretske is wrong, then, to imply that the answer to the question 'why did the dog salivate?' is one and the same with the answer to the question 'why did the dog salivate *instead of* jump?' (see § 3.3).

The triggering/structuring distinction is equally applicable to events and processes that are not actions, be they natural or consequences of a creature's behaviour. To illustrate, in an episode of the television comedy *Flight of the Conchords* one of two musicians spends $2.79 on a new mug, resulting in their having insufficient funds in their account to cover the phone-bill cheque. They are consequently charged an overdraft fee which causes their cheque for the gas bill to bounce, which in turn leads to their power being cut off. What triggers the overdraft fee is the phone-bill cheque. The process of its doing so may be structurally explained by the purchase of the mug, insofar as this purchase triggers the process of the phone-bill cheque's bouncing. However the underlying structural cause of why it does *this* will be whatever fact explains why the pair of musicians were so near their limit to begin with – viz. the facts that explain why it only took one mug to cause all this calamity. Conflating the two objects of explanation is no trivial matter. Indeed, the perils of identifying triggers as the causes of systematic failure are neatly captured by Nassim N. Taleb and Mark Blyth:

> Humans simultaneously inhabit two systems: the linear and the complex. The linear domain is characterized by its predictability and the low degree of interaction among its components, which allows the use of mathematical methods that make forecasts reliable. In complex systems, there is an absence of visible causal links between the elements, masking a high degree of interdependence and extremely low predictability. Nonlinear elements are also present, such as those commonly known, and generally misunderstood, as 'tipping points.' Imagine someone who keeps adding sand to a sand pile without any visible consequence, until suddenly the entire pile crumbles. It would be foolish to blame the collapse on the last grain of sand rather than the structure of the pile, but that is what people do consistently, and that is the policy error.
>
> U.S. President Barack Obama may blame an intelligence failure for the government's not foreseeing the revolution in Egypt (just as former U.S. President Jimmy Carter blamed an intelligence failure for his administration's not foreseeing the 1979 Islamic Revolution in Iran), but it is the suppressed risk in the statistical tails that matters – not the failure to see the last grain of sand.[13]

The question 'why did the sand pile collapse?' could be understood either as a question about what triggered the event of its collapsing or as a question regarding the underlying structure that enabled *x* to trigger it. These are two different objects of explanation. Analysts who provide 'tipping point' answers to questions about system failure are making a logical mistake that is hugely costly. Conversely, answers to questions such as 'why did *Harry Potter* become a best-seller?' or 'why did the young Bob Dylan achieve such fame?' that appeal solely to the qualities of the subjects in question point to structural causes which render the *explananda* intelligible, but cannot explain them without appeal to situational triggers (be they individual or collective).[14]

7.2   Structuring reasons

Dretske appeals to his distinction between triggering and structuring causes with the aim of showing how it is that psychological explanations of behaviour differ from non-psychological ones such as, for example, biological explanations. He concludes that intentional human behaviour is triggered by electro-chemical events but structured by so-called 'representational facts', facts about how we view the world.[15]

When we seek an explanation of intentional action in terms of an agent's reasons, Dretske maintains, we are always looking for a structuring cause that is internal, in other words, intrinsic to the system whose behaviour we are seeking to explain. Unlike plant behaviour, which is never intentional and whose structuring causes are always external – |that is, extrinsic to their system – human behaviour is to be, at least typically, explained in terms of the agent's beliefs and desires.[16]

There are some distracting similarities between this account and that made famous by Davidson: both allege that reasons are causes of behaviour and that these are further identifiable with the agent's beliefs and desires.[17] These are, however, fairly superficial. For not only do their accounts of action differ greatly, they also conceive of causes in radically different terms. According to Davidson the term 'cause' refers to that which 'causally explains' the event that is its 'effect',[18] whereas Dretske takes structuring causes to causally explain why something triggered the event that is the result of the entire triggering process. He maintains further that an agent's beliefs and desires – in the sense in which these may be called reasons for his behaviour – are not to be identified with psychological states or events. This is because explanatory reasons for action, on his view, are not reasons which cause the occurrence of a bodily movement but, rather, reasons for a person's bringing about a bodily movement. Dretske consequently holds that agential reasons are to be identified with so-called mental contents – viz. 'what a creature knows and wants'.[19]

In Chapter 6 I argued that agential reasons do not themselves explain action. In the same spirit Dretske makes it clear that the structuring causes that explain movements [M] are not agential reasons but rather (representational) facts *about* our psychology. These he contrasts to the triggering causes said to cause 'states' of desire (D):

> [W]hat makes it true to say that the rat presses the bar *in order to get food*, that getting food was the rat's *purpose* or *reason for pressing the bar*, that the rat pressed the bar because it *wanted* food, is that the rat's movements (M) are being caused, in part at least, by an internal state D, having food as its goal; and the explanation of *why* D is causing M, and hence an explanation of the behavior, is the fact that D has this goal, the fact that D is, specifically, a receptivity to *food*. It is this fact that explains D's recruitment as a cause of M and, thus, helps explain the rat's current behavior.
>
> The fact that a hungry rat, furiously pressing a bar in order to get food, occupies state D, a state that was recruited as a cause of bar-pressing movements because, *in the past*, these movements led to food does not, obviously, explain why D *now* exists, why the rat is *now* hungry. Nor does it explain why M is now occurring. D's having R as its goal, its being *for* R, is not a triggering cause of behavior. It is a *structuring* cause. It helps explain, not why D or M is occurring now, but why, now, D is causing M (rather than something else). Failure to appreciate the difference between bodily movements (or external changes) and the behaviour having those movements and changes as a product – hence, failure to appreciate the difference between a triggering and a structuring cause of behavior – is, I suspect, partly responsible for the mistaken idea that whatever triggers the behavior, whatever causes the beliefs (B) and desires (D) that (by causing M) constitute the behavior, must be the ultimate (causal) explanation of that behavior.

Triggering causes of behaviour, Dretske maintains, are neither agential reasons for our actions, nor causes of them. Rather, they are those (neural or perceptual) events which trigger beliefs and desires, thereby causing our movements M. Structuring causes of behaviour, by contrast, are both (a) things which we believe and (b) reasons for which we act. Reasons are causes then, but only of the structuring sort; the triggering causes of our behaviour are not reasons for which we act, as depicted in Figure 7.1 below (arrows signify – and reveal the direction of – a causal relation).

We saw in § 7.1 above that (on Dretske's account) behaviour – be it intentional or otherwise – is to be identified with the process that is

Triggering Causes (Events):
Stimulus (S) → Beliefs and Desires (B&D) → Bodily Movements (M)

|S————————→———— B&D ————————→————M|
S → B&D   B&D → M
(my coming to acquire certain   (my moving my body)
beliefs and desires)

Structuring Causes (Facts): Reasons which explain why B & D → M
(why my moving of my body occurred/why I moved my body)

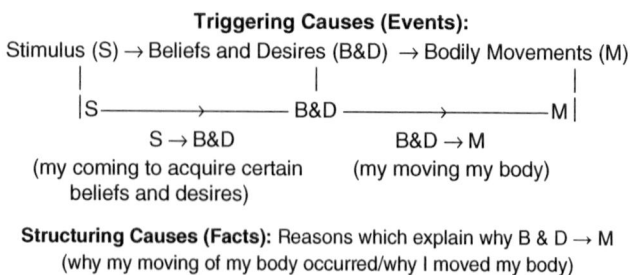

Figure 7.1   Moving my body

the *causing* of M.[20] In the case of *intentional* behaviour M will always be caused (triggered) by a belief (B) and desire (D). This is a necessary but insufficient condition, unless the explanation provided by the related structuring cause is teleological in nature. For Dretske, teleological explanations are ones wherein the reason which structurally causes the behaviour does so in virtue of the *meaning* of the 'representational contents' in question. Accordingly, action is intentional if and only if its structuring cause explains why B and D caused M by virtue of its meaning and not some other property.

   The point about meaning is not in itself new. Consider, for example, the following passage by the early modern philosopher William Wollaston:

> When I begin to move myself, I do it for some reason and with respect to some end. But who can imagine matter to be moved by arguments, or ever rankled syllogisms and demonstrations among levers and pulleys? Do we not see, in conversation, how a pleasant thing will make people break out into laughter, a rude thing into a passion, and so on. These affectations cannot be the physical effects of the words spoken because they would have the same effect, whether they were understood or not. It is therefore the sense of the words which is an immaterial thing, that by passing through the understanding, and causing that which is the subject of the intellectual faculties to influence the body, produces those motions in the spirits, blood and muscles.[21]

Wollaston's mistake is to conflate the structuring cause of an action (the meaning) with its triggering cause (the physical sounds). We may thus attribute to him the *Conflating View of Triggering Structures* (CVTS):

> Actions and/or events are causally triggered by their explanatory structures.

The materialist determinist Joseph Priestley responds to Wollaston's argument by equating the triggers of bodily movements with *reasons*:

> ...since it is a fact that reasons, whatever they may be, do ultimately move matter, there is certainly much less difficulty in conceiving that they may do this in consequence of their being the affection of some material substance, than upon their belonging to a substance that has no common property with matter. It is acknowledged that syllogisms and demonstrations are not levers and pullies, but neither are the effects of gunpowder, in removing the heaviest bodies, produced by levers and pullies, and yet they are produced by a material cause. To say that reasons and ideas are not things material or the affectations of a material substance, is to take for granted the very thing to be proved.[22]

Priestley thereby assumes the truth of the *Conflating View of Triggering Reasons* (CVTR):

> The reasons for which we act are the causal triggers of our actions.

CVTR is to be distinguished from the Davidsonian thesis that reasons causally explain action. The latter may well be so in some suitably weak sense, though not in the way that Davidson assumes (given the argument of Chapters 3 and 4).[23]

Pace both Wollaston and Priestley, Dretske has clearly shown that the sense of words can influence us purely materially, without the trigger of our action being an agential reason. The structuring causal role played by meaning here enables him to distinguish between explanations in which a belief–desire pair 'rationalises' an action (for instance when a climber loosens her hold *in order to* rid herself of the weight and danger) and ones where the same pair causes the same type of action in some non-rational manner (e.g. by making the climber nervous, which, in turn, causes her to loosen her hold). This successful method of meeting the challenge presented by so-called 'deviant causal chains' (in which belief–desire pairs cause the behaviour they rationalise in a non-rational manner) constitutes a serious theoretical advantage over causalist theories such as Davidson's, which cannot appeal to teleology here because they are in the business of providing a *reductive* account of what it is to act intentionally.[24]

The question remains, however, whether Dretske is right to maintain that in such cases agential reasons nonetheless function as the structuring causes of our actions. In what follows I answer this question negatively, raising an objection to his proposed necessary and sufficient conditions for an action being intentional. To anticipate, I shall conclude that, while Dretske's account of action explanation is superior to other causalist accounts, it remains based on a picture which ultimately fails to distinguish between intentional actions and instinctive non-intentional behaviour (of creatures); whose explanation is still teleological in nature – for example, actions that are neither intentional nor unintentional. Reflex actions are an obvious case in point, and it is to acts of this form that I now turn.

7.3   Enchanting causes

According to Dretske, the difference between instinctive non-intentional behaviour and intentional action is that, in the case of the former, our beliefs and desires (though present) play no *relevant* role in the production of our behaviour:

> Meaning, though it is there, is not relevantly *engaged* in the production of output. The system doesn't do what it does, C doesn't cause M, *because* of what C (or anything else) means or indicates about external conditions. Though C has meaning of the relevant kind, that is not a meaning it has *to* or *for* the animal to which it occurs. That, basically, is why genetically determined behaviours are not explicable in terms of the actor's reasons. That is why they are not *actions*. [25]

In other words, the structuring causes of reflex actions are external, and the explanation of instinctive behaviour is no different from the explanation of the behaviour of plants. This is surely right for certain non-intentional actions, but it is wrong for many others. The following case, for example, suggests that meaning may sometimes play a role in the explanation of involuntary, non-intentional action.

Suppose that I am walking down the street and somebody calls out 'Constantine'. Their doing so may cause me to turn my head toward the direction their voice is coming from. If asked why I turned my head that way, I will reply (rightly) that I heard someone call out my name. This reason (the fact that someone called out my name) causally explains why the sound they made in doing so triggered the event that

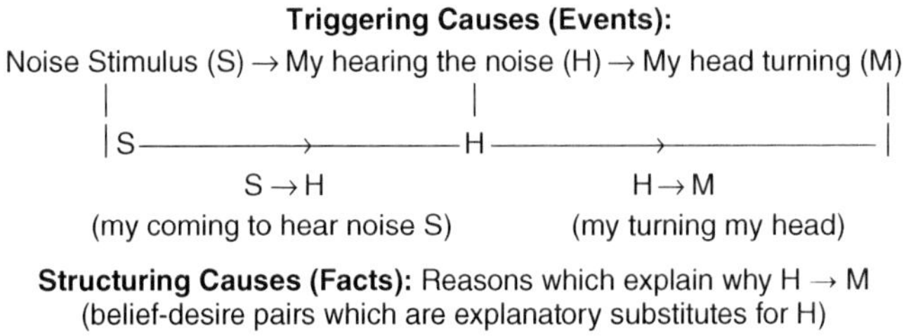

Triggering Causes (Events):

Noise Stimulus (S) → My hearing the noise (H) → My head turning (M)

| S————————→————————H————————→———————— |

S → H   H → M

(my coming to hear noise S)   (my turning my head)

Structuring Causes (Facts): Reasons which explain why H → M
(belief-desire pairs which are explanatory substitutes for H)

Figure 7.2   Turning my head

was my head turning around. As Figure 7.2 illustrates, the reason is the structuring cause of my behaviour whilst the noise stimulus exerted by the person calling my name is its triggering cause.

Hearing the noise causes me to turn my head because of the 'content' of the noise, because of what it means to me. It is because the word uttered is that of my name – or sounds like it to me – that I turn my head. If what is being uttered is given a purely physical (rather than a linguistic) description, then we will not ordinarily understand why these noises caused me to turn my head.[26] This fact (the reason why I turned my head) is therefore of great explanatory value to us – but it does not trigger anything. It is my hearing the noise that triggers the turning of my head, not what the noise stands for, what it means, or – in Dretske's terminology – what it represents.[27]

Nevertheless, it is in virtue of the meaning of the sounds uttered (and not the physical properties of the sound waves being transmitted) that this causal process takes place; the meaning of the sounds structures the (non-deviant) causation Moreover, it could have been sufficient (for my head to move) that I thought or believed that someone had called out my name (and that I had the relevant desire; see below). Suppose it turned out that what had actually been said was 'constantly'. The fact that my hearing this word being uttered caused me to turn my head (because I thought I heard 'Constantine') does not render my behaviour any more intentional.[28] Likewise, we may assume that I wanted to see who was calling my name. Had I been differently disposed (say that, for some reason, I wanted to be left alone), then my hearing my name (or my thinking that I heard my name) would not have caused me to turn my head (but perhaps to run, or hide). So it makes sense to think of my beliefs and desires as the structuring causes of my non-intentional behaviour. But what this means is that it is the fact that I have these beliefs and desires that is the structuring cause of my behaviour. There is a sense in which my beliefs and desires may be said to cause my head to move; however, what causally explains my moving my head (the reason why I moved it) is not a belief–desire pair itself but the fact that I have those beliefs and desires. Facts about our psychology may explain why we do certain things, and they may do so causally (in the sense that they point towards a cause), but it would be ontologically perverse to identify them with any mental episodes that trigger bodily movements of any kind.

My behaviour will count as intentional, on Dretske's view, if and only if this is so. Indeed, for Dretske, intentional behaviour *is* a movement being caused (in the 'right way') by a belief–desire pair. But although my wants and thoughts causally explained why I turned my head, I did not turn my head intentionally. Nor was I motivated to do it (and I certainly did not turn my head in the light of any reasons). To say that that you calling my name caused me to turn my head is just to say that my head turned when you called my name. I did not set out to turn it, nor did I turn it for an agential reason – though there is, of course, a reason which explains *why* I turned it. We should not, in such cases, conflate any teleological reasons we may give after the fact with our motivation (which will have been entirely absent in cases of non-intentional action).[29] We can, no doubt, imagine someone who, in turning his head, acts upon the consideration that someone called their name, perhaps taking this to be a good reason for turning his head. The point here is only that this need not be so when a person turns his head because someone has called out his name, or something that sounded like it.

Anscombe has persuasively noted that the attempted contrast between 'having hung one's hat on a peg because one's host said 'hang your hat on that peg' and 'turning around at hearing someone say Boo!' fails because whether or not we should view either action as one performed for a reason is to be decided by facts such as those relating to 'how sudden one's reaction was'.[30] Whether or not the triggering of any reaction is to be explained by a fact about what (if anything) the words meant to the person acting is neither here nor there. *Mutatis mutandis*, the question of whether one acted for a reason, or was merely caused to act, remains open in certain cases of actions that have exactly the same structure as the one which Dretske provides for intentional action. In the case of turning my head described above, some internal events – viz. my hearing, or my believing I heard, you call my name and my wanting to see who it was – in some way mediated between the initial triggering cause (calling my name) and the effect (my head turning), where this mediation played a causal role. Thus, the sound waves transmitted did not directly cause my head to turn (that would not have been a case of action at all – reflex or otherwise – but more like one's hair, or in the case of Mary Poppins her entire self, being blown by the wind), yet we could not confidently describe a sudden action of this type as being intentional.

Let me try a second example. In Gail Carson Levine's modern fairy tale *Ella Enchanted*, the imprudent fairy Lucinda casts a spell on Ella which causes her to 'always be obedient' – her behaviour triggered by 'commands' (typically uttered by her wicked half-sisters) which she literally cannot resist 'obeying'. Here is how Ella describes her own predicament in the novel:

> Anyone could control me with an order. It had to be a direct command, such as 'Put on a shawl,' or 'You must go to bed now.'... against an order I was powerless... I could never hold out for long. [31]

The nature of the curse entails that Ella's behaviour – which is without question beyond her immediate control – is non-intentional, i.e. neither intentional nor unintentional. Ella's behaviour is in no way *motivated* by the curse: she does not reason (consciously or otherwise) that she is under a spell and therefore has reason to obey. Crucially, the curse has the causal function of a desire without any accompanying desire-like phenomenology. The nature of the curse thereby entails that Ella's behaviour – described as being beyond her control – is non-intentional (i.e. neither intentional nor unintentional).

Levine's novel gives little detail as to whether Ella retains executive control over which means she uses to attain any given end, but it wouldn't be much of a spell if it left her free to choose the means most likely to fail in any given case.[32] I therefore stipulate, for the purposes of this thought-experiment, that her engagement in means–end reasoning is not properly practical: when ordered to kill the prince she loves then she does not desire to do anything that is likely to bring about his death, in either of the two senses of desire distinguished in § 4.3. She neither craves to kill him nor intends to, and yet she is behaviourally compelled to kill him.[33] If she is ordered to do x, and she believes that y is the most efficient way of bringing it about, Ella will involuntarily do both x and y without intending to do either (or, for that matter, anything else).[34] Accounts of the will in terms of second-order desires cannot help here, for Ella does not merely find herself acting upon first-order desires she would rather not have, she does things that she has absolutely no desire (of any order) to do, things that she despises with *all* her heart.[35]

The spell itself, whilst a structuring cause, does not operate as an agential reason of Ella's: her belief that she is under it plays no part whatsoever in determining the involuntary behaviour which the spell causes. The possibility of enchanted behaviour such as Ella's suggests that we should reject a purely behavioural account of what it is to act upon a reason, such as that offered by von Wright:

> An agent understands a knock as a reason for opening a door if, and only if, on hearing a knock he, normally, proceeds to opening the door unless he is physically prevented or has some stronger reason against doing this.[36]

The important factor here, omitted from von Wright's general analysis above, is that Ella is not following the commands given to her by her sisters but merely being caused to behave in a way which accords with them.[37] Indeed, we are told that Ella is constantly trying to stop herself from doing what she is told (and thereby caused) to do, it is just that the attempts always fail and she gets increasingly frustrated with this. In sum, the curse disposes her to do whatever she is told by paralysing her will to do otherwise.

Be that as it may, the causation is not of a brute kind, akin to that involved in reflex action or a nervous tic, for the *meaning* of any 'command' uttered to Ella (typically by one of her wicked half-sisters) plays a clear structural role in the causation of her behaviour. The expressions which cause Ella's behaviour are effective because of their (real or projected) *semantic* 'content', because Ella (who speaks American English) understands what the words used mean. Commands in languages that Ella does not understand are useless: they cannot make her do what the commander intends.

Both examples fit Dretske's account of intentional action as being *triggered* by physical events (e.g. of perception) but *structured* by the 'representational content' of what was seen or heard. If my characterisations of them are correct, Dretske's model cannot provide a criterion by which we can distinguish the explanation of intentional action from that of non-intentional behaviour. It is perhaps no wonder, then, that he also describes the behaviour of a bird avoiding a noxious type of bug as intentional,[38] a characterisation also favoured by Davidson's criteria.[39]

It may be objected that in both the head-turning case and that of Ella Enchanted, I have assumed an understanding of what makes an action intentional that others might find counter-intuitive.[40] Indeed, one anonymous reader asked if I would permit an objection to my argument in the form of 'a science fiction novel in which a creature named Ella Strange appears who lives in a cosmos in which logic, reality, truth, psychological experience, and so on, are all changed from that with which we are familiar'. How should one proceed from such an impasse? I believe that in the case of conceptual analysis, facts about logical possibility and ordinary usage trump all intuitions – regardless of whether they are thought to result from common sense or theory, be it *a priori* or empirical. A related strategy that has recently become very popular is that of conducting a conceptual survey or experiment. Investigations of this kind could reveal interesting facts about the conceptual and psychological intuitions of certain groups of people (and I shall be publishing my results in a separate paper), but I cannot see how this sort of experimental philosophy could possibly determine whether or not the intuitions are correct.[41]

A more promising, mutually compatible, suggestion is to view the very dispute as evidence for the possibility that we are here dealing with borderline cases that our everyday notions of 'intentional' and 'non-intentional' do not extend to one way or another. If so, the case would call for a conceptual decision rather than a discovery of some kind. I am not myself convinced that the examples I have given fall into this category, but the mere possibility of such cases suggests that whether or not an action is intentional is a matter of degree rather than of kind. This should in turn cast doubt on any theoretical attempt to spell out necessary and sufficient conditions for an action's being intentional.[42] Be that as it may, it remains possible that some (further specifiable) cases of a movement's being produced by one's beliefs and desires are indeed cases of intentional behaviour. For all I have shown, Dretske's analysis may have isolated necessary conditions for an action being intentional, despite failing to pick out sufficient ones.

7.4   Discontent with content

A different sort of response to the counterexamples offered in the previous section would be to narrow the Dretskean analysis of what it is for an action to be intentional by inserting the very notion of an agential reason straight into it. On such a revised view, intentional actions are processes of a bodily movements being caused by belief-desire pairs whose contents constitute agential reasons.

One potential obstacle to such a strategy is Hursthouse's counterexamples to the claim that all intentional actions are done for reasons; these include such actions as tearing one's hair or clothes in grief or clutching a picture or possession of a recently deceased loved one.[43] A second obstacle takes the form of challenges to the parallel assumption that all actions performed for reasons are intentional.[44] If either of these persuade, then reasons cannot be the mark of intentional behaviour. While in sympathy with both concerns, I remain neutral on these issues here, for I believe that the revised Dretskean analysis fails regardless. Let me illustrate with an example.

Suppose I raise my arm to wave to a friend. The Dretskean analysis of my behaviour can be pictured thus (Figure 7.3).

Suppose further that stimulus S constitutes my seeing my friend across the road, and that S causes me to acquire the belief that my friend is across the road, and the desire to wave to her, and that this belief–desire pair further causes my arm to rise. According to Dretske, the triggering cause of my behaviour (my raising my arm) is stimulus S, and the structuring cause is made up of the fact that – as I believe – my friend is across the street, and the further fact that I want to wave to her. Dretske himself illustrates such a point with a diagram of the sort depicted in Figure 7.4 below.[45]

In Dretske's terminology, B and D come to *represent* S (the structuring cause of M) by indicating S, and are consequently recruited as triggering

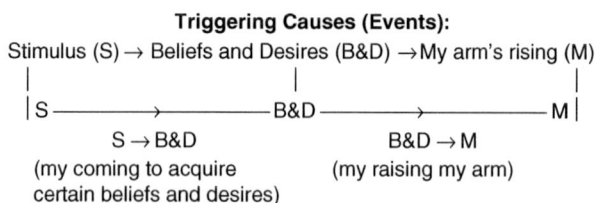

Triggering Causes (Events):

Stimulus (S) → Beliefs and Desires (B&D) → My arm's rising (M)

| S ————————→———————— B&D ————————→———————— M |

S → B&D   B&D → M
(my coming to acquire   (my raising my arm)
certain beliefs and desires)

Structuring Causes (Facts): Reasons which explain why B&D → M
(why my beliefs and desires caused me to raise my arm).

Figure 7.3   Raising my arm

causes of M. As we have already seen, my reason for acting on this view is not B and D, nor (typically) the fact B and D are true of me, but rather the 'content' of B and D. But now a problem arises: if M is triggered by my belief(s) and desire(s) proper, then – although it is causally relevant that these beliefs and desires have a (meaningful) content – I will have many other (competing) belief–desire pairs with meaningful content that may also be capable of rendering the same action intelligible. Content alone cannot tell us which belief–desire pair triggered the action, for – as we have already seen in § 3.3 – I may at any given time have several pairs whose content could render my action intelligible. In sum, the purported explanation of action provided by Dretske's structuring causes cannot reveal why one particular belief–desire pair triggered the action rather than another (with an equally suitable 'content'), and *a fortiori* cannot (by his own lights) determine which of her reasons were the ones she acted upon.

It won't do to respond that the belief–desire pair that triggered my bodily movement was whichever one was (motivationally) 'strongest', for the information required to settle such matters cannot be derived from a Dretskean structuring reason.[46] The challenge is that of distinguishing between being motivated to act upon some consideration and actually acting upon it, without falling into some version of CVMP.[47] On Dretske's account, our agential reasons are simply those related to whichever belief–desire pair leads us to action. The trouble is that mental 'contents' alone cannot pick these out. The account offers no method of determining *which* 'mental contents' constituted the reason(s) for which the agent acted, leaving us with no demarcating criterion for intentional action. As demonstrated in Chapters 4 to 6, facts *about* my psychology may indicate a triggering cause (thereby explaining why certain features of my psychology caused me to move my body) but 'mental contents' alone cannot do so. What I believe can, for instance, render my action of moving my arm intelligible without explaining why the movement was triggered by any one of an indefinite number of (internal or external) factors. Yet this is exactly what a Dretskean account of action explanation requires.[48]

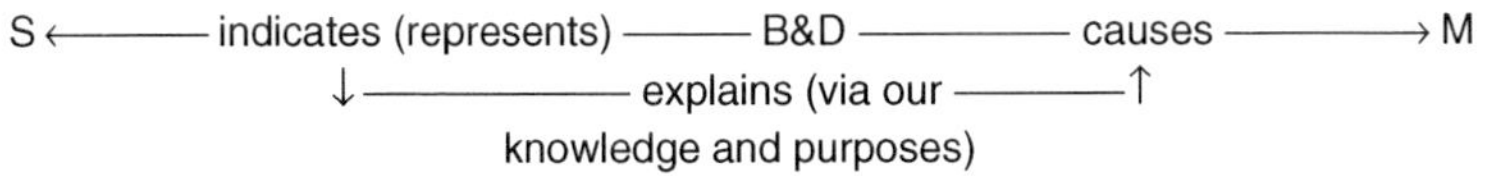

S ←——— indicates (represents) ——— B&D ——————— causes ——————→ M
      ↓ —————— explains (via our ————↑
                  knowledge and purposes)

Figure 7.4 Indicating stimuli

7.5   Explanatory compossibilities

The above does not demonstrate conclusively that the event of one's act-ing for a reason cannot be causally determined by a mental process, but it does suggest that we have yet to witness a plausible account of their compossibility. Regardless of whether or not such an account is avail-able, we may still allow that our beliefs and desires can *causally* explain why an action occurred and that they do so by picking out the elements of our psychology which moved us to action; for example, by causing us to see something as a reason – as suggested in Chapter 5. Such causal explanations will paradigmatically specify factors which increase the probability that any given action will occur.[49] It is thus amenable to the sort of science that Hume envisages for human action.[50]

The relative failure of psychological determinism, however, is cause enough for an investigation of alternative causal stories that are com-possible with everyday truisms about our agential reasons. A popular move, related to the distinctions covered in § 1.2, is to distinguish the causation of a (mere) bodily movement from that of an action. The former could no doubt be given in neuroscientific terms.[51] But, as D.G. Brown contends, it is equally 'intelligible and informative to say that a person's hand moved *because* he moved it'.[52]

Does this commit us to some sort of agent-causation? There are numer-ous answers that one can give here. One could, for example, claim that what is caused is not actions themselves but the bodily movements that they result in[53] maintaining further that causings are not events but rather 'instances of the relation expressed by the verb "cause"'.[54] An alternative option is to highlight the absurdity of thinking 'that some-thing should bring about the causing of an event',[55] or indeed that is A causes *x* there must exist some further event of A causing *x*,[56] in the robust sense in which such an event must itself have a cause. These sug-gestions may be further combined with a constitutivist view, according to which *in* raising my arm I make it the case that the process/event of my raising my arm occurs, without there being a distinct event of my doing so. Whether or not we are to count this as a case of 'causation' seems to me to be an arbitrary semantic choice.

Thankfully, the assessment of these and other proposals falls beyond the scope of this book. My chief aim in it has been to show that many disputes central to the theory of action and its explanation arise because those involved share a common mistaken assumption involving some kind of conflation between two or more objects of enquiry. The end result is a complex net of explanations that cannot be fully mapped out without knowledge across a large number of fields including biology, cultural studies, history, literature, neuroscience, philosophy, physiology, psychology, and social science. These may combine to give us a more complete picture of human nature, but there is no such thing as *the* complete explanation of a human action, any more than all the facts of the universe could serve as the complete explanation of an event. Indeed, there can be no clear understanding of human nature unless we cease to conflate different spheres of explanation. That said, I hope to have shown in this last chapter that knowledge belonging to one of these spheres can constrain the range of plausible explanations in another. Understanding these constraints better is vital for any prolegomena to interdisciplinary research.

Appendix I
The Ontology of Action

In which the metametaphysics of action is discussed with a particular focus on the work of Hornsby, Davidson, and Dancy.

So in philosophy all that is not gas is grammar.

Ludwig Wittgenstein[1]

1 That Thing You Do

According to Hornsby, when we talk of doing things we are ontologically committing ourselves to the existence of *things* we are doing. The term 'action', she maintains, is ambiguous because it can refer either to such things (e.g. raising one's arm), or to the events of our doing them (e.g. the raising of one's arm), which she equates with our doings. The latter appear to be particulars with spatio-temporal locations, whereas the former are not. The general line of thought here is one that I have been largely sympathetic to in this book. The event of one's doing something is typically denoted by nominals of the form 'my moving of my arm' or 'my moving my arm', whereas the things we are doing (which cannot be said to occur) are referred to by phrases of a slightly different form, such as 'moving my arm'. Accordingly, the sentence 'moving my arm was a mistake' expresses the same proposition as 'it was a mistake to move my arm', whereas 'my moving of my arm was a mistake' seems grammatically ill-formed and does not obviously express a proposition at all.[2] Be that as it may, I should like to voice some reservations about Hornsby's ontology of action. These will in turn also lead to criticisms of the Davidson's alternative.

In a footnote in her book *Actions*, Hornsby makes the following observation:

> It must be acknowledged that many phrases with a form superficially similar to that of 'his raising of his arm' do not denote events. I am inclined to think that some nominals (e.g. 'my eating of a cream bun') unambiguously denote events, and that, where such event-denoting nominals can be found, there are nominals of a slightly different form (in this case 'my eating a cream bun') which need not denote events. (Whether tokens of this other nominal denote events or not will usually be determinable in context).[3]

I have argued in §§ 1.1 and 2.2 that we should not equate my moving my arm with the event *of* my moving my arm. If Hornsby is right, the latter is best identified with my moving *of* my arm. Hornsby allows that phrases of the form 'my moving my arm' may *sometimes* denote an event, but what do they denote when this is not the case? She postulates certain entities – viz. things done – as the answer, suggesting that – unlike events – these entities cannot be particulars:

> [T]here are many philosophers, who, although they are explicit about believing that some nominals are true of events, seldom use nominals that are plausibly so: they are more likely to say [i] 'Anna's eating the apple' than [ii] 'Anna's eating of the apple'. Notice that of these two nominals, only [ii] (which I use) has any of the following three properties (a) it can be pluralized; (b) 'Anna's' in it can be replaced by an article, (c) the residual verbal element in it can be modified with adjectives (not adverbs). The fact that [i] has none of these properties makes it implausible that it stands for any *particular*, for any event.[4]

This passage leads Davidson to attribute to Hornsby the view that the things we do are universals, an outlook which he subsequently proceeds to criticise:

> Jennifer Hornsby wants to cling not only to the distinctions we usefully make in ordinary language but also to its surface ontology, whereas I am somewhat cavalier about departures from our common idioms when I think such departures make for semantic clarity. Most of her points depend on taking locutions like 'what Susan did' as *literally referring* to *entities* of some sort...she balks at saying the action (taken as a single event) is something Susan did, since 'She did an action', or 'She did an event' or 'She did Susan's firing of the gun' are not acceptable sentences of English...Well first of all there is a question of what sorts of entities these doings are. The only suggestion Hornsby makes is that they are they are universals, *sorts* of actions. This makes sense of the 'correspondence' between descriptions and doings: on my account our descriptions bring an action under a universal by *using* a predicate; Hornsby does it by *mentioning* the universal. She suggests that avoiding talk of universals may be a motive of mine in talking of descriptions, but this is not the case. I have no objections to referring to universals when it promotes some explanatory or semantic project. But does it here?
>
> There is something strange in the suggestion that when we ask what someone did we are asking for the *naming* of a universal. We don't say 'She did an action', but neither do we say 'She did a universal'. The things people do are in this world; they are not *Platonic abstractions*. Clearly expressions like 'set light to a fuse' or 'eat breakfast' are not referring expressions in English. Hornsby says these phrases refer to actions, but if so we need much more help than she gives us to see how to convert them to recognizable names or descriptions of anything, actions, kinds of action, or universals.[5]

A similar interpretation of Hornsby's distinction is offered by Dancy, who offers further criticism:

> I don't see the pressure to announce that things done are not particulars ... possible things done are not particulars, but actual things done are particulars (variously describable etc.) ... to think of things done as universals is of no help if we are trying to understand the sense in which what is done can be wrong. If

I say, in a given case, that what you did was wrong, am I predicating wrongness of a universal? I think that such predication is unintelligible. It might be that all instances of that universal are wrong, and wrong *as such*; but this would not make the universal itself wrong. A further question which I don't know how to answer is whether an action is to be thought of as a particular instance of a thing done – in fact, as an instance of many things done. If so, all Hornsby's distinction amounts to is a distinction between action-universals and particular actions. And though there is that distinction, it is odd to say that the relation between a doing and a thing done is the relation between particular and universal – the same relation as that between an object and a property.[6]

But Hornsby's view is considerably more complex than either Davidson or Dancy allow, albeit in a way that is by no means unproblematic. The trouble is that Hornsby has muddied the waters by maintaining that the things we do are frequently denoted by nominals such as 'my eating the cream bun'. Indeed, given the truism that if I am eating my cream bun then *what* I am doing is eating my cream bun and not *my* eating the cream bun, it would appear that Hornsby holds a *Conflating View of What is Done* (CVWD):

What I do when I *x* is my *x*-ing.

Unlike *what* I do when I eat a cream bun, *my* eating the bun may coherently be described as a particular. It is most likely CVWD, then, that leads Hornsby to make an otherwise perplexing 360-degree turn in her later writings and claim that the things we do *are* particulars:

Action, because it terminates in the objective world, is inherently particular. *What is done* is necessarily this particular act. No doubt similar changes might occur which are not deeds but natural happenings. But the deed which is the uprooting of this particular tree at this particular time under those particular conditions is dependent for its *occurrence* on human action. Apart from the acting this particular change would not have occurred.[7]

Pace Hornsby, what I do is *uproot* this particular tree not *the uprooting* of IT, though I may be engaged in its uprooting,[8] for – as Hornsby herself claims here – *the uprooting* of that tree is, by contrast, something which can *occur* (a process or event), marked by a nominal which meets all of Hornsby's own criteria for denoting a particular:

(a) It can be pluralised
(b) 'My' has been replaced by an article
(c) The residual verbal element in it can be modified with adjectives (not adverbs).

In rejecting the view that the things we do are particulars I do not mean to suggest that they are universals. One position one might take here is the one adopted by Hornsby in her 1980 book *Actions*:

I speak, as other English speakers do, as if we were committed to the existence of the things we do. Whether we accept that that gives us reason to think that there really are such universals as things done is on a par with the question whether we accept that there are things had because we find sentences like 'Wisdom is something he has'. I do not attempt to answer these ontological questions.[9]

In the later essay against which Davidson's comments above were directed, Hornsby similarly suggests that we should be prepared 'to introduce into theoretical generalizations about agency the locutions that are used every day, and save it for another occasion to decide whether all mention of universals needs to be banished'.[10] This seems right insofar as the denial that there are any things which we do is absurd, whatever our view of universals. But the question remains, and what better occasion to attempt to answer it than an appendix on the ontology of action?

Davidson's reservations about the things done being universals is as good a place to start as any. The crux of Davidson's worry above was that there is something problematic about taking our everyday sentences to refer to universals if these are surplus to the requirements of our explanatory scheme of things. He insists that the term 'action' *always* refers to an event because he has ontological qualms about there being any 'things' which we do:

> Much of our talk of action suggests that there are such *things* as actions and that a sentence like 'Jones buttered the toast in the bathroom with a knife' *describes* the action in a number of ways. 'Jones did it with a knife.' 'Please tell me more about it.' The 'it' here doesn't refer to Jones or the knife, but to what Jones did – or so it seems.[11]
>
> The word 'action' does not very often occur in ordinary speech, and when it does it is usually reserved for fairly portentous occasions. I follow a useful philosophical practice in calling anything an agent does intentionally an action, including intentional omissions. What is really needed is some generic term to bridge the following gap: suppose 'A' is a description of an action, 'B' is a description of something done voluntarily, though not intentionally, and 'C' is a description of *something* done involuntarily and unintentionally; finally suppose A = B = C. Then A, B, and C are the same – what? 'Action', 'event', 'thing done' each have – at least in some contexts – a strange ring when coupled with the wrong sort of description. Only the question, 'Why did you (he) do A?' has the generality required. Obviously, the problem is greatly aggravated if we assume, as Melden does, that an action (raising one's arm) can be identical with a bodily movement ('one's arm going up').[12]

For Davidson, then, the things we do intentionally are sometimes best described as actions, sometimes as things done and sometimes as events. Accordingly, if what we do is raise our arms, and our doing so (our raising our arm) is a bodily movement (event), then what we have done is an event, awkward as that may sound, indeed this seems to be Davidson's complaint against natural language. In sum, Davidson takes CVA to be true, carrying this view over to the explanation of action, as demonstrated by his claim that '[w]hat I am asked to explain is my shooting of the bank president',[13] thereby also committing himself to CVAE.

He does all this in the full knowledge that many will be tempted to draw a distinction between the things we do, and our doings of them:

> Jones did it slowly, deliberately, in the bathroom, with a knife, at midnight. What he did was butter a piece of toast. We are too familiar with the language of action to notice at first an anomaly: the 'it' of 'Jones did it slowly, deliberately, ...' seems to refer to some entity, presumably an action, that is then characterized in a number of ways. Asked for the logical form of this sentence, we might volunteer something like 'There is an action x such that Jones did x slowly and Jones did x deliberately and Jones did x in the bathroom...' and so on.[14]

Davidson believes that we should resist such temptations, maintaining instead that:

> The solution lies...not in distinguishing acts from events, but in finding a logical form for action sentences.[15]

Davidson argues that all talk of things we do can be captured by quantifying over events, without any loss in meaning. This supposedly confirms that expressions such as 'what you did' have no further referent, a strategy parallel to that which he makes in relation to expressions such as 'what you said'.[16] Davidson's overall aim here is to demonstrate that our ordinary talk does not commit us to the existence of entities named 'things we do' or 'things we say'. In § 7.5, focusing primarily on the notion of things we *believe*, I suggested that there is some truth to this view – not because such expressions refer to concrete particulars, but because there is an important sense in which they don't refer at all.

If Davidson's project were successful, it could hardly show that we never do things. The reduction of statements of one form to statements of another may show that we can carry on communicating as before without mentioning the things which the former statements quantified over, but this does not entail that the former statements were false. At most, a new conceptual scheme will have been developed, namely one which doesn't include reference to these things and yet still manages to communicate what was being said in the old language which had made reference to them.

The possibility of such a scheme involves no metaphysical revelations, but merely the withdrawal of meaning from certain (previously meaningful) phrases. The chief benefit of characterising the logical form of any given sentence is the clarification of original meaning, not metaphysical revelation. Bede Rundle puts it well:

> In characterizing the logical form of a sentence the concern is to lay bare those features which are relevant to the deductive interconnection of that sentence with others.... We may readily grant that a given sentence allows of a paraphrase in which a problematic term comes to function in a way that is no longer problematic, or in which the problematic term has been replaced altogether, but this may or may not serve to explain the behaviour of the term as it occurred in the original. Clearly, that question will remain untouched if it is admitted that the original use was problematic and that this is not the

use invoked in the translation … might not the translation … somehow serve to make clear the true structure of the original? Why shouldn't grammar be misleading as to logical form? Indeed, why shouldn't 'surface' grammar be misleading as to 'deep grammar'? We could, it is true, define a particular logical or grammatical function in such a way that whether or not a term had that function depended on there being the possibility of certain transformations of the sentence in which it occurred, so on moves which took us away from the original form of words. Thus if we wished to know whether 'ravishing' was intended verbally or adjectivally in 'He likes ravishing women', we might well ask whether the formulation, 'He likes women who are ravishing' would not be a close approximation to the sense of the original…. There is nothing amiss with definitions of this kind; it is just that it must be possible to say, given these transformations, that the term has the function in question in the original, and not just in a related sentence in which it may occur, since otherwise its role in the former is so far uncharacterised. Whether or not a noun is a grammatical object in a given sentence may depend on the legitimacy of a passive rendering of that sentence, but it is precisely the role in the original sentence that the possibility of the transformation establishes.[17]

M. Alvarez (1999) has convincingly argued that (a) the simplest way of formalising action sentences requires quantification over the results of actions, not actions themselves, and (b) even if it were true that action sentences are best formalised in the manner favoured by Davidson this would, in any case, not entail that actions are events. Further below (in § 3) I offer a new argument for why Davidson's project of paraphrasing all sentences mentioning things done with sentences quantifying over events instead cannot succeed. First, however, I should like to also lend support to Alvarez's second conclusion. I shall do so by reviving an old line of argument against the view that ordinary language harbours metaphysical commitments.

2 Grammatical movements

The temptation to think that talk of things we do commits us to the existence of entities of some sort (be they universals or particulars) stems from the false supposition that verbs like 'is' and 'are' carry metaphysical import. This is the sort of category mistake which Ryle warned us about in the opening chapter of *The Concept of Mind*:

> It is perfectly proper to say, in one logical tone of voice, that there exist minds, and to say, in another logical tone of voice, that there exist bodies. But these expressions do not indicate two different species of existence, for 'existence' is not a generic word like 'coloured' or 'sexed'. They indicate two different senses of 'exist', somewhat as 'rising' has two different senses in 'the tide is rising', 'hopes are rising' and 'the average age of death is rising'. A man would be thought to make a poor joke who said that three things are now rising, namely the tide, hopes, and the average age of death. It would be

just as bad a joke to say that there exist prime numbers and Wednesdays and public opinions and navies; or that there exist both minds and bodies.[18]

One need not agree that the example of minds is analogous to Ryle's other examples to appreciate the absurdity of the suggestion that to say that somebody did something is to postulate the existence of some kind of entity. The things we do are no more entities than are the indefinite number of descriptions we might fix to any given event. I do not share the Quinean dream of bare desert landscapes that motivates Davidson's ontological parsimony. Far from being led to metaphysical pluralism as a result, however,I maintain that expressions such as 'all I did was eat my breakfast' do not refer to any kind of entity (universal or otherwise) for which we have names (such as 'eat breakfast').

Likewise, although it is true that we do all sorts, kinds, or types of things, this does not mean that the things we do *are* sorts, kinds, or types, but only that they fall under them.

In § 7.5 I suggested that phrases of the form 'what I believe' have no referent: if I believe that it is raining and you pretend that it is raining, this does not entail that there exists a thing named 'that it is raining' that I believe and you pretend, be it a universal or a particular. By the same token, I now wish to suggest that phrases of the form 'what I did' have no referent either: if what I did (raise my voice) was impolite, that does not mean there exists some thing we term 'raised my voice' that was impolite and which I did, you remembered me doing, she resented, and so on. As with belief, this does not mean that there is no sense in which I may be said to refer to what I previously did, or am still doing. I am not, that is, making the negative existential claim that we never do (say, believe) anything, or that there is, strictly-speaking, nothing that anybody ever does. Indeed, it is a mistake to take our ordinary language to be ontologically committed – be it rightly or wrongly – to anything, and the existence of things we do is no exception. As Wittgenstein warned, we should not conflate statements made within a language-game with those aimed at elucidating its norms:

> You interpret the new conception as the seeing of a new object. You interpret a grammatical movement that you have made as a quasi-physical phenomenon that you are observing. (Remember, for example, the question 'Are sense-data the stuff of which the universe is made?'). But my expression 'You have made a "grammatical" movement' is not unobjectionable. Above all, you have found a new conception. As if you had invented a new way of painting; or again, a new metre, or a new kind of song... [when] one disapproves of the expressions of ordinary language (which, after all, do their duty), we have got a picture in our heads which conflicts with the picture of our ordinary way of speaking. At the same time, we're tempted to say that our way of speaking does not describe the facts as they really are. As if, for example, the proposition 'he has pains' could be false in some other way than by that man's *not* having pains. As if the form of expression were saying something false, even when the proposition *faute de mieux* asserted something true. For *this* is what disputes between idealists, solipsists and realists look like. The one party attacks the normal form of expression as if they were attacking an assertion; the others defend it, as if they were stating facts recognized by every reasonable human being.[19]

Wittgenstein's target here is perfectly real. D. H. Mellor, for example, explicitly subscribes to the methodology under attack (indeed he denies that there is any truth to *either* of the aforementioned claims, and in so doing helps us to understand how they are connected):

> It's true that you can unearth serious metaphysical assumptions hidden in our language, and it's important to do that. But the most important issues – for example in the metaphysics of time – do not arise just because language has been misused and cannot be settled just by not misusing it. Whether time really flows, for example, is a serious question, which cannot be settled that way. Ordinary language presupposes that it does, but that can be shown to be a mistake. The metaphysical assumptions of ordinary language are no more infallible than the Pope is.[20]

I have tried to suggest that Mellor is wrong to think that our ordinary language hides metaphysical assumptions, mistaken or otherwise. Rundle offers an insightful elaboration of the kind of error I have in mind:

> [M]uch contemporary 'ontologizing' proceeds as if based on something like the following recipe: you subject ordinary language to gross distortions, reading your own confusions into its innocent idioms; you then dismiss these idioms because of what you claim to have found them to imply, and you replace them by a formulation in which deviant uses of the vernacular are coupled with the symbolism of formal logic, presenting the result as a significant technical advance over the incoherences of ordinary language. A good example here is the way events are sometimes dealt with. The question, 'Are there events?', odd though it may strike us, is surely to receive the same answer as 'Does anything ever happen?' – an emphatic 'Yes'. However, there is a shift to an interpretation along the lines of 'Are events entities?', or 'Are there such entities as events?', and not surprisingly the inappropriate term 'entity' presents us with an issue whose sense is no longer clear and leaves the way open for a semi-formal version which retains the obscurity, or, alternatively, for an explicit rejection of the ordinary notion of an event.[21]

Rundle chose events as his example (earlier on in the same passage he talks of numbers) but he may as well have been talking about the things we do. Indeed, in a later book he does just this:

> Compare the inference from 'why he did it is clear' to 'something is clear'. The term 'something' is trivially allowable in lieu of the clause; its introduction does not require that the clause supplanted should *designate* something – which it plainly does not – nor that the clause itself should be what is affirmed to be clear. For one who seeks illumination as to what precisely is being said to be clear, it is to no avail to reiterate the given clause, 'why he did it', let alone the bare 'something', but we should look beyond the immediate grammatical form to a more perspicuous expansion: what is being said to be clear is the answer to the question, 'why did he do it?'[22]

We can similarly infer 'there was something he did' from 'what he did was reasonable', though neither phrase designates an entity, let alone one that is reasonable, sensible, etc. Such deflationist thoughts lead Jonathan Dancy to claim that actions cannot be described independently from the agents that perform them.[23] This suggestion, whose important ethical ramifications virtue-theorists have been reminding us of for some time, seems to me to hit the nail on the head. Dancy thus defends an adverbial approach to things done according to which 'he did the right thing for the wrong reasons' should be understood to mean something like 'he acted rightly, but for the wrong reasons'.[24] The term 'rightly' does not here characterise a way of acting but, rather, that he was right to do what he did. One can do the right thing in both a right and a wrong way: it might have been right (sensible, etc.) of him to move the carpet, but not to move it in the manner in which he did – i.e. he might not have moved it rightly (sensibly, etc.) even though he 'rightly, moved it'.[25] Indeed, it is quite commonplace to both praise and object to the *way* someone did something (tactfully, carelessly, etc.) as opposed to *what* they did. If what he did was to move a carpet, then to say that what he did was right is not to say that there was an entity named 'move a carpet' that was right but, rather, that it was right *of him* to move the carpet.

I part ways with Dancy, however, when he consequently denies that 'there really are such things as things done or actions in any sense beyond what one might call the grammatical', maintaining instead that 'both the acting and the thing done are more like grammatical constructs than items for which we need to find an independent place in our metaphysics'.[26] I have tried to show that the choice between metaphysical entity and grammatical fiction does not exhaust our options. Hans-Johann Glock, writing about verbs that take that-clauses, suggests that the word 'what' in the expression 'what I said' does not introduce the name of a thing but a propositional clause.[27] Presumably, this is not meant to imply what I said *is* a propositional clause, but only that it is *specified* by one.

Perhaps Dancy's grammaticalism can similarly allow that (i) we may legitimately talk of things we do and that in doing so (ii) we are not referring to grammatical clauses. What it rules out, so conceived, is a conception of *things* people do according to which *what was done* is analogous to *what was eaten* e.g. a cake (to steal Glock's example). *Pari passu*, to say 'I applaud what you did' is not to say that there is a thing called 'what you did' that is identical to another thing called 'what I applaud'.[28]

Part of the complication here is that the sense and extent to which conceptual clarification involves the location of items in our metaphysics depends on one's understanding of metaphysics, particularly in relation to whether conceptual questions can be completely separated from ontological ones (and vice-versa).[29] There is a great difference, after all between Collingwoodian and Strawsonian metaphysics, on the one hand, and Quinean and Davidsonian ones on the other – to say nothing of Lewisian and metaphysics. In final part of this appendix I revisit Davidson's attempt to demonstrate that all talk of things done can be captured by sentences that only qualify over people and events. To anticipate, I shall offer certain kinds of explanatory and normative sentences as counter-examples to Davidson's general thesis.

3   The logical form of reason sentences

Davidson claims to be able to show that all phrases of the form:

(a) A buttered the toast slowly, deliberately, in the bathroom, with a knife, at midnight.

are identical in meaning to phrases of the form:

(b) There is an event x, which was Jones's (slow and deliberate) buttering of the toast (with a knife), which occurred in the bathroom, at midnight.

It is by arguing that (b) captures the true logical form of action sentences that Davidson attempts to dispense with things done, consequently understanding all talk of our reasons for acting as talk of the reasons for which our actions (events) occur.[30] In doing so he embraces CVRA:

The reasons for which we act are reasons *for which* our actions occur.

When I say 'Jones buttered the toast in the bathroom' there is little doubt as to what I am asserting. Yet Davidson thinks that he has shown that this was just an elliptical way of saying that there was a buttering of the toast – by Jones, in the bathroom; for we cannot transform action sentences into logical notation without quantifying over *events*, yet we *can* do so without quantifying over things *done*. Even if such a thing were true, it could not follow that Jones did not do something – namely butter the toast in the bathroom. So there is nothing wrong with the suggestion that:

(c) There is an action x such that Jones did x slowly and Jones did x deliberately and Jones did x in the bathroom.

Does this not capture the logical form of (a)? Here is how Davidson describes the enterprise of getting the logical form of action sentences straight:

I would like to give an account of the logical or grammatical role of the parts or words of such sentences that is consistent with the entailment relations between such sentences and with what is known of the role of those same parts or words in other (non-action) sentences. I take this enterprise to be the same as showing how the meanings of action sentences depend on their structure.[31]

But we do not need to reveal any logical form to know what 'Jones buttered the toast in the bathroom' means. This should make us wonder whether Davidson's 'ontological reductions' are as important as he makes them out to be, but it doesn't show that they cannot be achieved. I now proceed to argue that for certain sentences his project is indeed bound to fail – i.e. that there are sentences about what we do which *cannot* be translated into statements about events.

Importantly – for our purposes – these are statements which mention reasons for action.

According to Davidson's remarks concerning the logical form of action sentences, all talk of action can be reduced to talk of events, including talk of our reasons for action. But now consider the following statement:

(a*) A's reason for buttering the toast in the bathroom was that the rest of the house was out of bounds.

According to Davidson, this is identical in meaning to:

(b*) There was an event x, which was Jones's buttering of the toast in the bathroom and which occurred because (he believed that) the rest of the house was out of bounds.

But (b*) doesn't capture the meaning of (a*) since (a*) is – but (b*) is not – a statement that explains why Jones did what he did – by pointing to the consideration which Jones acted upon, whereas (b*) can only be read as a statement attempting to explain why the particular event of Jones's buttering the toast in the bathroom occurred. Moreover, as Davidson himself would agree, the fact that the rest of the house was out of bounds does not even explain why the event in question occurred. We could of course insert a belief into (b*), as I have done above, but now what explains why the buttering occurred is not the actual consideration which Jones acted upon ('that the rest of the house was out of bounds'), but rather the fact that he had a certain belief (about the rest of the house being out of bounds).

Alternatively, Davidson could try and translate (a*) as:

(c*) There was an event x, which was Jones's buttering of the toast in the bathroom and which Jones did for a reason.

However this appeals to there being something which Jones did (an action) for a reason. So we might as well say that:

(d*) There was an event x such that Jones did x in the bathroom because the rest of the house was out of bounds.

The problem with (d*) is that to say this is to accept CVA:

A person's actions consist of the things she does e.g. her movings of her body.

Yet we have seen that we cannot coherently identify the things we do with the events of our doing them. Moreover, Davidson himself finds such sentences problematic because we 'need an appropriate singular term to substitute for x' and because 'there is no implication that any *one* action was slow, deliberate, and in the bathroom though this is clearly part of what is meant by the original'.[32] But this is clearly not what was meant in the original since it does not make sense to say that *what* Jones did (butter the toast in the bathroom) was slow or deliberate, but only that his doing it (his butter*ing* the toast in the bathroom) was slow and deliberate (i.e. that *he* did it slowly and deliberately). The trouble seems to be that Davidson accepts a version of CVD:

My doing *x* is identical to the event (process, etc.) of my doing *x*.

Attributing CVD to Davidson allows us to reconstruct his reasoning as follows:

P1. If I buttered the toast intentionally then *my buttering* the toast was intentional.

P2. We may talk of *the event of my buttering* the toast.

P3. The event of my buttering the toast is identical to my buttering the toast.

C. If my buttering the toast was intentional then the event of my buttering the toast was intentional (under some description).

We saw in §§ 1.2 and 2.2 why it is a mistake to identify the event of *x* with *x* itself.We can describe my buttering the toast as an action that was intentional, performed for a reason etc. But we cannot describe the event of my buttering the toast in this way. The latter is intentional-under-a-description if it is an event of my buttering the toast intentionally. It makes no sense to say that the event of my buttering the toast intentionally is itself intentional under-a-description, and yet Davidson is committed to saying that it is.[33]

I end this appendix with a different sort of example illustrating the same difficulty:

(a**) Jones was wrong to butter the toast in the bathroom.

If Davidson is right, we should be able to translate this into:

(b**) There was an event *x*, which was Jones's buttering of the toast in the bathroom, wrongly.

But what does 'wrongly' mean here? As we have already seen (in § 2) it cannot mean that Jones buttered the toast in the wrong way. Rather, we must take (b**) to be equivalent to:

(c**) There was an action *x* such that Jones did *x* in the bathroom and Jones was wrong to do it.

Or, if we must mention events to:

(d**) There was an event *x*, which was Jones's buttering of the toast in the bathroom, and which Jones was wrong to bring about.

I have already elaborated at length on why 'bring about' is something Jones does. This is of no help to Davidson, who needs something closer to:

> (e**) There was an event *x*, which was Jones's buttering of the toast in the bathroom, and which Jones was wrongly bringing about.

But (e**) is ambiguous as to whether Jones was wrong to bring about the event, or whether he was merely bringing it about in the wrong way. In order to disambiguate we must point to either (c**) or (d**), both of which appeal to the thing done. If we are to appeal to the thing done, we might as well stick to our original sentence and admit that we have failed to translate it. It would appear that Davidson himself recognises this, for in a later essay he uses expressions of the following form:

> (f**) It was intentional of Jones that there was an event of his *x*-ing.[34]

This is clutching at straws, for it makes no more sense to *intend* that an event occur any more than it does to *try* that an event occur. But suppose, *per impossibile*, that one could do such a thing. This would result in the following state of affairs:

> (g**) There was an event of Jones's *x*-ing that was intended by him.

Unless one's powers of intending are telekinetic or divine, all this could possibly amount to is an event of Jones's doing something that *fulfills* his intention (that such an event occur). But if this can be the case at all, it can be the case without the intention playing any causal role i.e. without Jones's *x*-ing being an action in any sense that Davidson could accept. There is a simple explanation for this: unless *x*-ing is something that Jones himself is *doing*, there cannot be an action of his *x*-ing.[35]

Appendix II
Thought and Motive in Historiography

In which a re-enactment of the thought of Hume and Collingwood illustrates mutually compatible ways in which historical explanation may succeed.

To explain history...means to reveal the passions of human beings, their talents, their active powers. This definiteness of providence is what is usually taken for its plan. Yet it is this very plan that is supposed to be hidden from our view, so that we would be presumptuous to want to understand it.

G.W.F. Hegel[1]

1   Hume's just medium

Actions, for Hume, are those bodily movements caused by the will, the latter having 'no more a discoverable connexion with its effects than any material cause has with its proper effect'.[2] As such, they are external objects which we can observe through the senses, though the senses cannot alone distinguish between mere bodily movement and action. Nevertheless, our knowledge of action is not *a priori* but empirical, mediated through perceptual impressions. Accordingly, Hume believes that purported explanations of action – be they singular or general – are to be tested through experience, either directly or through testimony; for 'we can give no reason for our most general and most refin'd principles, beside our experience of their reality'.[3] This does not entail that agential reasons are themselves external, observable, objects.[4] Rather, their existence is to be *inferred* from behaviour, the power of any given argument from analogy hanging on the proper degree and nature of philosophical scepticism about causal reasoning.

Reasons *why* people did or believed certain things figure on virtually every single page of all six volumes of *The History of England*. Hume also mentions such reasons in his philosophical works, be it explicitly[5] or implicitly.[6] He additionally describes reasons we *have* for acting[7], making no ontological distinction between the latter and the former kind of reason, whilst remaining highly alert to our tendency to over-rationalise actions, beliefs, and passions that are typically a matter of habit, custom, and sentiment.[8]

On Hume's account, we may acquire knowledge of another person's reasons or motives through a combination of inductive and analogical reasoning relating their behaviour to past instances:

> [I]n judging the actions of men we must proceed upon the same maxims, as when we reason concerning external objects. When any phaenomena are

155

constantly and invariably conjoin'd together, they acquire such a connexion in the imagination, that it passes from one to the other, without any doubt or hesitation. But below this there are many inferior degrees of evidence and probability, nor does one single contrariety of experiment entirely destroy all our reasoning. The mind balances the contrary experiments, and deducting the inferior from the superior, proceeds with that degree of assurance or evidence, which remains. Even when these contrary experiments are entirely equal, we remove not the notion of causes and necessity; but supposing that the usual contrariety proceeds from the operation of contrary and conceal'd causes, we conclude, that the chance or indifference lies only in our judgement on account of our imperfect knowledge, not in the things themselves, which are in every case equally necessary, tho' to appearance not equally constant or certain. No union can be more constant and certain; than that of some actions with some motives and characters; and if in other cases the union is uncertain, 'tis no more than what happens in the operations of body, nor can we conclude anything from the one irregularity, which will not follow equally from the other.[9]

The prediction and explanation of action thereby forms part of the science (i.e. systematic study) of human nature that Hume seeks to establish. Actions, for Hume, are no different from other events in being susceptible to empirical investigation (it is worth noting here that Hume's rare usage of the word 'event' is interchangeable with that of 'fact').[10] As with natural science, explanation in social science is inductive not deductive. If there is to be any such thing as a logic of history, then, it is to be an *inductive logic,* the limitations of which Hume famously exposed. Whatever one's philosophical position with regard to the validity of inductive reasoning (and Hume's exact take on it), explanation must always be a matter of informed *conjecture* based on patterns of reasoning and/or non-rational connections, in the face of varying degrees of uncertainty.[11] Such conjecture may be based on patterns of reasoning as well as patterns of non-rational connections and are to be confirmed or refuted through 'cautious observation of human life,'[12] the most systematic form of which is historiography:

> Mankind are so much the same, in all times and places, that history informs us of nothing new or strange in this particular. Its chief use is only to discover the constant and universal principles of human nature, by showing men in all varieties of circumstances and situations, and furnishing us with materials, from which we may form our observations, and become acquainted with the regular springs of human action and behaviour.[13]

Hume's work as a historian is geared towards revealing the motivating influence of character.[14] As Annette Baier notes, '[c]haracter is not some hidden inner constitution of a person' but 'the outward expressive face of that inner nature',[15] a point also emphasised by Collingwood.[16] Explanations in terms of character are to be *contrasted* with those that appeal to general facts about human nature.[17] Baier further suggests that explanation and evaluation are deeply entangled in Hume's writings, suggesting that Hume believes that the correct description of any given motive cannot be value-free.[18] If so, then Hume is the father of experimental philosophy of action in a very different way to that imagined by advocates of this methodological school, founded on an experiment that purports to show that our notion of 'intention' includes a moral component.[19]

Hume's early essay 'Of the Study of History' argues that impartial evaluative judgement requires an ethical sensitivity towards one's subject matter that is neither overly *involved* nor completely *disinterested*.[20] In the former case one is at risk of failing to interpret motives objectively, in the latter of not caring enough to be in a position to evaluate them at all (morality, for Hume, being a matter of feeling appropriate sentiments). The historian's distance from his subject enables him (and it is always a man in Hume's examples[21]) to adopt such a moderately stoic mean between *empathy* and *detachment*, thereby placing him in a privileged position with respect to the correct evaluation of his subjects' motives:

> When a man of business enters into life and action, he is more apt to consider the characters of men, as they have relation to his interest, than as they stand in themselves; and has his judgement warped on every occasion by the violence of his passion. When a philosopher contemplates characters and manners in his closet, the general abstract view of these objects leaves the mind so cold and unmoved, that the sentiments of nature have no room to play, and he scarce feels the difference between vice and virtue. History keeps in just medium betwixt these extremes, and places the objects in their true point of view. The writers of history, as well as the readers, are sufficiently interested in the characters and events, to have a lively sentiment of blame or praise; and, at the same time, have no particular interest or concern to pervert their judgement. [22]

For this reason, Hume begins *The History of England* by noting that he will not concern himself much with either distant or recent history, for the latter is temporally too far removed from our concerns to be of any interest, and the latter too close for us to keep an impartial distance. Hume's *History* thus begins after the Roman Invasions and ends with the glorious revolution of 1688, three-quarters of a century prior to the publication of its final volume in 1762[23] (a similar suggestion could easily be run for national and/or geographical location though Hume does not entertain this, possibly because his Scottish identity places him at a questionable emotional distance from English history). In keeping with this outlook, the aforementioned essay on History closes with a quotation from Lucretius' *De Rerum Natura* (III: 57–8) which roughly translates as 'only then are the words of truth drawn up from the heart'.[24] In Lucretius' original, the temporal adverb '*tum*' refers to times of great peril and adversity; by contrast Hume uses it to refer to that 'just medium' between *lively sentiment* and *personal disinterest* required for impartial judgement – a virtue he might have equally associated with Stoicism (elsewhere contrasted to apathy[25]), his notion of *sentiment* being sufficiently weak to include belief.[26]

The correct approach to historiography, on such a conception, consists in drawing appropriate inductive inferences from relevant information regarding the *character* of those concerned, it being a blatant falsehood that 'all characters and actions [are] alike entitled to the affection and regard of everyone'.[27] As we have just seen, Hume takes the proper assessment of character to require that a medium between *lively sentiment* and *personal disinterest. Pace* Hume, numerous writers on history including Croce, Knowles, and Carr have claimed that it is not the business of the historian to pass moral judgements on individuals, but only to explain why they acted as they did.[28] We have already noted that Hume, on the other hand, takes the understanding of action to be inextricably tied to the appreciation of character. *Pari passu*, a correct explanation of action appeals to the agent's *motives*, the discernment of which is necessarily evaluative: if you misjudge character you fail to explain action. A proper evaluation of character, Hume thinks, can determine whether any given event was more likely the result of *situation* or of *temper*. History tells us much about human nature and, conversely, the principles of human nature can (among other causal principles) help us to better interpret history. Hume's *History of England* thereby aims 'to provide an account of English history based on empirically plausible assumptions,'[29] as opposed to those histories which fruitlessly invoke miracles, prophecy, and revealed religion.

Hume is aware that actions may accord with more than one motive, just as Ducasse, Hempel, and Davidson would all later remind us that actions may accord with one or more of the agent's reasons. We saw earlier that Davidson's criterion for determining which of the numerous reasons an agent might have for acting is the one she actually acted for is causal (in a way which has proved to be highly problematic due to the possibility of deviant causal chains, whose challenge Davidson concedes to be problematic).[30]

Hume, by contrast, takes the more pragmatic view that the correct method for attributing motives to any given individual is to ask which ones(s) would reveal him as acting *characteristically*, a fact to be determined on purely empirical grounds of past regularity:

> No union can be more constant and certain; than that of some actions with some motives and characters...the *union* betwixt motives and actions has the same constancy, as that in any natural operations...a spectator can commonly infer our actions from our motives and character; and even where he cannot, he concludes in general, that he might, were he perfectly acquainted with every circumstance of our situation and temper...in judging the actions of men we must proceed upon the same maxims, as when we reason concerning external objects.[31]

What neither reason nor human nature can explain is thereby attributed to character, which divides human beings into sorts (including stereotypes). The more surprising an action, the more fine-grained divisions need to be, extreme cases requiring particularistic accounts:

> The most irregular and unexpected resolutions of men may frequently be accounted for by those who know every particular circumstance of their character and situation.[32]

Hume's science of humanity is thus non-Humean to the extent that it centres around considerations of motive and character, as opposed to beliefs and desires.

Indeed, there is an overwhelming amount of evidence demonstrating that when Hume argued that 'reason alone can never be a motive to any action of the will'[33] he was not equating reason (which he *contrasts* to sentiment) with belief (which he *defines* as a kind of sentiment).[34]

Christine Korsgaard has objected that the suggestion that agent-causation may be achieved 'when the person's character serves as a kind of filter in the causal chain, making the outcome turn one way rather than another' seems to 'lose track' of the 'fact' that 'nothing counts as an *action*', unless a person 'is the cause of an intentional movement, or something of that sort'.[35] It is true that as a philosopher Hume says nothing of agents causally determining intentional movements. As a historian, however, he takes it for granted that a strong character may determine the course of history, and he may have well agreed with the Sellars–Davidson thesis that an action may be caused without its agent being caused to perform it.[36]

None of this makes Hume oblivious to competing non-psychological causes of human action, as made clear in the following remark on from his essay 'That Politics May Be Reduced to a Science':

> So great is the force of laws, and of particular forms of government, and so little dependence have they on the humours and tempers of men, that consequences almost as general and certain may sometimes be deduced from them, as any which the mathematical sciences afford us.[37]

To understand all is to be able to fully demarcate between the effects of character and those of situation as they relate to human and natural laws. The case of law and government renders political events as close as human behaviour can come to naturally approximate events observed in controlled experiments, though Hume's deterministic science of behaviour must here be understood in the light of his much-debated notions of causation and necessity.

Human behaviour is as much the product of an unobservable causal necessity as any other natural event. The only difference between them is *epistemic*: our knowledge of the principles of human nature that bind motion to action is less precise than that of the 'universally allowed' deterministic laws which bind physical force to motion.[38] This is partly due to the fact that the former laws are considerably more complicated, but it is equally a result of the fact that it is all but impossible to perform extensive controlled experiments involving human action (though Hume would have certainly been interested in the work of Benjamin Libet). Be all this as it may, our imperfect psycho-physical knowledge is nonetheless sufficient to enable us to predict individual and social behaviour in an indefinite number of situations.[39]

Good historiography, then, seeks to *narrow* the scope of chance elements by gathering as much information as possible. Such information may be synchronic as well as diachronic. It may relate to past patterns and traditions and general tendencies in practical reasoning (including irrational ones) but it might also involve particular information about both situational context and any given individual's psychology (itself established through a form of *holistic induction*). While historians do not, as a general rule, explicitly apply *probability calculus* (it makes for bad narratives), some form of probabilistic reasoning must inform any historical conjecture if it is to be valid. As Hume remarks, ideal historiography provides the reader with entertainment as well as instruction.[40]

2   Collingwood's thought

Collingwood has great admiration for 'so determined and profound a thinker' as Hume, whose greatest philosophical achievement he takes to be 'the demonstration that history was a legitimate and valid type of knowledge, more legitimate in fact than most others because not promising more than it could perform and not depending on any questionable metaphysical hypotheses'.[41] His only complaint against him is that he embraced a 'substantialistic view of human nature that was really quite inconsistent with his philosophical principles'[42]:

> [H]is attack on the idea of spiritual substance should, if successful, have demolished this conception of human nature as something solid and permanent and uniform; but it did nothing of the kind because Hume substituted for the idea of a spiritual substance the idea of constant tendencies to associate ideas in particular ways, and these laws of association were just as uniform and unchanging as any substance.[43]

Collingwood here underplays Hume's emphasis on the differences between individual characters, but is nonetheless alive to a real difference between their philosophies. He Collingwood maintains, under the influence of Hegel's evolutionary philosophy of history and in opposition to that of Hume, that 'the historical development of the science of human nature entails an historical development in human nature itself'.[44] Collingwood accordingly he takes the correct balance between empathy and detachment to rest not on the *evaluation* of the past actions and motivational springs of people we share a common nature with, but on the ability to *understand* associations of thought quite different to our own – a skill that Collingwood explicates in terms of his infamous notion of re-enactment. Collingwood takes the re-enactment of past thought processes to be the key to achieving a *scientific* history of human nature, and actions that emerge from it. The notion of a science employed here is the same as Hume's – viz. that of any systematic or orderly thought about a topic. Collingwood takes the most fundamental of these to be metaphysics, understood not as that about which we can say nothing meaningful but, rather, as the historical science of our absolute presuppositions.[45] Their unfolding throughout history is mirrored in our ever-evolving (and, arguably, essentially contested) concepts, including those of 'science', 'cause', 'event', or indeed 'metaphysics'.

Mark Bevir has argued that Collingwood slides between an *acceptable* (weak) understanding of re-enactment and an *unacceptable* (stronger) one – the latter requiring the historian to literally relive the mental lives of his subjects – and assigns to empathy the role of facilitating this process. Bevir himself endorses a detached notion of history as re-enactment which he identifies with the former strategy, thereby defending an account of historical explanation that might be termed *rationalistic*, for lack of a better term:

> [H]istorians ascribe beliefs and pro-attitudes to people, but they do not do so on the grounds that they have relived the mental lives of the people

concerned. Indeed, too great a concern with empathy rests on a mistaken analysis of objectivity. The problem is that even the most scrupulous proponents of history as re-enactment, such as R.G. Collingwood, slide from a weak to a strong account of empathy. A correct, weak concern with empathy asserts only that historians should not attempt 'to emulate the scientist in searching for causes or laws of events' since to understand any action we have to discover 'thought expressed in it'. An erroneous, strong concern with empathy asserts that to discover the thoughts expressed in past actions we have to 're-enact the past' in our own mind, we have to 'go through the process the [actor] did in deciding on this particular [action]'.[46]

A weak concern with empathy simply prepares to locate the original thought(s), intention(s), or, indeed, emotion(s), that motivated the action in question. This is not done with the further aim of explaining some historical event by subsuming it under a causal law – for to discover the thought expressed in any action, on this view, just *is* to understand it. Bevir continues:

> [I]f objectivity depended on pure perceptions, historians of ideas might have to re-enact the mental processes of the authors they study in order to have a pure experience of the viewpoints of these authors. Actually, however, because objectivity rests on a practice of comparison, the worth of all the histories we tell does not depend on our successfully having identified with our subjects. Indeed, as with most logics of discovery, a preoccupation with empathy would be a useless hindrance to the historian. If a historian succeeded in entering into the psyche of his subjects so as to go through their mental processes, he would find he could not refer to their pre-conscious and unconscious beliefs, so he would be unable to transcend the limits of the accounts his subjects would give of their own works. Thus, because pre-conscious and unconscious beliefs sometimes do constitute part of the meaning of a work, successful psychic identification would be a barrier to our understanding of the past.[47]

This account relies heavily on folk psychology, emphasising that its notions are constrained by principles of rationality that have no equivalent in the natural sciences. On this model, historical explanation differs from scientific explanation because it deals with psycho-physical relations that are not strictly nomological (there are no strict laws bridging the psychological to the physical). Bevir thus endorses Davidson's anomalous monism, using it to side with Dray versus Hempel in the first debate about whether the explanation of human action is deductive-nomological, but we saw in chapter three that Davidson himself most adamantly sides with Hempel (contra Dray) when it comes to models of action explanation.[48] Bevir allows that folk psychological explanation requires knowledge of the mental life of agents, but no literal re-enactment of it. If there are no strict psycho-physical laws we cannot expect our psychological knowledge to yield explanations of the same sort as those advanced in natural sciences. This is not to rule out a *logic* of history that is probabilistic rather than deductive, and based upon inferences to the best explanation.[49]

Such a deflationist adoption of historical re-enactment contrasts sharply with that put forward by Karsten Stueber, who assigns empathy the role of *uncovering* the thought in question – or, at the very least, testing the mental postulates of folk psychology:

> [W]e must reject the purely psychological conception of the interpretative process ... Still ... part of the proper account of grasping the larger historical significance of various individual actions includes understanding those intentions of the agent ... to grasp such reasons involves empathetic abilities ... it is only in the light of such capacities that we can recognize whether an interpretive hypothesis in the folk-psychological idiom is a plausible contender for being the correct one in the first place.[50]

Stueber criticizes Bevir for not taking empathy more seriously as a first person perspective. On his view, we should treat empathy as being epistemically central for our folk psychological understanding of historical agents. Mere knowledge of a person's individual thoughts, we are told, is not sufficient to understand their *reasons*. This is because we need to acquaint ourselves with their general psychological framework in order to understand the precise function of any isolated thought, and this requires empathetic re-enactment.[51] He concedes, however, that empathy has its limitations and that this creates a need for additional theoretical strategies. The historian of thought must consequently perform a fine balancing act between re-enactive empathy and more theoretically informed interpretations.[52] It is perhaps no accident that the cover of Stueber's book, *Rediscovering Empathy*, depicts an agile tight-rope walker.[53] But is the walk being suggested that of a just medium or one of perilous empathy?

Collingwood's own method strikes a fine balance between distanced and empathetic understanding, not unlike the one recommended by David Hume. Like Hume before him, Collingwood often speaks of the explanation of historical *events* without the term with the precise ontological sense bestowed upon it. Unlike Hume, however, he sees actions as *expressions* of thought and intention. If I raise my arm with the aim of opening the window, then my action (if things go as planned) is one of opening the window. If I raise my arm and my intention is to signal to someone, it is one of signalling, on pain of failure. On such a view actions are not identified through – let alone *with* – bodily movements, but by the thought(s) which they express. Inspired by Hegel, Collingwood frequently speaks of actions having an interior aspect that events lack. Arguably, this is just a metaphorical (albeit misleading) way of expressing the more obvious, Aristotelian, point that in attempting to understand any given action we may ascribe a practical syllogism to its agent. Such syllogisms are reconstructed reasonings which help to explain the agent's action by disclosing *what* she was doing. They need neither accompany nor precede the act, which they are not entirely separable from.[54] Hence, Collingwood's claim that, when historians know *what* happened they already know *why* it happened:

> ... for the historian there is no difference between discovering what happened and discovering why it happened.[55]

This thought would later be echoed by Anscombe in her account of explanation through redescription:

> The description of something as a human action could not occur prior to the existence of the question 'Why?', simply as a kind of utterance by which we were *then* obscurely prompted to address the question.[56]

It remains a moot point whether or not Collingwood recognises that explanation is sensitive to description.[57] What *is* clear, however, is that he anticipates Anscombe in taking his point about specification to debunk a causalist approach to explanation that had already begun to gain prominence:

> This does not mean that words like 'cause' are necessarily out of place in reference to history; it only means that they are used there in a special sense. When a scientist asks 'Why did that piece of litmus paper turn pink?' he means 'On what kinds of occasions do pieces of litmus paper turn pink?' When an historian asks 'Why did Brutus stab Caesar?' he means 'What did Brutus think, which made him decide to stab Caesar?' The cause of the event, for him, means the thought in the mind of the person by whose agency the event came about: and this is not something other than the event, it is the inside of the event itself.[58]

More importantly, for our purposes, we can attribute to Collingwood the view that 'inner' thoughts do not lie behind actions (causally preceding them) without requiring him to be a simulation theorist. Thoughts, for Collingwood, are but aspects of the actions which can be used to characterise them:

> The historian, investigating any event in the past, makes a distinction between what may be called the outside and the inside of an event...By the inside of an event I mean that in which it can only be described in terms of thought: Caesar's defiance of Republican law, or the clash of constitutional policy between himself and his assassins...an action is the unity of the outside and inside of an event...[the historian's] main task is to think himself into this action, to discern the thought of its agent...For history, the object to be discovered is not the mere event, but the thought expressed in it. To discover that thought is already to understand it. After the historian has ascertained the facts, there is no further process of inquiring into their causes. When he knows what happened, he already knows why it happened.[59]

Collingwood's philosophy of history here follows directly from his Hegelian philosophy of action. If action is ontologically inseparable from thought then one cannot even begin to understand and/or explain action without understanding the thoughts which form part of its constitution:

> The processes of nature can...be properly described as sequences of mere events, but those of history cannot. They are not processes of mere events but processes of actions, which have an inner side, consisting of processes of thought; and what the historian is looking for is these processes of thought. All history is the history of thought.[60]

Given this account of the relation between thought action the question of whether beliefs and 'pro-attitudes' are *causes* of intentional behaviour does not even arise. Dray captures this aspect of Collingwood's philosophy of mind and action perfectly:

> ...far from considering explanatory thoughts as unobservable events, he regarded them as having no existence at all apart from the events which expressed them. In this connection, his views are much closer to those of his successor in the Chair of Metaphysical Philosophy of Oxford, Gilbert Ryle, than has always been supposed. Suggestive in this connection is his vigorous attack on what he called 'the metaphysical theory of mind' – the conception of it as a non-physical substance, rather than a complex of activities.[61]

It makes no sense to look for nomological relations between the inner and outer aspects of one and the same event. One may find interesting patterns of association between various inner and outer characterisations e.g. 'outer bodily movements of form x are typically expressions of inner thoughts of form y,' but the outer movements are not what the historian is trying to explain – for the job of the historian is to explain *action* (and thereby also *thought*), not mere movements of material bodies.[62]

off the mark .com   by Mark Parisi

I NEVER KNOW WHAT'S GOING ON INSIDE HIM...

A unified account of neuroscientific explanations of every single bodily movement of some person does not constitute a biography.[63] The explanation of past action requires an understanding of past thoughts, to be achieved through a reconstruction of the reasoning that led up to them. Without it, the historian's knowledge is limited to that of the occurrence of mere bodily movements.[64] Collingwood explicates:

> The history of thought, and therefore all history, is the re-enactment of past thought in the historian's own mind. This re-enactment is only accomplished, in the case of Plato and Caesar respectively, so far as the historian brings to bear on the problem all the powers of his own mind and all his knowledge of philosophy and politics. It is not a passive surrender to the spell of another's mind; it is a labour of active and therefore critical thinking. The historian not only re-enacts past thought, he re-enacts it in the context of his own knowledge and therefore, in re-enacting it, criticizes it, forms his own judgment of its value, corrects whatever errors he can discern in it. This criticism...is an indispensable condition of the historical knowledge itself...the thought which re-enacts past thoughts...criticizes them in re-enacting them.[65]

What does re-enactment consist of? A clue is provided in the following passage:

> Suppose, for example, [the historian] is reading the Theodosian Code, and has before him a certain edict of an emperor. Merely reading the words and being able to translate them does not amount to knowing their historical significance. In order to do that he must envisage it as that emperor envisaged it. Then he must see for himself, just as if the emperor's situation were his own, how such a situation might be dealt with; he must choose to see the possible alternative, and the reasons for choosing one rather than another; and thus he must go through the process which the emperor went through in deciding on this particular course. Thus he is re-enacting in his own mind the experience of the emperor; and only in so far as he does this has he any historical knowledge, as distinct from a merely philological knowledge, of the meaning of the edict.[66]

Sans re-enactment, we can only capture a record of statements which *chronicle* events. Likewise, with no knowledge of the intention whose expression is the meaning of any historical text, a contextualist reader will at most understand its sentence or *expression* meaning, but not what Grice called the utterer or *speaker* meaning – viz. what the author meant to convey.[67] In claiming that one may 'know the language in a philological sense' without 'understanding the passage as a historian of philosophy' Collingwood is effectively making the proto-Gricean point that one can uncover (b) the *expression* meaning of a text while completely misinterpreting (a) its *speaker* meaning, thereby failing *qua* historian of ideas. But the information missing is not a thought or intention that hides behind an otherwise clear meaning. In the case of a philosophical text, for example, its meaning can only be understood once one has seen 'what the philosophical problem was, of which his author is here stating his solution...rethinking for himself the thought of the author'.[68] To achieve this, we must 'come prepared with an experience sufficiently like his own to make those thoughts organic to it'.[69]

In what sense are we supposed to go through the same process of thought as the person we are trying to understand? Collingwood does not tell us what he has in mind, forcing the reader to adopt strategies of re-enactment in order to find out what re-enactment actually is. It should immediately strike her that it is impossible to go through the same *particular* process, at which point she may adopt the more modest goal of undergoing a thought process of the same type. One way of attempting to do so is via some kind of (empathetic) simulation. This could indeed help, but it is neither necessary nor sufficient for understanding. As for whether historical explanation requires empathy or detachment, there is room for both a weak and a strong understanding of what Bevir calls the *strong* concern with empathy. It is not clear whether Bevir would object to both understandings or just the (doubly) strong one, which is not obviously attributable to Collingwood, for whom the re-thinking of a thought is nothing more (or less) than its critical consideration.[70] Collingwood writes:

> The dilemma rests on the disjunction that thought is either pure immediacy, in which case it is inextricably involved in the flow of consciousness, or pure meditation, in which case it is utterly detached from that flow.[71]

His response is not that we should reject both horns of the dilemma, but that we should *accept* them both:

> [Thought] is both immediacy and mediation. Every act of thought, as it actually happens, happens in a context out of which it arises and in which it lives, like any other experience, as an organic part of the thinker's life…in addition to actually happening it is capable of sustaining itself and being revived or repeated without loss of its identity…what we think is not altered by alterations of the context in which we think it…in their immediacy, as actual experiences organically united with the body of experience out of which they arise, Plato's thought and mine are different. But in their mediation they are the same.[72]

> When I read Plato's argument in the *Theaetetus* against the view that knowledge is merely sensation, I do not know what philosophical doctrines he was attacking; I could not expound these doctrines and say in detail who maintained them and by what arguments. In its immediacy, as an actual experience of its own, Plato's argument must undoubtedly have grown up out of a discussion of some sort, though I do not know what it was, and been closely connected with such a discussion. Yet if I not only read his argument but understand it – follow it in my own mind by re-arguing it with and for myself – the process of argument which I go through is not a process resembling Plato's, it actually is Plato's so far as I understand him correctly.[73]

Collingwood here explicitly rejects the still-dominant view that identity – as opposed to mere resemblance – is either a matter of strict numerical (token/token) identity, or of an instantiation of a universal type. Instead, he maintains that one may go through the *very same* thought process as Plato just by reasoning in exactly the same way as he did. A thought process, after all, is but a reasoning process and it is a tautology – in no need of any theoretical support – that two people can at different times and places, reason in exactly the same way. To reason in similar (as opposed to identical) ways is to have at least slightly different thoughts. However, two people's thoughts (headaches, feelings, etc.) cannot be classified as being different simply on the grounds that they belong to different people. To suggest otherwise is to beg the question against those who, like Collingwood, wish to allow that two people can have the same belief. There is no genuine dispute here which might be resolved through metaphysics, logic, science, or analysis. Rather, as Wittgenstein was keen to point out, we are being presented with two different language games, neither of which is *in itself* justified or unjustified, correct or incorrect, though their comparative proximities to everyday parlance are instructive.[74]

Re-enactment, for Collingwood, is not merely rationalistic. Nor does it involve the sort of taking on of a persona that we might associate with a Stanislavskian method actor taking on the role of Hamlet or some dressed-up amateur in the midst of a battle re-enactment.[75] Why should re-enactment require *identification* at all? Can one not properly capture another's process of reasoning without adopting it? To consider what someone's feelings may have been is not to attempt to *reproduce* them in oneself; it may be acceptable within the acting profession to simulate madness or jealousy, but the thought of a historian having to constantly do so is laughable. To discover and understand a thought is not the same thing as *having* that thought, or any accompanying feelings. Does one not, in understanding a thought, come to *think* the thought in question? Not at all. I may perfectly understand that Plato thought that *x* was the case without agreeing with him, and if I don't agree with him then I don't share his thought. What we will share is what Hume called a 'simple conception' or idea, but we may *conceive* that *x* is the case without being 'persuaded of the truth of what we conceive'[76] – i.e. without *believing* or *thinking* that *x*. To fully understand Plato's thought is to have the very same *ideas* before one's mind. This need not (though it may) involve the sharing of any thoughts, only conceptions.[77]

3   True histories

Good historiography seeks, *inter alia*, to narrow the scope of chance elements by gathering as much information as possible. Such information may be synchronic as well as diachronic. It may relate to past patterns and traditions and general tendencies in practical reasoning (including irrational ones) but can also involve particular information, be it about situational context or individual psychology. This requires both holistic induction and the re-enactment of thought. Whilst historians rarely have good reason to explicitly apply probability calculus, some form of probabilistic reasoning must inform historical conjecture. Historiography is not merely a matter of relating facts, events, and/or states of affairs, but of doing so under descriptions that reveal narratives that would have remained hidden if the same facts were related under different descriptions. One could correctly state that Cleopatra VII married Ptolemy XIV without revealing that in so doing she married one of her brothers, and vice versa.

It is the historian's duty not only to describe events in ways that do not obscure relevant facts, but to ensure that these facts are themselves described in appropriate ways. Psychological, behavioural, and sociological facts are accordingly woven together to produce a picture that could never be produced through mere attendance to bodily movements and physical laws.[78] Moreover, as Hume points out, *ideal* historiography provides the reader with entertainment as well as instruction.[79] It thereby distances itself equally from both fables and chronicles, as well as from reductive science.

Notes

1 Objects and Objectives of Action Explanation

1. From 'The Elephant's Child', in Kipling (1902).
2. Cziko (2000: 14).
3. Unlike philosophers, scientists tend not to distinguish between causal relata and causal explanations, though some arguably conceptualise the former as proximate causes and the latter as ultimate causes (see § 1.4).
4. See § 1.2 for distinctions.
5. Mook (1986: 4).
6. Gross (1996: 114).
7. Ibid.: 109.
8. E.g. Nietzsche (1868/1973: § 264) v. J.B. Watson (1924: 82).
9. E.g. Clark and Grunstein (2000: 253–70) and Pinker (2002: viii & 114).
10. I return to Freud and other revelators of our 'real' reasons in Chapter 5.
11. See, for example, Fodor (1968: xxi).
12. Weiner (1992: 3–4).
13. See, for example, Schreier (1957: 42).
14. Thierry (2004: 1182–3).
15. Kimble (1996: x).
16. Gross (1996: 98).
17. von Wright (1998: 97).
18. See, for example, Watson (1919: 19ff). For an early history of the molar/molecular distinction see Tolman (1932: ch. 1).
19. Schreier (1957: xiii).
20. I address aspects of the debate in *Appendix I*.
21. Hornsby (1980: ch. 1 & 1986: 93–4). See *Appendix I*, § 1 for why, *pace* Hornsby, I do not take the preposition 'of' to here mark an important ontological distinction.
22. See von Wright (1963).
23. Cf. Stoutland's distinction between (i) the event of the moving of M's hand and (ii) the *action* of M moving his hand (Stoutland 1968: 473–4, n. 10).
24. Ewing (1938: 91). For motivated resistance see Bach (1980) and Lowe (2010).
25. E.g. Dretske (1988b & 2009) and Alvarez and Hyman (1998).
26. See, for example, Stout (1996:155ff. & 2005: ch. 6); cf. Aristotle (1989a: bk III, 201a10–11) and Charles (1984). For the claim that Aristotle has no ontology of action see Ackrill (1978).
27. Near-exhaustive catalogues are collectively provided by O'Shaugnessy (1972: 222), McCann (1979), Steward (1997: ch. 3) and Stout (1996: 46–62 & 1997).
28. See Anscombe (1957, § 23: 39).
29. Thanks to David Charles for pointing this out to me. For the relation between events and facts (as well as states of affairs) see P. F. Strawson (1950) and Austin (1954), as well McCann (1979); von Wright (1963: 39) is happy to identify the results of actions with both events and facts.
30. See, for example, Kim (1982: 64); cf. Hornsby (1986) and Lennon (1990: 161).

31. von Wright (1963: 41), emphasis in the original. For a different distinction between acts and activities inspired by Aristotle see Ruben (2003: 42–3).
32. David Dolby has persuaded me that the property of being red is not 'being red' but redness; we use the term 'Europe' as shorthand for 'the continent of Europe', but Europe is not a continent in the sense in which continental Europe (viz. 'the continent') is. We may similarly talk of the Economic Union of Europe, and so on.
33. To think otherwise is to adopt what (in Chapter 2, § 2.2) I shall call the *Conflating View of Doings* – viz. the view that my doing *x* is identical to the event (process, etc.) of my doing *x*.
34. Mourelatos (1978: 423).
35. For further argument see Kennett and Smith (1996: 80).
36. von Wright (1971: 67). His identification of things done with the results of actions eventually leads him to a logical tangle that culminates in his acceptance of backwards causation (Ibid.: 76ff.).
37. von Wright (1971: 66).
38. Hacker (2007: 153ff.) answers the question negatively. By contrast, Melden (1961: ch. 5), Danto (1963 & 1965a: 44–5), Chisholm (1964), White (1968: 2–3), and Alvarez and Hyman (1998) all claim that, as White puts it, 'things may be brought about either directly or by means of other things', though Danto denies that the former is a case of causation. The debate is closely linked with various contrasting notions of what it is for an act to be basic (see Sandis 2010a: 10–13). For example, von Wright's early view that for *most* cases to act is to bring something about *at will* (1963: 35) leaves space for his later suggestion that basic actions are not to be included within the range he had in mind (1971: 66–9), though the waters are muddied in an endnote in which he adds '[a]s far as I can see, there exists no directly performable action whose result could not *also* be brought about by doing something else' (1971: 199, fn. 38, emphasis in the original).
39. von Wright (1971: 67) takes such (intrinsic) connections to be mutually exclusive with causal (extrinsic) ones.
40. For the Fregean application of this distinction to things we think, perceive, believe, think, and mean, see Frege (1918–19), White (1972), McDowell (1996: 27) and Hornsby (1997). I shall not concern myself with disanalogies here, for the general point is neutral with regard to specific ontologies of things done, believed, perceived etc. We don't do our own doings any more than we desire our desirings, believe our believings, suspect our suspectings, perceive our perceivings, and so on.
41. Macmurray (1938: 74–6), emphasis in the original.
42. Austin (1954: 164), Brown (1968: 28–9), Thalberg (1977: 55), Hornsby (1980: ch. 1), and Clark (1989).
43. Macmurray (1938: 79).
44. Cf. Clark (1989).
45. For adverbial approaches to these distinctions see *Appendix I* (§ 2).
46. For the view that all actions are inner mental acts see Hornsby (1980: ch. 1)
47. I use Husserl's expression for the way in which a thing may strike us, though it has nowadays become more fashionable to express this idea in the somewhat narrower terms of action description, as inherited from Anscombe (1957) and Davidson (1963).

48. Achinstein (1975: 11–18). For complications relating to emphasis and illocutionary force see Achinstein (1983: 76–81). The similar but weaker thesis that an explanandum is only fixed under sentential representation is briefly discussed by Kim (1989: 275–6) who attributes the view to Hempel (1965: 421–2), with reference to Dretske's related suggestion that we may refer to 'event alomorphs', akin to *aspects* of events (Dretske 1977).
49. Achinstein (1983: 102).
50. A point famously brought home by Anscombe (1957).
51. Thankfully, most academics and scientists do not shed their layskins completely.
52. Hornsby (1993: 142), my emphasis.
53. I explore the ontological details of Hornsby's own account in *Appendix I* (§ 1).
54. For applications see Huxley (1916), Thompson (1917), Baker (1938), and Mayr (1961), Alessi (1992), and Alcock and Sherman (1994).
55. Aristotle (1989b: bk V, 1013a). See also Aristotle (1989a: bk II).
56. A neat exegetical overview is provided by Falcon (2011: § 2).
57. For examples of heated disputes within this common framework see D.W. Thompson (1917), Francis (1990), Armstrong (1991), and Alcock and Sherman (1994). Those who reject the dichotomy (e.g. Thierry 2004) do so on grounds of integration rather than pluralism.
58. There are some overlaps between the arguments that follow and those of Anscombe (1983).
59. Rose (1997: 10–14).
60. Ibid.: 14.
61. Ariew (2003: 559–64), emphasis in the original.
62. The original versions of some of the answers that follow may be found on internet sites such as www.whydidthechickencrosstheroad.com. Many thanks to Dan Hutto and Arto Laitinen for additional suggestions (see also Hutto 1991).
63. G. Taylor (1976: 164).
64. Hutto (2008) provides an account of the explanatory importance of folk-psychological narratives that I am in huge sympathy with. Hutto further maintains – against both 'theory theory' and simulation theory – that the basis of this ability is socio-cultural rather than inherited. I shall not be engaging with this debate about so-called ultimate causes, though I explore the explanatory role of empathy in *Appendix II* (§ 2).
65. Moore (1903: vi), emphasis in the original.

2 Conflation in Action

1. Shakespeare (1603–6/1996: Act I, Sc. iv).
2. Weiner (1992: 3–4).
3. Ibid.
4. C. Taylor (1964), Harré and Secord (1972), Stoutland (1976), and Dretske (1988b), to name a few.
5. von Wright (1963 & 1971) arguably avoids holding CVRA by maintaining that actions are never events but the doings and bringings about of events. Things are complicated, however, by the fact that while he never explicitly

addresses the possibility of there being events *of* doing and/or bringing about things, he seems to equate the things we do with both (a) events and (b) the bringing about of bodily movements (see § 1.2). This certainly commits him to CVA if not CVRA as well.

6. Schueler (2001: 254), my emphasis.
7. Ibid.: 255.
8. Vendler (1984: 371).
9. Ibid.: 372, my emphasis.
10. Smith (2003: 152).
11. Dancy (2000: 172).
12. Cf. Dancy (2000: 131).
13. See Collins (1987: 125–8).
14. Pietroski (2000: 1).
15. Stout (1996). T. Nagel similarly talks about 'a reason for something simply to occur' (1970: 120, fn. 1). I address Nagel's claims in § 2.7.
16. Stout (1996: 2).
17. Ibid., emphasis in the original.
18. Ibid.: 3–5.
19. Ibid.: 1.
20. Ibid.: 40 and 44.
21. MacMurray writes: 'But how can we disprove the contention of a theistic hypothesis that all events, in the last analysis are acts of God? At the most we could perhaps show that we have no grounds for supposing this; though in fact I believe that even that is not demonstrable. Our certainty about action is of a higher order than our knowledge of events' (1938: 80–1).
22. Hegel (1849/1988: 12ff.).
23. For a plausible analysis of divine action see Ward (2007: 18ff.); cf. Hegel (1849/1988: 16), quoted at the outset of *Appendix II*, and Werther (2007). The more extreme view that 'everything we do is God's creative action' may be found in Rumi's poem 'Emptiness' (1995: 26).
24. Davidson (1971b: 43) rightly claims that stumbling can be deliberate under some description, for my stumbling may be identical to my going home. But I don't stumble *for* whatever reason explains by stumbling.
25. Broome (2004: 34).
26. I borrow the term from Hacker (2009); cf. Hieronymi (2011). Agential reasons, or reasons of our *own*, are a subset of motivationally operative reasons that are the reasons we act upon. The remaining subset is that of 'defeated motivators' (Dancy 2000: 4), also a subset of the reasons that we *don't* act upon or 'con-reasons', to use David-Hillel Ruben's terminology (Ruben 2009: 63–4).
27. Typically, these conflations are not explicitly held by anyone, for they involve a failure to see that there is a distinction to be made. An exception is Donald Davidson who consciously rejects the possibility of an ontological distinction, for relatively Quinean reasons (see Milgram 2009: chs. 8 & 9).
28. Whilst I make some additional historical connections both here and throughout the book, my project is not one of philosophical archaeology so details will be limited. I say next to nothing, for example, about the influence of Aristotle, Aquinas, and Wittgenstein on Anscombe (for this see Teichmann 2008).
29. Ross (1930: 42 & 47).

30. Sandis (2010b) explores the ways in which this was anticipated by Hegel.
31. This involves a version of what I shall introduce as the *Conflating View of Normative Reasons* (see § 4.1).
32. Anscombe (1958: 9, fn.1).
33. Anscombe (1957: § 19).
34. Ibid., my emphasis.
35. Ibid.: § 29, emphasis is in original.
36. Thompson (2008: 136, fn. 17).
37. Anscombe (1957: § 23), emphasis is in original.
38. In Sandis (2006 & 2010a) I argue that some killings are of this nature, and that certain puzzles about their spatio-temporal location disappear once we acknowledge this.
39. White (1968: 3) and von Wright (1963: 41).
40. Hornsby (1980: 3), emphasis is in original. For an exploration of Hornsby's metaphysics see *Appendix I* (§ 1).
41. Anscombe (1979: 209).
42. Of course Oedipus does also sorts of other things in killing the old man, e.g. contract his muscles, raise his arm, upset the gods, and so on.
43. Kripke (1980: 35–8).
44. cf. Lennon (1990: 148–151). I should emphasise here that descriptivism does not remove the *de re/de dicto* ambiguity since that relates to modes of presentation more generally.
45. See Sandis (2010b: 51).
46. This is betrayed by the fact that Davidson himself asserts that 'felt as guilty as if he had intentionally married his mother and killed his father', in the very passage in which he is trying to convince the reader than Oedipus' action was indeed intentional under some description (Davidson 1985: 297).
47. This point is taken up by von Wright (1963: 36), though he remains guilty of equating an individual act that 'is done on a certain occasion' with an individual act that is 'the doing of a generic act' (Ibid.: 36–7).
48. Ricœur (1990/1992: 62–3, see also 60 & 70).
49. The imagery is that of Ricœur (1990/1992: 67–74).
50. I discus some of the details of Davidson's argument in *Appendix I*. For Quine's ontological influence on Davidson see Millgram (2009: chs 8 & 9)
51. Lepore and McLaughlin (1985) and Vermazen and Hintikka (1985) provide excellent starting points, though much has happened since.
52. Davidson (2001a: dust cover), the emphasis is mine.
53. This is Davidson's term for 'the reason why an agent did something' where this is understood as a 'reason that rationalizes an action' (Davidson 1963: 4).
54. Ibid.: 3–4 and 9.
55. Ibid.: 8, emphasis in the original.
56. Ibid.: 9.
57. See Davidson's foreword to Donagan (1994: vii–ix) and Davidson (1971).
58. Smith and Pettit (1997: 73), mainly my emphasis. We may here ignore the question of whether Smith and Pettit take their theory of rationality to be substantive or merely procedural. Their account of action explanation is discussed in § 3.5.
59. I elaborate on this point in Chapter 4.
60. Hornsby (1993: 134–5).

61. See Davidson (1967a).
62. T. Nagel (1970: 47).
63. See Chisholm (1964).
64. T. Nagel (1970: 47).
65. T. Nagel (1986: 114–5), emphasis in the original.
66. Hornsby (1993: 46).
67. A different argument for a related form of pluralism about action is advanced by Millgram (2010).

3   What Makes an Action Explanation Proper?

1. Pope (1734: Bk II).
2. Taleb (2010: 95).
3. See Holloway (2008).
4. For overviews and further context of the debate I summarise below see Borger and Cioffi (1970), Ryan (1970), Vesey (1971) and Gardiner (1974).
5. E.g. by Skinner (1972). For reasons why 'naturalism' may be a misleading term see Hornsby (1997).
6. Mill (1843/1973: 388–406/3.8.1–7). For Mill's influence on Hempel see Ruben (1990: 110).
7. Mill (1843/1973: 388–454–5/1.3.5).
8. Mill (1865/1976) and B. Russell (1948).
9. Mill (1843/1973: 354–5/3.5.11).
10. Hempel (1942: 5.2).
11. I discuss nested explanations in Chapter 5.
12. Dray (1962: 68–70).
13. For examples of the continuing prominence of the second debate see Aguilar and Buckareff (2010) and D'Oro. (2012a). Bitttner, Hempel, von Wright, and D'Oro participate in both debates. Much of D'Oro's work explicitly highlights important connections between the two.
14. Ducasse (1925: 150ff.).
15. Hempel (1942).
16. Davidson (1976: 262).
17. Karl Popper likewise defends the hypothetico-deductive model of action explanation while rejecting (for a variety of reasons including the denial of determinism) the more general thesis that social science can be modelled on the natural sciences (Popper 1957: § 15).
18. Bittner (2001: 88–9).
19. Taylor (1964: 3).
20. I address this issue in Chapter 7.
21. Passmore (1958: 275), emphasis in the original.
22. Hempel (1963: 102 & 105).
23. I owe this example to Michael Smith.
24. Smith goes for the state rather than the fact because he thinks of reasons as producing action. This is because he thinks they must motivate it and a psychological fact, unlike a belief, cannot motivate us.
25. It is no accident that Hume takes personality to be so crucial to the explanation of historical action (see *Appendix II*, § 1).
26. I explore the notion of a consideration one acts upon in depth in Chapter 4.2.

27. It could even reveal why she took something else to be an appropriate consideration. I discuss such nested explanations in Chapter 5.
28. For the same sort of point see Baier (2008b: 14/250).
29. For the distinction between natural and non-natural meaning see Grice (1989: 88–93). I return to the relation of non-natural meaning to action explanation in Chapter 7.
30. See §§ 2.3 and 4.3 .
31. Ayer (1956: 275).
32. G. Strawson (1986/2010: 35ff./29 & 31).
33. T. Nagel (1986: 114–6), emphasis in the original.
34. T. Nagel (1986: 114–7), my emphasis. In a footnote, Nagel adds that 'Lucas notices this but is not, I think, sufficiently discouraged by it: "There remains a tension between the programme of complete explicability and the requirements of freedom. If men have free will, then no complete explanation of their actions can be given, except by reference to themselves. We can give their reasons. But we cannot explain why their reasons were reasons for them ... Asked why I acted, I give my reasons: asked why I chose to accept them as reasons, I can only say 'I just did'" [Lucas (1970: 171–2)]'.
35. My criticism here is inspired by – but also digresses from – Hornsby (2003: 143ff.).
36. I tackle such nested explanations in Chapter 5.
37. Not all who accept CVAE and CVR further conflate questions of the form 'why did event A occur?' with questions of the form 'why did the event of her A-ing for reason *x* occur rather than the event of her B-ing for reason *y*?' Consequently, they are not all as pessimistic as Nagel about the possibility of our reasons for action being capable of explaining the latter. For example we shall see in § 4.3 that Michael Smith believes that (statements about our) belief-desire pairs care capable of explaining action teleologically. If Smith is right, Nagel is wrong to suppose that *nothing* can explain our actions.
38. Toulmin (1964: 96).
39. I take it that Weber's 'ideal type' interpretive causal explanations (*verstehende erklaerung*) would also fall into this category.
40. Davis (1979: 85), emphasis is in original.
41. cf. D'Oro (2008: 145).
42. A detailed argument for why a causal connection is neither necessary nor sufficient is provided by Anscombe (1989: 110–1); for commentary see Vogler (2002: 213–22). Whilst I am sympathetic to the spirit of Anscombe's account, its couching in the terminology of CVA and CVRA makes it incredibly difficult to diagnose.
43. I develop these thoughts more fully in Chapter 7, suggesting that a corollary of it is that the considerations upon which we act cannot explain action.
44. See Sandis (2009b).
45. Chapter 7 is devoted to such matters, including the question of what causes the events of our acting.
46. von Wright (1971: 16).
47. It is worth asking here whether this distinction extends to teleological explanation concerning non-intentional agents such as acids (contrast Sandis 2004 to Martin, Sugarman & Thomson 2003). If so, then we should expect the explanation of 'why liquid A burnt the carpet' to be different from that of 'why the

event of liquid A's burning (of) the carpet occurred'. And indeed it will be, for the explanation of the former might be 'because liquid A is an acid', whilst the explanation of the latter might be something like 'because liquid A was dropped on it'. Now, as it happens, in this case both explanations rely on causal laws, but only the former renders something intelligible, and everyone is in agreement that to render something intelligible is not necessarily to provide a deductive–nomological explanation of it. In the case of agency, we might add, it may well be the case that the explanation of why someone or something did something will only be deductive–nomological when there was no intention present e.g. when we are explaining a reflex action. To deny this possibility from the outset is to beg the question against the anti-causalist.

48. Louch (1966: 5).
49. D'Oro (2009: 144–5).
50. See Taleb (2007) and Taleb and Pilpel (2010).
51. For diverse examples see Lippmann (1922), Bernays (1928/2005 & 1945), Packard (1957/2007), Charlton (1988), A.O. Rorty (1988: III.11–13), Gosling (1990), Hurtshouse (1991), Sutherland (1992), Schor (1998) Chomsky (2002), K. Taylor (2004), Elster (2007: 232–245), Ariely (2008), Brafman and Brafman (2008), Cialdini (2008), Thaler and Sunstein (2008/9), and J. Lehrer (2009). Chapters 4 and 5 offer templates for the surgical removal of some of the conflations that hinder the insights behind a number of these writings.
52. See *Appendix II* (§ 1).
53. Bernays (1928/2005: 76).
54. Dray (1963: 88), emphasis in the original.
55. For examples of different historiographical methods the relations between them see *Appendix II*.
56. Weber (1975: 125ff.). For exegesis see Allen (2010).
57. The conflations lead Jardine (2000: 259ff.) to identify Weber as a straight-forward causalist when in truth his position cuts across both camps in a helpful manner.
58. Williams (1980: 106–7), emphasis in the original. Famously, Williams' larger project is to show that unless someone is capable of being motivated to perform a certain action he has no good (no external) reason to do so, but this take on the much debated 'ought implies can' principle need not concern us for the moment.
59. The meta-theoretical approach of this chapter has much in common with that of J. L. Martin (2011), published after this book went into production. But whereas Martin's diagnosis of where explanatory theories go wrong is chiefly motivated by differences between first person (actor) and third person (observer) responses (cf. Jones and Nisbett 1972), mine has focused on the distinctness of different objects of explanation. For some interesting empirical data on actor/observer assymetries in the explanation of behaviour which I take to lend support Martin's main thesis see Knobe and Malle (2002).

4   The Operation of Reasons

1. Dancy (2000: 168).
2. Ramsey (1925: 115–6).
3. Pascal (1670/1966: III: 233).

4. Kavka (1983).
5. See § 1.1.
6. Proponents include G. Strawson (1986), Mele (1992), M. Smith (1994) and Lenman (1996). I distinguish between different senses of desire in § 4.4. For the notion of alief see § 5.5 in which I query whether such things (whatever their precise characterisation) are ever agential reasons and, if so, whether talk of them is sometimes reducible to talk of thoughts *about* and/or *as* surface strikings or appearances. For the purposes of the current chapter, however, I use the term 'belief' in a sense loose enough to include what Gendler calls 'aliefs' without presuming a positive answer to this question.
7. Proponents include (1970), Foot (1972), McDowell (1978 & 1979), McNaughton (1988) and Gendler (2008b: 558).
8. Proponents include Parfit (1997 & 2011) and Dancy (1993 & 2000).
9. Proponents include P.F. Strawson (1986), T. Nagel (1970) and Mele (1992), M.Smith (1994) and Brink (1997).
10. Proponents include Dancy (1995a & 2000) and Collins (1997). Hints of this are also evident in Williams (1980) and T. Nagel (1986: 142 & 1997: 112ff.). The anti-psychologism about normative reasons plugged into it is defended by realists of various stripes including Broome (1997), Raz (1986), Scanlon (1999), Dancy (2000) and Quinn (1993), as well as by the 'cognitive irrealist' Skorupski (2011) .
11. Clinton (1998), my emphasis.
12. Dylan (1966: 197).
13. For a taxonomy of some of these sense see Alvarez (2010: chs. 3 & 5).
14. Audi (1986: 75–6), emphasis in the original.
15. Ibid.: 77.
16. Ibid.; cf. Stoutland (1998). I explore the notion of a 'real' reason in § 5.4. Whether or not all the reasons we act for are 'proper' according to Audi's criteria is a matter of some dispute. It might be thought, for example, that considerations of duty are neither grounded upon nor sources of purpose of any kind.
17. Goetz (2009: 49).
18. M. Smith (1994: 104).
19. Skorupski (2010: 57ff.); cf. von Wright (1988, § 3: 83), who conflates the subset with the larger one and consequently offers very weak conditions for what it is to understand something as a reason (quoted in § 7.3). Skorupski (2010: 233ff) defends an account of 'Rational explanation' as one which takes actions to be caused by recognition of warrant. This has more in common with Balgay (1729/34: 559/85; see n. 69 below) than with any of the positions outlined in Chapter 3.
20. For a defence of this view of animal action and related cognition see Sandis (2010e & 2011c) and Bortolotti *et al.* (2012). In § 7.3 (note 37) I tentatively suggest that the required capacity is that of rule-following.
21. Dancy (2000: 1–5).
22. For detailed explorations of ontological matters relating to normative reasons see Skorupski (2010) and Parfit (2011: part I).
23. Williams (1980).
24. For the original distinction see Smith (1992: 329). It is worth noting that Smith has since distinguished between two different senses of 'good reason', contrasting rational grounds (facts) with rational springs (psychological states),

see Smith and Pettit (1997: 297ff.). Dancy's normative constraint is concerned with the former sense. While Smith concedes that we may act upon reasons so conceived, he denies that they have any explanatory power (which he takes to be part of the notion of a 'motivating reason').

25. Dancy (2000: 101).
26. Ibid.: 103.
27. Dancy (1995a), though this is not due to the worry of it being concerned with a distinct kind of object of explanation.
28. I borrow the term 'operative' from Moyar (2010).
29. http://www.btlife.bt.com/do-more-online/ten-reasons-to-try-twitter-today. Retrieved 11 April 2011
30. See Dancy (2004b).
31. http://www.btplc.com/careercentre/whyjoinbt/whyjoinbt.htm.   Retrieved 11 April 2011
32. http://www.goethe.de/lrn/prj/zgd/en867247.htm . Retrieved 11 April 2011.
33. D. G. Brown (1968: 9–10). A minor objection to Brown's claim that there are no relevant but neutral considerations would be the conceivability of what Dancy calls 'enabling conditions' (Dancy 2000: 127–30), but this does not affect his overall message.
34. http://persianoad.wordpress.com/2007/06/02/ten-good-reasons-to-eat-organic-food. Retrieved 11 April 2011.
35. See Sandis (2010c & 2011a) for issues surrounding the question of whether philosophers such as Williams (1980), Frankfurt (2004), and M. Schroeder (2007) are right to think that all normative reasons require the presence of some sort of passion, care, or desire in order to get going. Parfit (2011: part I) answers this question negatively.
36. Plato (1952), translated by Hackforth as 'fancy not being able to distinguish between the cause of a thing and that without which the cause would not be a cause!' and by Gallop as 'fancy being unable to distinguish between two things: the reason proper and that without which the reason could never be a reason!' See also Dancy (2004a: 45).
37. For the challenging view that acting for the reason that p is the exercise of the ability that is knowledge that p, see Hyman (1999, 2010 & 2011); cf. Dancy (2011).
38. For a detailed investigation of ways in which we can act in ignorance or with false beliefs see Parfit (2011: Vol. I, 150–164).
39. http://labouryes.org.uk/why-vote-yes. Retrieved 11 April 2011.
40. http://www.no2av.org. Retrieved 11 April 2011.
41. Various forms of this distinction may be found in Wittgenstein (1921/1969: § 1 & 1953/2009: §§ 95 & 429), Frege (1818–19), White (1972), McDowell (1995: 27), Hornsby (1997), and Dancy (2009b). I call for further refinement in § 6.4.
42. M.Smith (1994: 96), emphasis in the original.
43. Davidson (1963: 3–4 & 9).
44. M.Smith (1994: 206–7) We can take this general point on board without agreeing with his further claim that this can only be so when an agent is 'perfectly rational'.
45. Ibid.: 131, emphasis in the original.
46. Ibid.
47. Ibid.

48. The further specification rill depend on one's response to worries about deviant causal chains of the sort envisioned by Davidson (1973: 79).
49. See Bennett and Hacker (2003: 29 & 68ff.).
50. It is worth noting in relation to this that Smith (1994: 102) insists that his argument need not rely on a causal theory of action *explanation*, but only a causal theory of *action*; see Ancombe (1983: 101) and Ruben (2003: 113ff.) for this distinction. In Sandis (2009b) I argue that commitment to the latter view is what separates modern causalists from the fatalism of the ancient Greeks.
51. Davidson (1973: 65) and Sellars (1966: 144 & 156). I critically explore this thesis in Sandis (2009b: 363ff.).
52. There may be cases when 'the fact that I wanted something' and 'my wanting something' refer to one and the same, but not always so; see P.F. Strawson (1950) for an attack of the view that events can be facts, and Austin (1954) for a criticism of Strawson's arguments.
53. Smith (1994: 95), emphasis in the original.
54. Ibid.: 131. What Smith appears to mean by 'my normative reasons' is something like 'the reasons I take (perhaps mistakenly) to be normative'. Does Smith allow that I can act for these? Yes, but he also insist that they can't be my reasons for action if these reasons are meant to *explain* why the action occurs, let alone produce it. For the same reason, Smith also claims that we can't be motivated by them.
55. T. Nagel (1970: 27–9). For illuminating exegesis see Schueler (1995: ch. 1).
56. Hursthouse (1991).
57. E.g. Heuer (2004) and Raz (2009).
58. Hornsby (1993a: 134), emphasis in the original.
59. Raz (1999: 109–10); cf. Schueler (1995: 29–37).
60. T. Nagel (1970: 30) takes the presence of such desires to be a logically necessary condition of being motivated. By contrast Dancy (2000: 14) argues for the phenomenological reality of such desires, on the grounds that that to have a desire simply *is* to be motivated.
61. Frankfurt (1971: 12) famously divides thick desires into *first* and *second* order ones; Frankish (2004: xii–6) distinguishes between non-conscious, dispositional *basic* desires and representational, linguistically structured *super* desires. I think it is overall best to conceive of this distinction as one between different types of (first or second order) 'thick' desire, but aspects of it seem to also map onto Raz's thin/thick distinction.
62. In Sandis (2009c & 2011d) I argue that not even Hume believed this.
63. Skorupski (2010: 235ff.).
64. Darwall (2003: 436).
65. Dancy (2000: 8).
66. Chapter 6 attempts to demonstrate that this last claim of Dancy's is strictly speaking false, but my argument here does not rest on this conclusion.
67. I first raised this issue in Sandis (2007); cf. Hieronymi (2011). As I write this no citable version of this paper exists, so I shall not dwell on the differences and similarities between my specific approach and that of Hieronymi, save to say that the former are greater than the latter.
68. M. Smith (2003: 460–3).
69. Dancy (2003b: 487).
70. Dancy (2000: 2–6), my emphasis.

71. Not with Hume but with Balgay (1729/34: 559/85) who distinguished between 'exciting reasons' for choice and 'justifying reasons' for approbation. Balgay argued – contra Hutcheson – that our *approbation* of virtuous action is a sufficient exciting reason for it, Hutcheson (1725/6: 444/400ff.) having previously distinguished between rational and instinctive approbation. For context and commentary to this and other Early Modern debates on moral motivation see Darwall (1995).
72. Dancy (2003b: 489); cf. Prichard (1949), Falk (1948: 24–5), Frankena (1976: 51), and Raz (1986: 141). Falk's terminology is also inherited by T. Nagel (1970: 5–7) who helped put the theory of motivation on the meta-ethical map by famously announcing that he conceives of ethics as 'a branch of psychology' relating to the 'ultimate motivational basis' and that 'psychology, specifically motivation theory, may therefore be the appropriate field in which to make progress in ethical theory'. It should come as no surprise, therefore, that philosophers writing after him on this topic have also come to inherit this terminology and, consequently, some of the confusions which accompany it.
73. J.S. Brown (1961: 24).
74. Wallace (2003: 430 & 435); cf. Everson (2010).
75. Dancy (2003b: 470). I discuss various sorts of nesting explanations in Chapter 5.
76. Dancy (2003b: 481) does not think so, because he maintains, contra Wallace, that 'that something is the case can explain action, by standing as the reason for which it was done'. I argue against this thesis in Chapter 7.
77. For a related point about deliberation see Blackburn (1998: 250–6). We might also ask whether Dancy's understanding of motivation here is the same as the one he assumes in discussing the debate between motivation internalism and externalism (Dancy 1993: ch. 1).
78. Wallace (2003: 431), emphasis is in original.
79. In Sandis (2009b & 2011d) I argue that this is in fact also Hume's own position.
80. For this point see also Alvarez (2010).

5   Nested Explanations

1. Wittgenstein (1953/2009: §§ 126–9), emphasis in the original.
2. Nestroy (1847).
3. Cf. Stoutland (1998).
4. Dancy (2000: 173).
5. See Cabanac (1979).
6. See Sandis (2008).
7. See § 6.2 for clarification.
8. See Sandis (2009b).
9. See Hume (1777/1974: 244/app. I.18) and Wittgenstein (1953/2009: §§ 474–85 & 1969: §§ 599–613).
10. On this last point see Pink (2009).
11. See Bennett and Hacker (2003: 364–5).
12. Peculiar cases, such as that of behaviour caused by hypnotic suggestion, may differ, but these are defective or at best borderline cases of action, and not obviously intentional (see, for example, S. Schroeder 2010: 460).
13. Freud (1933/1971: 248).

14. Davidson (1976:261). Strictly speaking the current refers to those books published in R. F. Holland's edited series *Studies on Philosophical Psychology* (see Davidson 1963: fn.1) which included Peters (1958) and MacIntyre (1958). But many other critiques, such as Flew (1956) and Peters (1969), were written in the same vein.
15. Davidson (1982: 172).
16. As Bouveresse (1995:78) observes, Freud did not seek to extend the range of phenomena subject to reason explanations but, rather, to extend the methods of causal explanation employed in the natural sciences so that they could be applied to psychological phenomena.
17. I remain neutral here on whether or not psychoanalysis could in principle qualify as a science. For a recent argument in favour of a moderately positive answer to this question see Lacewing (2011) which tackles the earlier debate between Grünbaum (1984) and Hopkins (1988).
18. See, for example, Nietzsche (1868/1973: § 6), Freud (1901/1966), Bernays (1928/2005), and Packard (1957/2007).
19. Bernays (1928/2005: 75 & 77).
20. The proof for this is in the counterfactual pudding.
21. Ibid.: 75.
22. Packard (1957/2007: 39–40).
23. For more on implicit bias see § 5.4.
24. Indeed, in the next chapter I provide an argument in defence of this.
25. Packard (1957/2007: 243–4).
26. Ibid.: 231.
27. Ibid.: 257.
28. Ibid.: 232.
29. Ibid.: 231.
30. Ibid.: 249.
31. Regarding the subjects' alleged denial of 'a possible effect of the position of the article' one would like to know more about the exact question they were asked: an effect on *what* exactly?
32. Nisbett and Wilson (1977: 233).
33. See also §§ 3.3 and 4.2.
34. For a situationist versions of this thesis which frequently claim to have moral significance see the literature referred to in § 5.3 above.
35. I shall return to similar examples in § 5.5.
36. Strictly speaking it is also fallacious to infer (i) from (ii) since *a* reason for *x* need not be *the* (only) reason for *x*. In Chapter 6 I argue further that we cannot even infer from (ii) that this was *a* reason for her choosing since explanations, unlike reasons, are factive.
37. See § 4.2.
38. Cf. von Wright (1988: 89).
39. Freud (1971: 285).
40. See, for example, Reeves (1962: 70–4) and Ogilvy (1963).
41. Bouveresse (1995: xx); cf. Wittgenstein's remarks as recorded in Malcolm (1968: 44–5).
42. The notion of an implicit association should be distinguished from Gendler's (2008a & b) concept of an alief, which may be either implicit or explicit. For the relation between the two notions see Gendler (2008b: 574–85).

43. See the research papers conducted in conjunction with *Project Implicit*, all archived at http://www.projectimplicit.net/articles.php. For a sceptical interpretation of what the tests show see Egloff *et al* (2005). An indication of further debates has been captured by Tierney (2008).
44. Fricker (2007).
45. Jolls and Sunstein (2006: 946).
46. Ibid.: 967.
47. Bloom (2010)
48. This is not to say that environmental factors are never required to explain the considerable differences in our tastes.
49. Gendler (2008a: 642).
50. Gendler (2008b: 557).
51. Ibid.: 555.
52. Ibid.: 556–7.
53. Gendler (2008a: 659).
54. Gendler (2008b: 557).
55. Ibid.: 558.
56. Gendler (2008a: 650).
57. This much is unquestionably true of Bernays (1928/2005), Packard (1957/2007) Thaler and Sunstein (2008/9), etc., whatever one makes of their ethics and politics.
58. See Kuhn (1962).

6   The Structure of Agential Explanation

1. Frankfurt (2006: 15).
2. As Dancy notes, there is 'more than one way in which things can go wrong. The agent can be wrong about whether *p*, or wrong about whether if it were the case that *p*, that would be a reason for acting' (Dancy 2008: 267; cf. 2000: 140, and Parfit 2011: Vol. I, 150–64). I do not concern myself with the second way here, though my suggestions are compatible with its possibility. Mele (1997) argues that non-psychologists such as Dancy should take the possibility of agents performing actions which they mistakenly think of as being 'objectively favoured' to show that not all 'intentional, deliberate, purposeful' actions are performed for reasons, unless the concept of a reason geared towards action explanation is different from that geared towards evaluation (Mele's own view is that such conceptual matters should be experimentally informed).
3. Dancy (2000: 131).
4. Peacocke (2008), though this is not to side with realists such Peacocke and Boghossian (2006) against pragmatists such as Rorty (1998) and Dummett (2006), but merely noting that we frequently use 'explanation' as shorthand for 'true explanation'; this is so whatever the precise relation of truth to justification, meaning, and belief. Indeed, I am here agreeing with Rorty that 'the resolution of these debates will have no bearing on practice' (Rorty & Engel 2007: 34).
5. Cf. Achinstein (1983: 19 & 116ff.). Ruben (2003:185–6) is right to point out that 'poor' may also be used as a relative term, both objectively and subjectively.

For the perils of conflating the analysis of explanation with the pragmatics of giving explanations see Ruben (1990: 21).
6. See G. Strawson (1986/2010: 35–6/29–31).
7. Lenman (2009: § 6).
8. Cf. Searle (2001: 100–1). Mark Lance pointed out to me that Dancy is not committed to the view that *theoretical* explanation can be non-factive. This renders his stance less counter-intuitive than it might at initially appear to be. Be that as it may, I see no reason to limit the thought that all genuine explanations are factive to the theoretical domain. If it is false that JD likes to shop for leather trousers, then the statement 'JD went to the Milan conference because he likes to shop for leather trousers' cannot explain why JD went to the Milan conference (even if he ended up buying several pairs during his visit). The same applies to teleological explanation: if it is false that he intended to purchase any leather trousers, then we cannot explain his going to Milan by stating that he went there *in order* to do so.
9. Lenman (2009, § 6), emphasis is in original.
10. See Chapter 4.
11. In what follows I shall use 'non-psychologism' as shorthand for this view about agential reasons, to distinguish it from the view in the theory of motivation described as 'anti-psychologism' in Chapter 4.
12. Dancy (2003b: 469).
13. Dancy (2008: 267).
14. Dancy (2003a: 427).
15. Davis (2003b: 455).
16. Ibid.: 480.
17. Ibid.: 481.
18. Hempel and Oppenheim (1948). Dancy (2011) claims that 'if we take the whole sentence to be the *explanans*, then of course all explanation is factive, but trivially so'. But we might equally complain that reasons explanation is trivially non-factive if we take *reasons* to be the *explanantia*. In what follows I argue that we should not even think they form a *part* of any given *explanans*.
19. Achinstein (1983: 102).
20. Cf. Ruben (1990: 23ff.).
21. Hence Anscombe's characterisation of intentional actions as 'those to which a certain sense of the question "Why?" is given application' (Anscombe 1957: § 5).
22. Dancy (2003a: 426–7).
23. Ibid.: 427.
24. This contrasts sharply with the knowledge case that Dancy claims is analogous. For in the knowledge case what is false is the very thing that is being put forth as a truth/knowledge/fact, whereas here the truth claim/assertion is not 'that *p*' but 'that his reason was that *p*' (Dancy 2000: 131–2).
25. Dancy (2000: 134); see also Knobe and Malle (2002).
26. Ibid.: 137.
27. Dancy (2004: 25).
28. Ibid.: 25.
29. Ibid.: 26.
30. Dancy (2000: 132–7).
31. Ibid.: 134.

32. Hyman (1999: 443).
33. Dancy (2008: 274).
34. Ibid.: 270.
35. See Davis (2003: 458) and M. Smith (2010: 155–6).
36. M. Smith (1998: 158).
37. According to Dancy, Smith's line of argument lends no support to psychologism, but only to the 'new theory' that motivating reasons are facts *about* our psychological states, and not the states themselves (Dancy 2000: 121ff.; see also 2003b: 469). Smith, by contrast, sees no great tension, taking 'motivating reasons' to be explanatory (Dancy 2003: 152) and argues that all explanations of intentional action appeal to psychological states (Smith 1998, esp.155–8; see also Mele forthcoming).
38. Dancy (2000: 127).
39. Ibid.
40. Ibid.: 131.
41. I am grateful to David Dolby for ongoing conversations on the matters which follow, upon which we have come to share a bundle of interrelated thoughts which can no longer be individuated on any basis of original ownership. Unsurprisingly, some of the distinctions that follow mirror those made with regard to action in § 1.2.
42. Davis (2003: 454–5).
43. Dancy (2003b: 481).
44. Dancy (2009b: 289).
45. White (1970: 16). In *Appendix I* (§ 2) I suggest that we might also think of things do in the same way as things believed, etc.
46. Quine (1960: 216), Prior (1963 & 1971: 16–22) and Davidson (1968); cf. Millgram (2009: 149–76). For objections to the Quine-Prior thesis see White (1972: 80), Rundle (1979: 286–7) and Künne (2003: 68–9).
47. Kenny (1963: 127).
48. See, for example, B. Russell (1919), Ayer (1940: § 10), and Moore (1953: 59ff. & 1966: 133–43). I owe these references to White (1970: 14), a text to which the main thrust of the argument in this section is indebted, even when White himself is under the line of attack.
49. I thus part company with White when he states that, across the board, 'to read, take down, print, preserve, alter, or destroy what is said is to read, take down, print, preserve, alter, or destroy what is uttered or written' (White 1970: 16.) Such passages suggest to me that White ultimately remains committed to identifying 'that *p*' with 'what is conveyed by a sentence', though, if so, he seems somewhat reluctant to announce this (see White 1970: 11, 14, 24 & 1972: 69 & 71). Of course I *can* write down what you said, but not in a sense in which this can be destroyed.
50. White (1972) ; cf. Bennett and Hacker (2003: 172ff. & 268).
51. Cf. Everson (2009).
52. Dancy himself encourages such considerations (e.g. Dancy 2009b: 286); see also *Appendix I* (§ 2).
53. Davidson briefly looks into French usage but with an altogether different aim. In doing so, however, he tellingly misreads the 'que' in 'dit que' as a demonstrative (Davidson 1968: 98–9).
54. I owe this example to Arto Laitinen.

55. Dancy (2000: 147).
56. See, for example, Dancy (2003a: 427) and S. Schroeder (2010: 559ff.).
57. A refreshing exception is Alfred Mele (forthcoming) who argues that 'even if all reasons for action are true propositions and true propositions can cause nothing, it cannot be inferred from this that causalism about action explanation is false'.
58. Dancy (1995b).
59. Dancy (2008: 270).
60. Alvarez (2010: 177, fn 11); cf. Dancy (2000: 134). Alvarez's disjunctivist account of agential reasons should be distinguished from disjunctivist accounts of *acting* for a reason, for it does not follow from the view that I acted for the reason that *p if* a, b, or c that my reason (that *p*) *was* either a, b, or c. According to non-disjunctivism about reasons, acting upon the false belief that *p* just *is* acting for the reason that *p*. As Dancy (2008: 268ff) has noted, this best coheres with disjunctive or trisjunctive accounts of acting for a reason; see Dancy (2000: 140) for an earlier suggestion.
61. Alvarez (2010: 178).
62. Ibid. (174, fn. 8; cf. 6.2.3).

7 Spheres of Explanation

1. von Wright (1988: 83)
2. Dretske (1988b: 15), emphasis in the original.
3. See Dretske (2009).
4. See von Wright (1963) and Davidson (1963 & 1969).
5. Dretske (1988b: 42–5), emphasis in the original. See also Dretske (2010).
6. See Dretske (1983) for his defence of representationalism. The identification of true beliefs with facts is persuasively challenged by Rundle (1993). Such conceptions of facts undermine the notion of a 'representational fact' as employed by Dretske. Further worries about Dretske's notion of representation content have been voiced by Hutto (2001). To highlight these and other difficulties I keep the term 'content' within inverted commas throughout this chapter. There is little in Drestke's account of action explanation, however, which renders it hostage to this particular detail of his presentation.
7. Dretske (2004: 170–1).
8. Dretske (1988b: 114–5).
9. Ibid.: 43, emphasis in the original.
10. Ibid., emphasis in the original.
11. Ibid.: 43–4.
12. A structuring cause need not be a reason for which an agent acts in order to explain why a stimulus elicited a particular piece of behaviour.
13. Taleb and Blyth (2011: 35–6).
14. See § 3.3.
15. See, for example, Dretske (1993, 2004 & 2010)
16. Dretske (2004: 172–6).
17. Compare, for example, Davidson (1963) to Dretske (1988b: 44).
18. See, for example, Davidson (1967b).
19. Dretske (1988b: 32 & 1988a: 40–3).

20. See also Dretske (1988b: 15 & 2009).
21. Wollaston (1722/1750: 355), as quoted in Priestley (1777: § 8.3/85–6).
22. Priestley (1777: § 8.3/86).
23. cf. Toulmin (1970), Tanney (1995), Hutto (1999), S. Schroeder (2001a & 2010), and D'Oro (2012a).
24. This point is nicely emphasised by Sehon (1997). Davidson himself confesses that the possibility of causal deviancy forms an 'insurmountable' challenge to his view and that he despairs of 'spelling out … the way in which attitudes must cause actions if they are to rationalize the action' (Davidson 1973: 79).
25. Dretske (1988b: 94–5), emphasis in the original; cf. Dretske (1988b: 80).
26. On some non-anomalous physicalist views, an *extra*ordinary (neurobiological) understanding may be possible given a considerable amount of knowledge about relevant correlations. Dretske (1988a: 31–2) explicitly rejects such a possibility, claiming that he 'doesn't share these advanced ideas.
27. Dretske (1988b: ch. 3).
28. In primary school I would frequently flinch when an angry teacher used the word 'constantly'.
29. Many thanks to Jack Marr for bringing the point to my attention. This particular form of rationalisation should be distinguished from those involved in (i) the 'unconscious factor' cases described in Chapter 5 and (ii) cases where we *concoct* explanations after a fact whose occurrence may have been random (see Taleb 2007).
30. Anscombe (1957: §15); cf. von Wright (1988).
31. Levine (1997: 9). Ella occasionally suggests that the curse itself (as opposed to any 'command' she is given) is the triggering cause: 'Father had told me to, and the curse was tugging at me to obey' (Ibid.: 16). This doesn't threaten the idea that the curse can only cause her to do whatever she is ordered to in virtue of the meanings of the words spoken to her.
32. Ella talks of not being able to 'hold out for long', but we can easily stipulate a scenario in which she is not able to hold out *at all* and perhaps cannot even *try* to do otherwise, though trying couldn't, in any case, help action-based-theories unless one conceiving of all actions as tryings; cf. Hornsby (1980).
33. This should make us sceptical of any behaviourist or functionalist accounts of desire according to which to desire *p* is 'to be disposed to act so as to bring about *p*' or, at the very least, 'to be disposed to take whatever actions [one] believes are likely to bring about *p*' (T. Schroeder 2009; cf. M. Schroeder 2007: 195).
34. It would be misguided to maintain that her action is non-voluntary (but still intentional under some description), for there is a crucial difference between being coerced or otherwise forced to do something and being under a spell of compulsion; as Sartre (1958: 433ff.) was keen to point out, the former still leaves room for an element of choice.
35. Ella is no wanton, for she cares very much about what she wills, and is arguably bad news for revealed preference theorists. Her case suggests that the 'content' of an attitude cannot be determined in terms of *actual* causal relations. A *counterfactual* analysis might be more promising, for whether or not she desires to do something (in a sense that would render any action of hers that followed from such a desire intentional) is better understood in terms of

how she *would* act if she had a choice (where this could include the choice to give in to duress or coercion). I here side with Knox (1968: 63) who suggests that 'choice implies rejection'. To say 'no' to desire is 'to be liberated from its compulsiveness', though we frequently also reject the option of *not* giving in to our desire, without being under any kind of compulsion to do so.

36. von Wright (1988: 83).
37. This distinction between following rules and merely acting in accordance with them is arguably crucial in determining whether certain animals have agential reasons. See MacIntyre (1999: 53ff.) and Glock (2010: 387ff.).
38. Dretske (2004: 174).
39. For its relation to the various identification mechanisms of the kind offered by offered by Frankfurt (1978) see Sandis (2009b: 366–7).
40. I trialled my initial thoughts about the Ella Enchanted scenario on the *Flickers of Freedom* blog. Both the original post and the discussion that followed may be found here (retrieved 18 February 2011): http://agencyandresponsibility. typepad.com/flickers-of-freedom/2011/02/enchanting-causes.html
41. See Sandis (2010d) for a critical appraisal of what I take to be the limited value of such experiments; cf. Papineau (2011).
42. Cf. O' Brien (2007: 129–58).
43. Hursthouse (1991), cf. von Wright (1988: 89). For a Humean response to Hursthouse see M. Smith (1998: 158–61).
44. See, for example, Knobe and Kelly (2009).
45. See Dretske (1988b: 88).
46. For controversies regarding the very notion of motivational strength compare Thalberg (1985) to Mele (2010).
47. Cf. von Wright (1988: 281).
48. A similar objection can also be raised against Davidson's model of action explanation. Indeed Frankfurt (1978 & 1988) and Velleman (1992) do just this, though Velleman's worry is one about agency tout court and Frankfurt does not clearly separate it from the altogether different questions of free will and responsibility. Frankfurt's response is to claim that intentional behaviour is caused by second-order desires to be actuated by our motives, whilst Velleman concludes that intentional behaviour is caused by desires to act in accordance with considerations which constitute good reasons for acting. But we must now ask ourselves whether or not these desires function as triggering causes. If so it is unclear why we should regard any behaviour caused by them as intentional. If not a suitable structural story needs to be told.
49. On some accounts, such as that of Mellor (1995), this is all causation amounts to. For a counterfactual theory of causal explanation that requires no explicit generalisations (and might not even need implicit ones) see Ruben (2003: 185–217).
50. See *Appendix II* (§ 1).
51. See von Wright (1971: 76–82) and Bennett and Hacker (2003: 364–5).
52. Brown (1968: 134).
53. Human and Alvarez (1998); cf. von Wright (1971:67).
54. Hyman (2002: 309).
55. O'Connor (2000: 61).
56. See Ruben (2003: 155ff.)

Appendix I – The Ontology of Action

1. Wittgenstein (1980: 112).
2. It is worth noting that the terms 'doings' and 'things done' simply do not have set meanings in ordinary language. For one, things we can be said to be *doing* fall in the category of *things we do* (as opposed to our *doing* these things). In addition the term 'deed', with which both Hornsby and Macmurray contrast 'doings' (Macmurray 1938: 74 & Hornsby 1993a: 142) can denote actions in both the sense of things which can *occur* as well as hat of things which we *do*. But *what* I might be *doing* is not the same as *my doing* (of) it. Still, there is clear *conceptual* space for the distinction in question, even if we have to place a straightjacket on certain aspects of everyday usage in order to capture it. As Hornsby herself writes: 'There are many uses of "what he did" which refer to particulars; or at least it may be that philosophers have so often used "what he did" meaning it to refer to his doing what he did that we now sometimes understand "what he did" as referring to a particular. If that is so, there is an ambiguity in "what he did" and then my claim will be that it is worth taking the pains to disambiguate' (Hornsby 1980*:* 4, fn. 3, my emphasis).
3. Hornsby (1980: 4, fn. 3).
4. Hornsby (1999: 624, fn. 5).
5. Davidson (1999: 636–7), my emphasis.
6. Dancy (2009: 401), emphasis in the original.
7. Hornsby (1993a: 142), my emphasis.
8. Thanks to Galen Strawson for pointing this out to me. When engaged in the process of uprooting the tree I may be said to be uprooting it, but I am not doing *my* uprooting it (as we saw when we rejected CVTD in § 2.2).
9. Hornsby (1980: 4, fn .4).
10. Hornsby (1999: 625).
11. Davidson (1967a: 108), emphasis in the original.
12. Davidson (1963: 5, fn. 2), my emphasis. For an interpretation of that Davidson according to which he shares Melden's assumption see Sandis (2004b).
13. Davidson (1967a: 109).
14. Ibid.: 105.
15. Ibid.: 114.
16. According to Davidson (1968) what we are pointing to when we use the expression 'he said that' is an uttered or written token. But see § 6.4.
17. Rundle (1979: 8–11); see also Hacker (1982) who offers a persuasive argument against the very idea that philosophy could confirm or disconfirm the existence of any 'posited entities'.
18. Ryle (1949: 24).
19. Wittgenstein (1953/2009: §§ 401–2); see also Wittgenstein (1974: IV & X; 1975: I–VI) and Hacker (1996: 214–45).
20. Pyle (1999: 104).
21. Rundle (1979: 188–9).
22. Rundle (1993: 17). Cf. Hacker (1998: 94).
23. Dancy (2009).
24. Ibid.: 409.

25. Ibid.: 410.
26. Ibid.: 404.
27. Glock (1997: 98).
28. See § 6.4.
29. See D'Oro (2005b, 2007 & 2012a,b).
30. See § 4.3.
31. Davidson (1967a: 105).
32. Ibid.
33. Indeed many talk of intentional events as if the notion was unproblematic, thereby betraying commitment to CVA. See, for example, Malle (2006: 12).
34. Davidson (1971a: 195).
35. See Hyman (2001: § 5) for complications relating to the proposal that agents are the *subjects* of events.

Appendix II – Thought and Motive in Historiography

1. Hegel (1849/1988: 16).
2. Hume (1739–40/1978: 632/ appendix to 1.3.14.13).
3. Ibid.: xviii/Int. 10.
4. See Baier (2008c: 230) for the trouble this creates in relation to both *Treatise* definitions of a 'cause'. Baier also notes that Don Garrett and Peter Millican have suggested that the dropping of principle of contiguity from the definitions in his first *Enquiry* might have occurred to allow for mental causation. Its absence would also seem to allow for action at a distance.
5. See, for example, Hume (1739–40/1978: 358/2.2.5.4 & 379/3.2.1.9).
6. Ibid.: 83/1.3.4.2.
7. Ibid.: 133/1.3.9.13.
8. See, for example, Hume (1739–40/1978: 351/2.2.3.9 & 97/1.3.7.6). Indeed, Hume's naturalist concept of what contemporary philosophers call *normative* reasons is proto-Wittgensteinian insofar as it is to be explained by human forms of life and associated tendencies and practices (expectation, induction, prediction, and so forth) rather than the other way round; see Hume (1739–40/1978: 88/1.3.6.3), P.F. Strawson (1985/2005: 11ff.), Garrett (2007: 4–5), and Sandis (2009c: 151–2 & 2011d).
9. Hume (1739–40/1978: 403–4/2.3.1).
10. Ibid.: 83/1.3.4.2.1; see also Austin (1961: 156).
11. So construed, it is symmetric to informed prediction (see § 3.4).
12. Hume (1739–40/1978: xix/Int. 10).
13. Hume (1777/1974: 83/8.1.7).
14. See, for example, Hume (1739–40/1978: 316/2.1.11.1).
15. Baier (2008b: 4/242).
16. See *Appendix II* § 2.
17. Baier (2008b: 14/250).
18. Ibid.: 7/243.
19. Knobe (2003a & b). For the view that experimental philosophy is a continuation of Hume's philosophical psychology see Appiah (2008: 1 & 9–11). My worry with Appiah's position is that it takes Hume's words seriously out of context. For example, Appiah quotes Hume as writing that 'the study of

history confirms the reasonings of true philosophy' when what he actually wrote in this passage (which Appiah omits to provide a precise reference for) is '... in this particular [viz. the role of bigotry and superstition in the establishment of rights], the study of history confirms the reasonings of true philosophy' (Hume 1739–40/1978: 562/3.2.10.15).

20. I take the essay to be evidence that Hume's philosophical and historical work are not as distinct as was once supposed, thereby also adding credence to Hume's remark to Stewart that he is not 'such a Sceptic as you may, perhaps, imagine' (letter to Stewart, February 1754).

21. Baier reminds us that his essay 'Of the Study of History' was 'later withdrawn, because of its condescending tone to women, whom he had urged to read history rather than novels and romances' (Baier: 2008b: 5/242).

22. Hume (1777/1985: 567–8). See also A. Baier (2008b); cf. Knowles (1963: ch.1).

23. Hume (1739–40/1978: 3–4/1).

24. Hume (1777/1985: 568).

25. Ibid.: 151.

26. Hume (1739–40/1978: 97/1.3.7.7).

27. Hume (1777/1974: 169–70/73.2). This interest character is temporarily forgotten in his discussion 'of personal identity' (Baier 2008b: 242ff.), but the important role it plays throughout the rest of his work suggests that it would be myopic for any account of Hume on the self to ignore the question of character (cf. P. Russell 1995: 95). Hume would have agreed, for instance, with David Knowles' pronouncement that 'a life is not a bundle of acts; it is a stream or a landscape; it is the manifestation of a single mind and personality that may grow more deformed or more beautiful to the end' (Knowles 1963: 10). One way out would be to follow Christine Korsgaard's suggestion that perhaps Hume's 'notion of the person as the object of pride or love is not the same as the notion of the person as a bundle of successive perceptions' (Korsgaard 2008: 290).

28. Croce (1941: 47) and Knowles (1963: 4–5), both quoted in Carr (1961: 77).

29. Merrill (2008: 138).

30. Davidson (1978: 87).

31. Hume (1739–40/1978: 403–4/2.3.1–2).

32. Hume (1777/1974: 88/ 8.1.15); see also Baier (2008b: 12/249).

33. Hume (1739–40/1978: 413/2.3.3.1).

34. See Hume (1777/1974: 134/1.3 & App. 3/624). I build a case for an anti-Humean reading of Hume's understanding of agential reasons in Sandis (2009c & 2011d); see also Korsgaard (1997: 24) and Baier (2008 & 2010).

35. Korsgaard (2008: 292).

36. See § 4.3.

37. Hume (1777/1985: 16).

38. It is worth noting just how weak Hume's definitions of 'cause' and 'necessity' actually are: 'I define necessity in two ways, conformable to the two definitions of cause, of which it makes an essential part. I place it either in the constant union and conjunction of like objects, or in the inference of the mind from one to the other' (1739–40/1978: 409/2.3.2). For a full exploration of Hume's causal language see Sandis (2011b).

39. None of this prevents Hume from pursuing his 'reconciling project' of demonstrating that necessity (as he has defined it) is compatible with free will,

which Hume equates to the liberty of *spontaneity* to do as one desires. Far from being an obstacle moral responsibility, the necessity which binds character to action is *required* for its existence, at least given Hume's account of the virtues, according to which the viciousness or virtue of any given act arises from 'some *cause* in the character and disposition of the person who performed them' (1777/197: 8.2.29/98); see also Millican (2011).

40. Hume (1778/1983: 3–4).
41. Collingwood (1946/1994: 73 & 75).
42. Ibid.: 76.
43. Ibid.: 83.
44. Ibid.: 84.
45. Collingwood (1940/1998: part I, esp. part VI).
46. Bevir (1999: 157–8). Bevir's quotations are from Collingwood (1946/1994: 214).
47. Ibid.: 158.
48. But see Stoutland (1999) for ways in which Davidson remains an 'intentionalist'.
49. See Bevir (1999: 125).
50. Stueber (2006:197–204).
51. Ibid.: 152–72. Stueber is thereby also committed to a moderate form of intentionalism, according to which 'an agent's or author's intentions are relevant for the interpretive practice of the human sciences' (Stueber 2009: 290).
52. Ibid.: 214–8.
53. Shinn (1924). Subsequent to my initially suggesting this interpretation (in Sandis 2011e) Stueber let me know that he did not conceive of the cover art in this way, but simply chose it because Theodor Lipps followed Adam Smith in illustrating empathy through the example of bystanders 'twisting this way and that as they watch the tight-rope walker' (Smith 1759: i.1.3). Stueber added, however, that he much prefers my own take on it and that this just shows that interpretation is not always guided by an author's intentions.
54. Dray (1995: 44–50).
55. Collingwood (1946/1994: 177).
56. Anscombe (1957: § 46).
57. Dray (1995: 49, n. 29).
58. Collingwood (1946/1994: 214–5). For an alternative way of capturing the nature of action explanation which does not resort to the inside/outside metaphor, see Collingwood (1940/1998: 285–89). Many thanks to Giuseppina D'Oro for this reference.
59. Collingwood (1946/1994: 213–4).
60. Ibid.: 215.
61. Dray (1980:12); see also D'Oro (2003 & 2005a). Further parallels between Hegelian and Wittgensteinian approaches to mind and action are explored in C.Taylor (1979 & 1983); see also Laitinen and Sandis (2010b: 6–7).
62. Dray (1995: 22–4).
63. See Bennett and Hacker (2003: 364–5).
64. See Collingwood (1946/1994: 302–14).
65. Ibid.: 216–7.
66. Ibid.: 283.
67. Grice (1989: 117).
68. Collingwood (1946/1994: 283); see also Collingwood (1939: 53–76).

69. Bevir (1999: 300).
70. See Browning (2010: 355).
71. Collingwood (1946/1994: 300).
72. Ibid.: 300–1.
73. Ibid.: 301.
74. See Wittgenstein (1953/2009: §§ 253–4), Collingwood (1946/1994: 12ff.), Hacker (1990: 21), and Browning (2010: 355).
75. See Sandis (2011e).
76. Hume (1739–40/1978: 96–7, n.1/1.3.7.5, n.20; see also 623–5/App. 2 & 3).
77. Happily, Hume's distinctions are detachable from his account of the difference between simple conceptions and beliefs as one of mere firmness in the conception.
78. This was part of Weber's point, as introduced in § 3.5.
79. Hume (1778/1983: 3–4).

Bibliography

Achinstein, P. (1975), 'The Object of Explanation' in Körner, pp. 1–45.
—— (1983), *The Nature of Explanation* (New York: Oxford University Press).
Ackrill, J. L. (1978), 'Aristotle on Action', *Mind*, Vol. 87, No. 348 (Oct.), 595–601.
Aguilar, J. H. and Buckareff, A. (eds) (2009), *Philosophy of Action: 5 Questions* (Birkerød: Automatic Press).
—— (eds) (2010), *Causing Human Actions: New Perspectives on the Causal Theory of Action* (Cambridge MA: MIT Press).
Alcock, J. and Sherman, P. (1994), 'The Utility of the Proximate-Ultimate Dichotomy in Ethology', *Ethology*, Vol. 96, No. 1 (Jan.–Dec.), 58–62.
Alexander, P. (1962), 'Rational Behaviour and Psychoanalytic Explanation', *Mind*, LXXI. Reprinted in Care and Lendesman (1968: 159–78) to which any page numbers given refer.
Alessi, G. (1992), 'Models of Proximate and Ultimate Causation in Psychology', *American Psychologist*, Vol. 47, No. 11 (Nov) (Special Issue: *Reflections on B. F. Skinner and Psychology*), 1359–70.
Allen, K. (2010), 'Weber', in O'Connor and Sandis, pp. 546–53.
Allen, K. and Stoneham, T. (eds) (2011), *Causation and Modern Philosophy* (London: Routledge).
Alvarez, M. (1999), 'Actions and Events: Some Semantical Considerations', *Ratio*, XII (Sept), 213–39.
—— (2010), *Kinds of Reasons: An Essay in the Philosophy of Action* (Oxford: Oxford University Press).
Alvarez, M. and Hyman, J. (1998), 'Agents and their Actions', *Philosophy*, 73, 218–45.
Anscombe, G. E. M. (1957), *Intention* (Oxford: Blackwell).
—— (1958), 'Modern Moral Philosophy', *Philosophy*, 33, 1–19.
—— (1979), ' "Under A Description" ', *Noûs* 13. Reprinted in her *Metaphysics and the Philosophy of Mind* – Collected Papers Volume II (Oxford: Blackwell), 208–19, to which any page references refer.
—— (1983), 'The Causation of Action', in (ed.) C. Ginet, *Knowledge and Mind* (Oxford: Oxford University Press), 174–90. Reprinted in Geach and Gormally (2005: 89–108), to which any page numbers given refer.
—— (1989), 'von Wright on Practical Inference', in (eds) P.A.Schilpp and L.E. Hahn, *The Philosophy of Georg Henrik von Wright* (La Salle IL: Open Court Press), 377–404. Reprinted as 'Practical Inference' in Geach and Gormally (2005: 109–47), to which any page numbers given refer.
Appiah, K.A. (2008), *Experiments in Ethics* (Boston MA: Harvard University Press).
Ariely, D. (2008), *Predictably Irrational: The Hidden Forces That Shape Our Decisions* (London: Harper).
Ariew, A. (2003), 'Ernst Mayr's "Ultimate/Proximate" Distinction Reconsidered and Reconstructed', *Biology and Philosophy*, Vol. 18, No. 4, 553–65.
Aristotle (1989a), *Physics*: Books I–IV, revised edition, trans. P. H. Wicksteed and F. M. Cornford (Harvard MA: Loeb Classical Library).

—— (1989b), *Metaphysics*: Books I–XI, revised edition, trans. H. Tredennick (Harvard MA: Loeb Classical Library).

Armstrong, D. P. (1991), 'Levels of Cause and Effect as Organizing Principles for Research in Animal Behaviour', *Canadian Journal of Zooolgy*, Vol. 69, No. 4, 823–29.

Atkinson, J. L. (1969), 'Change of Activity: A New Focus for the Theory of Motivation', in Mischel (1969: 105–35).

Atkinson. R. L., Atkinson, R. C, Smith, E. E., Bem, D. J., and Hilgard, E. R. (eds) (1996), *Introduction to Psychology*, 12th edition (Florida: Harcourt Brace College Publishing).

Audi, R. (1986), 'Acting for Reasons', *Philosophical Review*, 95. Reprinted in Mele (1997: 75–105) to which any page numbers given refer.

—— (1993), *Action, Intention, and Reason* (Ithaca, NY: Cornell University Press).

Austin, J. L. (1954), 'Unfair to Facts', *Proceedings of the Aristotelian Society*, Supplementary Vol. XXIV. Reprinted in Austin (1961: 154–74), to which any page numbers given refer.

—— (1961), *Philosophical Papers*, 3rd edition (1979), (eds) J. O. Urmson and G. J. Warnock (Oxford: Oxford University Press).

Ayer, A. J. (1940), *Foundations of Empirical Knowledge* (London: Macmillan & Co.).

—— (1956), 'Freedom and Necessity', in his *Philosophical Essays* (London: Macmillan & Co.), 271–84.

—— (1964), *Man as a Subject for Science* (London: Athlone).

Bach, K. (1980), 'Actions are not Events', *Mind*, Vol. 89, 114–20.

Baier, A. C. (2008a), *Death and Character: Further Reflections on Hume* (Boston MA: Harvard University Press).

—— (2008b), 'Acting in Character' in Baier (2008a: 3–21) and Sandis (2009: 241–56). References are to both editions, in chronological order.

—— (2008c), 'The Energy in the Cause', in Baier (2008a: 224–36).

—— (2010), 'Hume', in O'Connor and Sandis (2010: 513–20).

Baker, J. R. (1938), 'The Evolution of Breeding Seasons', in (ed.) G. R. de Beer, *Evolution: Essays on Aspects of Functional Biology* (Oxford: Clarendon Press), 161–77.

Balguy (1729/34), *Foundation of Moral Goodness*, 3rd edition [as included in *A Collection of Tracts Moral and Theological*] (London: J. Pemberton).Any references are by section number, followed by the page number(s) in Selby-Bigge (1897).

Bennett, M. R. and Hacker, P. M. S. (2003), *Philosophical Foundations of Neuroscience* (Oxford: Blackwell).

Berkowitz, L. (ed.) (1977), *Advances in Experimental Social Psychology*, Vol. 10 (New York: Academic Press).

Berlin, I. (1960), 'The Concept of Scientific History', in *History and Theory*. Reprinted in Berlin (1998: 17–59), to which any page numbers given refer.

—— (1969), *Four Essays on Liberty* (Oxford: Oxford University Press).

—— (1974), 'The Divorce between the Sciences and the Humanities' in Berlin (1998: 326–59).

—— (1998), *The Proper Science of Mankind* (London: Pimlico).

Bernays, E. (1928/2005), *Propaganda*, new edition (New York: IG Publishing).

—— (1945), *Public Relations* (Boston, MA: Bellman Publishing Company).

Bevir, M. (1999), *The Logic of the History of Ideas* (Cambridge: Cambridge University Press).

Bindra D. and Stewart J. (eds) (1966), *Motivation: Selected Readings* (London: Penguin).

Binkley, R., Bronaugh, R., and Marras, A. (eds) (1971), *Agent, Action, and Reason* (Oxford: Oxford University Press).

Bittner, R. (2001), *Doing Things for Reasons* (Oxford: Oxford University Press).

Black, M. (ed.) (1965), *Philosophy in America* (London: Allen & Unwin).

Blackburn, S. (1998), *Ruling Passions: A Theory of Practical Reasoning* (Oxford: Clarendon Press).

Bloom, P. (2010), *How Pleasure Works: The New Science of Why We Like What We Like* (New York: Norton).

Bolles, R. C. (1975), *Theory of Motivation* (New York: Harper Row).

Bolton, N. (ed.) (1979), *Philosophical Problems in Psychology* (London: Methuen).

Borger, R. and Cioffi, R. (eds) (1970), *Explanation in the Behavioural Sciences: Confrontations* (Cambridge: Cambridge University Press).

Bortolotti, L., Blassime, A, and Sandis, C. (2012) 'With Power Comes Vulnerability', forthcoming in (eds) M. Quigley and S. Chan, *Humans and Other Animals: Challenging the Boundaries of Humanity* (Bloomsbury Academic).

Bouveresse, J. (1995), *Wittgenstein Reads Freud – The Myth of the Unconscious*, trans. C. Cosman (Princeton NJ: Princeton University Press).

Brafman, R. and Brafman, O. (2008), *Sway: The Irresistible Pull of Irrational Behavior* (London: Doubleday).

Brand M. and Walton D. (eds) (1976), *Action Theory* (Dordrecht: D. Reidel Publishing Company)

Brandt R. and Kim, J. (1963), 'Wants as Psychological Explanations of Actions', *The Journal of Philosophy*, LX. Reprinted in Care and Landesman (1968: 199–213), to which any page numbers given refer.

Bransen, J. and Cupyers, S. (eds) (1998), *Human Action, Deliberation, and Causation* (Dordrecht: Kluwer Academic Publishers).

Brink, D. O (1997), 'Moral Motivation', *Ethics*, Vol. 108, 4–32.

Broome, J. (2004), 'Reasons', in Wallace et al. (2004: 28–55).

Brody, N. (1983), *Human Motivation – Commentary on Goal-Directed Action* (New York: Academic Press).

Brown, D. G. (1968), *Action* (London: George Allen & Unwin).

Brown, J. S. (1961), *The Motivation of Behavior* (New York: McGraw-Hill Book Company, Inc.).

Browning, G. (2010), 'Agency and Influence in the History of Political Thought: The Agency of Influence and the Influence of Agency', *History of Political Thought*, Vol. 31, No. 2 , 345–66.

Cabanac, M. (1979), 'Sensory Pleasure', *Quarterly Review of Biology*, Vol. 54, 1–29.

Care, N. S. and Landesman, C. (eds) (1968), *Readings in the Theory of Action* (Bloomington: Indiana University Press).

Carr, E. H. (1961), *What is History?* (London: Penguin).

Charles, D. (1984), *Aristotle's Philosophy of Action* (London: Duckworth)

Charlton, W. (1988), *Weakness of the Will: A Philosophical Introduction* (Oxford: Blackwell).

Chisholm, R. (1964), 'The Descriptive element in the Concept of Action', *Journal of Philosophy*, 61, 613–24.

Chomsky, N. (2002), *Media Control*, 2nd edition (Seven Stories Press: New York).

Cialdini, R. B. (2008), *Influence: The Psychology of Persuasion*, revised edition (New York: Harper Collins)

Clark, R. (1989), 'Deeds, Doings and What is Done: The Non-extensionality of Modifiers', Noûs, Vol. 23, No. 2, 1989 A.P.A. Central Division Meetings (Apr.), 199–210.

Clark, W. R. and Grunstein, M. (2000), *Are We Hardwired?: The Role of Genes in Human Behavior* (Oxford: Oxford University Press).

Clinton, B. (1998), 'Speech to the Nation', August 17. Retrieved from http://www.cnn.com/ALLPOLITICS/1998/08/17/speech/transcript.html on 20 May 2011.

Collingwood, R.G. (1939), *An Autobiography* (Oxford: Oxford University Press).

—— (1946/1994), *The Idea of History*, revised edition (Oxford, Clarendon Press).

—— (1940/1998), *An Essay on Metaphysics*, revised edition (Oxford: Clarendon Press).

Collins, A. W. (1987), *The Nature of Mental Things* (Notre Dame Ind.: University of Notre Dame Press).

—— (1997), 'The Psychological Reality of Reasons', *Ratio*, Vol. 10, No. 2, 108–23.

Croce, B. (1921), *History: Its Theory and Practice*, trans. D. Ainslee (New York: Harcourt, Brace and Co.).

—— (1941), *History as the Story of Liberty*, trans. S. Sprigge (London: George Allen & Unwin).

Cziko, G. (2000), *The Things We Do: Using the Lessons of Bernard and Darwin to Understand the What, How, and Why of our Behavior* (Cambridge MA: MIT Press).

Dancy, J. (1993), *Moral Reasons* (Oxford: Blackwell).

—— (1995a), 'Why There is Really No Such Thing as the Theory of Motivation', *Proceedings of the Aristotelian Society*, Vol. 95, 1–18.

—— (1995b), 'Arguments from Illusion', *The Philosophical Quarterly*, Vol. 45, No. 181, 421–38.

—— (ed.) (1997), *Reading Parfit* (Oxford: Blackwell).

—— (1999), 'Motivation, Dispositions and Aims', *Theoria*, Vol. LXV, 212–24.

—— (2000), *Practical Reality* (Oxford: Oxford University Press).

—— (2003a), 'A Précis of Practical Reality', *Philosophy and Phenomenological Research*, Vol. 67 , No. 2, 423–28.

—— (2003b), 'Replies', *Philosophy and Phenomenological Research*, Vol. 67, No. 2, 468–90.

—— (2004a) *Ethics Without Principles* (Oxford: Oxford University Press).

—— (2004b), 'Enticing Reasons', in Wallace et al. (2004: 91–118).

—— (2005) 'Two Ways of Explaining Actions', forthcoming in *Philosophy* and to be reprinted in (eds) J. Hyman and H. Steward, *Action and Agency* (Oxford: Oxford University Press).

—— (2008) 'On How to Act Disjunctively', in (eds) A. Haddock and F. Macpherson *Disjunctivism: Perception, Action, Knowledge*, (Oxford: Oxford University Press), 262–80.

—— (2009a), 'Action in Moral Metaphysics' in (ed.) Sandis (2009a: 398–417).

—— (2009b), 'Action, Content and Inference' in (eds) H. J. Glock and J. Hyman, *Wittgenstein and Analytic Philosophy: Essays in Honour of P.M.S. Hacker* (Oxford: Oxford University Press), 278–98.

—— (2011) 'Acting in Ignorance', *Frontiers of Philosophy in China*, Vol. 6, No. 3, 345–57.

Danto, A. C. (1963), 'What We can Do', *The Journal of Philosophy*, LX. Reprinted in Care and Landesman (1968: 113–26), to which any page numbers given refer.
—— (1965a) 'Basic Actions', *American Philosophical Quarterly* 2, 141–8. Reprinted in White (1968: 43–58), to which any page numbers given refer.
—— (1965b), *Analytic Philosophy of History* (Cambridge: Cambridge University Press).
—— (1973), *Analytic Philosophy of Action* (Cambridge: Cambridge University Press).
Darwall, S. (2003), 'Desires, Reasons, and Causes', *Philosophy and Phenomenological Research* Vol. 67 , No. 2, 436–43.
—— (1995), *The British Moralists and the Internal 'Ought':1640–1740* (Cambridge: Cambridge University Press).
Davidson, D. (1963), 'Actions, Reasons, and Causes', *Journal of Philosophy*, Vol. 60: 685–700. Reprinted in Davidson (2001a: 3–19), to which any page numbers given refer.
—— (1967a), 'The Logical Form of Action Sentences, in (ed.) N. Rescher, *The Logic of Decision and Action* (University of Pittsburgh Press). Reprinted with 'Cricicism, Comment, and Defence', in Davidson (1980/2001: 105–148), to which any page numbers given refer.
—— (1967b), 'Causal Relations', *Journal of Philosophy*, Vol. 64. Reprinted in Davidson (2001a: 149–62), to which any page numbers given refer.
—— (1968), 'On Saying That', *Synthese* 17, 304–23. Reprinted in Davidson (2001b: 17–36), to which any page numbers given refer.
—— (1969), 'The Individuation of Events', in (ed.) N. Rescher, *Essays in Honour of Carl. G. Hempel* (Dordrceht: R. Reidel), 216–34. Reprinted in Davidson (2001a:163–80), to which any page numbers given refer.
—— (1970a), 'How is Weakness of the Will Possible?', in (ed.) J. Feinberg, *Moral Concepts* (Oxford: Oxford University Press). Reprinted in Davidson (2001a: 21–42), to which any page numbers given refer.
—— (1970b), 'Events as Particulars', *Noûs* 4. Reprinted in Davidson (2001a: 181–7), to which any page numbers given refer.
—— (1971a), 'Eternal vs. Ephemeral Events', *Noûs* 5. Reprinted in Davidson (2001a: 198–203), to which any page numbers given refer.
—— (1971b), 'Agency', in (eds) R. Binkley, R. Bronaugh and A. Marras, *Agent, Action and Reason* (Toronto: University of Toronto Press). Reprinted in Davidson (2001a: 43–61), to which any page numbers given refer.
—— (1973), 'Freedom to Act', in (ed.) T. Honderich, *Essays on Freedom of Action* (London: Routledge & Kegan Paul). Reprinted in Davidson (2001a: 63–82), to which any page numbers given refer.
—— (1974), 'Psychology as Philosophy', in (ed.) S. C. Brown, *Philosophy of Psychology* (London: Macmillan). Reprinted with 'Comments and Replies' in Davidson (2001a: 229–44), to which any page numbers given refer.
—— (1976), 'Hempel on Explaining Action', *Erkenntnis* Vol. 10, 239–53. Reprinted in Davidson (2001a: 261–75), to which any page numbers given refer.
—— (1978). 'Intending', in (ed.) Y. Yovel, *Philosophy of History and Action* (D. Reidly and The Magnes Press). Reprinted in Davidson (2001a: 83–102), to which any page numbers given refer.
—— (1982), 'Paradoxes of Irrationality', in (eds) R. Wollheim and J. Hopkins, *Philosophical Essays on Freud* (Cambridge: Cambridge University Press), 289–305. Reprinted in Davidson (2004: 169–87), to which any page numbers given refer.

—— (1985), 'Adverbs of Action', in Vermazen and Hintikka (1985: 230–41). Reprinted in Davidson (2001a: 293–304), to which any page numbers given refer.

—— (1987), 'Problems in the Explanation of Action' in Pettit, Sylvan and Norman (1987, 35–8). Reprinted in Davidson (2004: 101–116), to which any page numbers given refer.

—— (1999), 'Reply to Jennifer Hornsby', in Hahn (1999: 636–40).

—— (2001a), *Essays on Actions and Events*, 2nd revised edition (Oxford: Clarendon Press).

—— (2001b), *Inquiries into Truth and Interpretation*, 2nd revised edition (Oxford: Clarendon Press).

—— (2004), *Problems of Rationality* (Oxford: Clarendon Press).

—— (2005a), *Truth, Language, and History* (Oxford: Clarendon Press).

Davis, L.(1979), *Theory of Action* (New Jersey: Prentice-Hall, inc).

Davis, W. A. (1984), 'A Causal Theory of Intending', *American Philosophical Quarterly*, Vol. 21, 43–54l. Reprinted in Mele (1997: 131–48) to which any page numbers given refer.

—— (2003), 'Psychologism and Humeanism', *Philosophy and Phenomenological Research*, Vol. 67, No. 2, 452–9.

Descartes, R. (1970), *Philosophical Letters*, ed. and trans. by A. Kenny (Oxford: Clarendon Press).

Dilthey, W. (1961), *Patterns and Meaning in History: Thoughts on History and Society*, ed. H. P. Rickman (London: Harper Row).

Dollard, J. and Miller, N. E. (1950), *Personality and Psychotherapy: An Analysis in Terms of Learning, Thinking, and Culture* (New York: McGraw-Hill).

Donagan, A. (1962), *The Later Philosophy of R.G. Collingwood* (Oxford: Clarendon Press).

—— (1987), *Choice* (London: Routledge).

—— (1994), *The Philosophical Papers Volume II - Action, Reason, and Value* (Chicago: University of Chicago Press).

Doris, J. M. (1998), 'Persons, Situations, and Virtue Ethics', *Noûs*, 32, 504–30.

—— (2002), *Lack of Character: Personality and Moral Behavior* (Cambridge: Cambridge University Press).

D'Oro, G. (2003), 'Collingwood and Ryle on the Concept of Mind', *Philosophical Explorations*, Vol. VI, No. 1, 18–30.

—— (2005a), 'Collingwood's Solution to the Problem of Mind-Body Dualism', *Philosophia* 32, 349–63.

—— (2005b), 'In Defence of the Agent-Centred Perspective', *Metaphilosophy*, 36, 652–67.

—— (2007), 'Two Dogmas of Contemporary Philosophy of Action', *Journal of the Philosophy of History*, Vol. 1, 11–26.

—— (2008), 'Historiographic Understanding', in (ed.) A. Tucker, *A Companion to the Philosophy of History and Historiography* (Oxford: Wiley-Blackwell), 142–51.

—— (2011), 'Davidson and the Autonomy of Human Sciences', in (ed.) J. Malpas, *Dialogues with Davidson: New Perspectives on his Philosophy* (Boston MA: MIT Press).

—— (2012a) (ed.), *Reasons and Causes: Causalism and Anti-Causalism in the Philosophy of Action* (Basingstoke: Palgave Macmillan).

—— (2012b), 'Reasons and Causes: The Philosophical Battle and the Meta-Philosophical War', *Autralasian Journal of Philosophy*, 15 June (iFirst): 1–15.

Dray, W.H. (1957), *Laws and Explanation in History* (Oxford: Clarendon Press).

—— (1963) 'The Historical Explanations of Actions Reconsidered', in (ed.) S. Hook (1963: 105–35). Reprinted in Gardiner (1974: 66–89) to which any page numbers given refer.

—— (1980), *Perspectives on History* (London: Routledge & Kegan Paul).

—— (1995), *History As Re-Enactment: R.G. Collingwood's Idea of History* (Oxford: Clarendon Press).

Dretske, F. (1977), 'Referring to Events' in French (1977).

—— (1983), 'The Epistemology of Belief', *Synthese*, 55, 3–19. Reprinted in his *Perception, Knowledge and Belief: Selected essays* (2000: 64–79). Cambridge: University Press.

—— (1988a). 'The Explanatory Role of Content', in (eds) R. H. Grimm and D. D. Merrill, *Contents of Thought* (Tucson: University of Arizona Press), 31–43.

—— (1988b), *Explaining Behavior: Reasons in a World of Causes* (Cambridge MA: MIT Press).

—— (1993), 'Mental Events as Structuring Causes of Behavior', in Heil and Mele (1993: 121–36).

—— (2004), 'Psychological vs. Biological Explanations of Behaviour', *Behavior and Philosophy* 32, 167–77.

—— (2009), 'What Must Actions be for Reasons to Explain Them?', in Sandis (2009a: 13–21).

—— (2010), 'Triggering and Structuring Causes', in O'Connor and Sandis (2010: 139–44).

Ducasse, C. J. (1925), 'Explanation, Mechanism, and Teleology', *Journal of Philosophy*, 22, 150–5.

Dummett, M. (2004), *Truth and the Past* (New York: Columbia University Press).

—— (2006), *Thought and Reality* (Oxford: Oxford University Press).

Dylan, B. (1966), 'I Want You', in *Blonde on Blonde* (New York: Columbia Records). Lyrics reprinted in his *Lyrics 1962–2001* (London: Simon & Schuster, 2004), 196–7, to which any page numbers given refer.

Egloff, B., Schwerdtfeger, A., Schmukle, S. C. (2005), 'Temporal Stability of the Implicit Association Test-Anxiety', *Journal of Personality Assessment*, Vol. 84, No. 1, 82–8.

Elderedge, N. (2004), *Why We Do It: Rethinking Sex and the Selfish Gene* (New York: W.W. Norton).

Elster, J. (2007), *Explaining Social Behavior: More Nuts and Bolts for the Social Sciences* (Cambridge: Cambridge University Press).

Enç, B. (2003), *How We Act – Causes, Reasons, and Intentions* (Oxford: Oxford University Press).

Everson, S. (2009), 'What Are Reasons for Action?', in Sandis (2009a: 220–47).

—— (2010), 'Motivating Reasons', in O'Connor and Sandis (2010: 145–52).

Ewing, A. C. (1938), 'What is Action?', *Proceedings of the Aristotelian Society*, Supplementary Vol. XVII, 86–101.

Falcon, A. (2011), 'Aristotle on Causality' (substantially revised version), in (ed.) E.N. Zalta, *The Stanford Encyclopedia of Philosophy* (Spring Edition), http://plato.stanford.edu/archives/spr2011/entries/aristotle-causality/.

Falk, W. D. (1948), 'Ought and Motivation', in *Proceedings of the Aristotelian Society* 1947–8, 492–510. Reprinted in Falk (1986: 21–41), to which any page numbers given refer.

—— (1963), 'Action-Guiding Reasons' in *Journal of Philosophy*, 60, 702–18. Reprinted in Falk (1986: 82–98), to which any page numbers given refer.

—— (1986), *Ought, Reasons, and Morality: The Collected Papers of W.D. Falk* (Ithaca NY: Cornell University Press).

Feigl, H. and Scriven, M. (eds) (1956), *Minnesota Studies in the Philosophy of Science* (Minneapolis: University of Minnesota Press).

Flew, A. (1956), 'Motives and the Unconscious', in Feigl and Scriven (1956).

Flyvbjerg, B. (2001), *Making Social Science Matter: Why Social Enquiry Fails and How it Can Succeed Again,* trans. S. Sampson (Cambridge: Cambridge University Press).

Fodor, J. A. (1968), *Psychological Explanation: An Introduction to the Philosophy of Psychology* (New York: Random House).

Foot, P. (1972), 'Reasons for Action and Desires', *Supplmententary Proceedings of the Aristotelian Society,* 61. Reprinted in Foot (1978: 148–56) to which any page numbers given refer.

—— (1978), *Virtues and Vices (and Other Essays in Moral Philosophy)* (Oxford: Blackwell).

Francis, R. C. (1990), 'Causes, Proximate and Ultimate', *Biology and Philosophy,* Vol. 5, No. 4, 401–15.

Frankena, W.K. (1976), *Perspectives on Morality,* ed. Goodpaster, K. (Indiana: University of Notre Dame Press).

Frankfurt, H.G. (1969). Alternate Possibilities and Moral Responsibility, *Journal of Philosophy* 66, 829–39. Reprinted in Frankfurt (1988: 1–10), to which any page numbers given refer.

—— (1971), 'Freedom of the Will and Concept of a Person', *Journal of Philosophy,* 68. Reprinted in Frankfurt (1988: 11–25), to which any page numbers given refer.

—— (1977), *'Identification and Externality'* in (ed.) A. Rorty, *The Identities of Persons.* (Berkeley CA: University of California Press). Reprinted in Frankfurt (1988: 58–68), to which any page numbers given refer.

—— (1978), 'The Problem of Action', *American Philosophical Quarterly,* 155, 157–62. Reprinted in Frankfurt (1988: 69–79), to which any page numbers given refer.

—— (1988), *The Importance of What We Care About* (Cambridge: Cambridge University Press).

—— (2004), *The Reasons of Love* (New Jersey: Princeton University Press).

—— (2006), *On Truth* (New York: Alfred A. Knopf).

Frankish, K. (2004), *Mind and Supermind* (Cambridge: Cambridge University Press).

Freedman, J. L. (1982), *Introductory Psychology,* 2nd Edition (Reading MA: Addison-Wesley Publishing Company).

Frege, G. (1918–19), 'Der Gedanke' ('The Thought') in *Eine logische Untersuchung,* in *Beiträge zur Philosophie des Deutschen Idealismus I*: 58–77. Published in an English translation (by Peter Geach and R.H. Stoothoff) as 'Thoughts' in ed. B.F. McGuinness (1984), Frege's *Collected Papers on Mathematics, Logic, and Philosophy* (Oxford: Blackwell), 351–72, to which any page numbers given refer.

French, P. A., Uehling, T. E. Jr., and Wettstein, H. K. (eds) (1977), *Contemporary Perspectives in the Philosophy of Language* (Minneapolis: University of Minnesota Press).

Freud, S. (1933/1971), *New Introductory Lectures on Psychoanalysis,* trans. J. Strachey, ed. A. Richards (London: Pelican).

—— (1901/1966), *The Psychopathology of Everyday Life*, trans. A. Tyson, ed. J. Strachey, A. Richards and A. Tyson.

Frey, R. and Morris, C. (eds) (1993), *Value, Welfare, and Morality* (Cambridge: Cambridge University Press).

Fricker, M. (2007), *Epistemic Injustice: Power and the Ethics of Knowing* (Oxford: Oxford University Press).

Gardiner, P.(1952), *The Nature of Historical Explanation* (Oxford: Oxford University Press).

—— (ed.) (1974) *The Philosophy of History* (Oxford: Oxford University Press).

Garrett, D. (2007), 'Reasons to Act and Believe: Naturalism and Rational Justification in Hume's Philosophical Project', *Philosophical Studies*, 132: 1–16.

Geach, M. and Gormally, L. (eds) (2005), *Human Life, Action and Ethics – Essays by G.E.M. Anscombe* (Exeter: Imprint Academic).

Gendler, T.S. (2008a), 'Alief and Belief', *Journal of Philosophy*, Vol. 105, No. 10, 634–63.

—— (2008b), 'Alief in Action (and Reaction)', *Mind & Language*, Vol. 23, No. 5, 552–85.

Gilbert, D. T. and Jones, E. E. (1986), 'Peceiver-Induced Constraint: Interpretations of Self-generated Reality', *Journal of Personality and Social Psychology*, 50, 269–80.

Ginet, C. (1989), 'Reasons Explanation of Action: An Incompatabilist Account', *Philosophical Perspectives* 3, 17–46. Reprinted in Mele (1997: 106–30) to which any page numbers given refer.

—— (1990), *On Action* (Cambridge: Cambridge University Press).

Glock, H. J. (1997), 'Truth Without People?', *Philosophy*, 72, 85–104.

—— (2010), 'Animal Agency', in O'Connor & Sandis (2010: 384–92).

Goetz, S. (2009), Interview in Aguilar and Buckareff (2009: 45–58).

Goldman, A. I. (1970), *A Theory of Human Action* (New Jersey: Princeton University Press).

Gosling, J. (1990), *Weakness of Will* (London: Routledge).

Greenwald, A. G. and Krieger, L. H. (2006), 'Implicit Bias: Scientific Foundations', *California Law Review*, Vol. 94, No. 4 (July), 945–67.

Grice, H. P. (1989), *Studies in the Way of Words* (Cambridge MA: Harvard University Press).

Gross, R. (1996), *Psychology: The Science of Mind and Behaviour*, 3rd edition (London: Hodder and Stoughton).

Grünbaum, A. (1984), *The Foundations of Psychoanalysis* (Berkeley, CA: University of California Press).

Hacker, P. M. S. (1982), 'Events, Ontology and Grammar', *Philosophy*, 57, 477–86.

—— (1990), *Meaning and Mind: Exegesis 243–247 Pt. II: Volume 3 of an Analytical Commentary on the Philosophical Investigations* (Oxford: Blackwell).

—— (1996), *Wittgenstein: Mind and Will: An Analytical Commentary on the Philosophical Investigations, Volume 4* (Oxford: Blackwell).

—— (1998), 'Davidson on the Ontology and Logical Form of Belief', *Philosophy*, 73, 81–96.

—— (2001), *Wittgenstein: Connections and Controversies* (Oxford: Clarendon Press).

—— (2007), *Human Nature: The Categorial Framework* (Oxford: Blackwell).

—— (2009),'Agential Reasons and the Explanation of Human Behaviour', in Sandis (2009: 75–93).

Hahn, L. E. (ed.) (1999), *The Philosophy of Donald Davidson*, Library of Living Philosophers (Illinois: Open Court Publishing).

Haidt, J. (2001), 'The Emotional Dog and its Rational Tail: A Social Intuitionist Approach to Moral Judgement', *Philosophical Review*, Vol. 108, No. 4, 814–34.

Harré, R. and Secord, P. F. (1972), *The Explanation of Social Behaviour* (Oxford: Blackwell).

Heider, F. (1958), *The Psychology of Interpersonal Relations* (New York: Wiley).

Heil. J. and Mele, A. R. (eds) (1993), *Mental Causation* (Oxford: Oxford University Press).

Hegel, G.W.F. (1849/1988), *Introduction to the Philosophy of History*, trans. L. Rauch (Indiana: Hackett).

Hempel, C. G. (1942), 'The Function of General Laws in History', *Journal of Philosophy*, Vol 39.

—— (1962), 'Rational Action', in *Proceedings and Addresses of the American Philosophical Association*, XXXV 5–24. Reprinted in Care and Lendesman (1968: 281–305) to which any page numbers given refer.

—— (1963), 'Reasons and Covering Laws in Historical Explanation', in (ed.) S. Hook (1963: 143–63). Reprinted in Gardiner (1974: 90–105) to which any page numbers given refer.

—— (1965), *Aspects of Scientific Explanation and Other Essays in the Philosophy of Science* (New York: Free Press).

Hempel, C. G. and Oppenheim, P. (1948), 'Studies in the Logic of Explanation', *Philosophy of Science*, XV, 135–75.

Heuer, U. (2004), 'Reasons for Actions and Desires', *Philosophical Studies*, Vol. 121, No. 1, 43–63.

Hieronymi, P. (2011), 'Reasons for Action', *Proceedings of the Aristotelian Society*, Vol. CXI, Part III.

Holloway, R. (2008), *Between the Monster and the Saint* (Edinburgh: Canongate Books).

Hook, S. (ed) (1963) *Philosophy and History: A Symposium* (New York: University Press).

Hopkins, J. (1988), 'Epistemology and Depth Psychology', in (eds) P. Clark and C. Wright, *Mind, Psychoanalysis and Science* (Oxford: Blackwell), 33–60.

Hornsby, J. (1980), *Actions* (London: Routledge and Kegan Paul).

—— (1986), 'Physicalist Thinking and Behaviour', in (eds) J. McDowell and P. Pettit, *Subject, Thought and Context* (Oxford: Oxford University Press).

—— (1993a), 'Agency and Causal Explanation', in Heil and Mele (1993: 161–88). Reprinted Hornsby (1997a: 129–53) to which any page numbers given refer.

—— (1993b), 'On What's Intentionally Done', in (eds) S. Shute, J. Gardner, and J. Horder, *Action and Value in Criminal Law* (Oxford: Clarendon Press).

—— (1997a), *Simple Mindedness: In Defense of Naive Naturalism in the Philosophy of Mind* (Cambridge MA: Harvard University Press).

—— (1997b), 'Truth: The Identity Theory', *Proceedings of the Aristotelian Society*, XCVII.

—— (1997c), 'Thinkables', in (ed.) M. Sainsbury, *Thought and Ontology* (Milan: Franco Angeli), 63–80.

—— (1999), 'Anomalousness in Action' in L. E. Hahn (1999: 623–35).

Hull, C. L. (1943), *Principles of Behavior: An Introduction to Behavior Theory* (New York: D. Appleton).

Hume, D. (1757/1989) *A Dissertation on the Passions*, in (ed.) T.H. Green and T.H. Grose, *The Philosophical Works of David Hume* (London : Longmans, Green, and Co.), Vol. II, 139–66.

—— (1739–40/1978), *A Treatise of Human Nature*. 2nd edition, ed. P. H. Nidditch (Oxford: Oxford University Press). References to *page numbers given* in 2nd edition followed by original book, part, section, and paragraph numbers.

—— (1777/1974), *Enquiries Concerning Human Understanding and Concerning the Principles of Morals*, eds. L. A. Selby-Bigge and P. H. Nidditch, 3rd edition (Oxford: Oxford University Press). References are to *section* numbers in 3rd edition followed by original book, section, and paragraph numbers.

—— (1777/1985), *Essays: Moral, Political, and Literary*, revised edition, ed. E. F. Miller (Indianapolis: Literary Fund).

—— (1778/1983), *A History of England*, Vol. 1 (New York: Liberty Classics).

Hursthouse, R. (1991), 'Arational Actions', *Journal of Philosophy*, 88, 57–68.

Hutcheson, F. (1725/6), *An Inquiry Concerning the Original of Our Ideas of Virtue or Moral Good*, 2nd edition (London: J. Darby). Any references are by section number, followed by the page number(s) in Selby-Bigge (1897).

Hutchinson, P., Read, R., and Sharrock, W. (2008), *There is No Such Thing as a Social Science: In Defence of Peter Winch* (Aldershot: Ashgate).

Hutto, D. D. (1991), 'Presence of Mind', *Philosophy Now*, No. 2 (Winter).

—— (1999), 'A Cause for Concern: Reasons, Causes and Explanations', *Philosophy and Phenomenological Research*, Vol. 59, No. 2 (June), 381–401.

—— (2001), 'Consciousness and Conceptual Schema', in (ed.) P. Pllykkänen, *Dimensions of Conscious Experience* (Amsterdam: John Benjamins),. 15–43.

—— (2008), *Folk Psychological Narratives: The Sociocultural Basis of Understanding Reasons* (Cambridge MA: MIT Press).

Huxley, J. S. (1916), 'Bird-watching and Biological Science: Some Observations on the Study of Courtship in Birds', *Auk*, 33, 142–61.

Hyman, J. (1999), 'How Knowledge Works', *Philosophical Quarterly*, Vol. 49, No. 197 (Oct), 433–51.

—— (2001), '-ings and -ers', *Ratio*, Vol. 4, No. 4, 298–317.

—— (2010), 'The Road to Larissa', *Ratio*, Vol. 23, No. 4, 393–414.

—— (2011), 'Acting for Reasons: Reply to Dancy', *Frontiers of Philosophy in China*, Vol. 6, No. 3, 358–68.

Jardine, N. (2000), *The Scenes of Inquiry: On the Reality of Questions in the Sciences*, revised 2nd edition (Oxford: Oxford University Press).

Jolls, C. and Sunstein, C. R. (2006), 'The Law of Implicit Bias', *California Law Review*, Vol. 94, No. 4 (July), 969–96.

Jones, E. E. and Harris, V. A. (1967), 'The Attribution of Attitudes', *Journal of Experimental Social Psychology*, 3 ,1–24.

Jones, E. E., and Nisbett, R. E. (1972), 'The Actor and the Observer: Divergent Perceptions of the Causes of Behavior', in (eds) E. E. Jones, D. Kanouse, H. H. Kelley, R. E. Nisbett, S. Valins and B. Weiner, *Attribution: Perceiving the Causes of Behavior* (Morristown, NJ: General Learning Press), 79–94.

Kavka, G.S. (1983), 'The Toxin Puzzle', *Analysis*, 43 (1), 33–6.

Kennett, J. and Smith, M. (1996), 'Frog and Toad Lose Control', in *Analysis*, 56, 63–73. Reprinted in Smith (2004: 73–83), to which any page numbers given refer.

Kenny, A. J. P.(1963), 'Oratio Obliqua', *Proceedings of the Aristotelian Society*, Supp. Vol. xxxvii, 127–146.

Kim, J. (1981), 'Causes as Explanations: A Critique', *Theory and Decision*, 13, 293–309.

—— (1982), 'Psychophysical Supervenience', *Philosophical* Studies, Vol. 41, No. 1 (Jan - Essays in Honor of James Welton Cornman), 51–70.

—— (1989), 'Mechanism, Purpose, and Explanatory Exclusion', *Philosophical Perspectives*, 3, 77–108. Reprinted in Mele (1997: 256–82), to which any page numbers given refer.

—— (1993), *Supervenience and Mind* (Cambridge: Cambridge University Press).

Kimble, G. A. (1996), *Psychology: The Hope of a Science* (Cambridge MA: MIT Press).

Kipling, R. (1902), *Just So Stories* (London: Macmillan & Co.).

Knobe, J. (2003a), 'Intentional Action and Side Effects in Ordinary Language', *Analysis*, 63, 190–3.

—— (2003b), 'Intentional Action in Folk Psychology: An Experimental Investigation', *Philosophical Psychology*, 16, 309–24.

Knobe, J., and Kelly, S. D. (2009). 'Can One Act For a Reason Without Acting Intentionally?', in Sandis (2009a: 169–83).

Knobe, J. and Malle, B. (2002), 'Self and Other in the Explanation of Behavior: 30 Years Later', *Psychological Belgica*, *42*, 113–30.

Knowles, D. (1963), *The Historian and Character* (Cambridge University Press).

Knox, M. (1968), *Action* (London: George Allen and Unwin).

Körner, S. (ed.) (1975), *Explanation* (Oxford: Blackwell).

Korsgaard, C. (1997) 'The Normativity of Instrumental Reason' in (eds) G. Cullity and B. Gaut, *Ethics and Practical Reason* (Oxford: Oxford University Press).

—— (2008), *The Constitution of Agency: Essays on Practical Reason and Moral Psychology* (Oxford: Oxford University Press).

Kripke, S. (1980), *Naming and Necessity* (Oxford: Blackwell).

Kuhn, T. S. (1962), *The Structure of Scientific Revolutions* (Chicago: University of Chicago Press).

Künne, W. (2003), *Conceptions of Truth* (Oxford: Clarendon Press).

Lacewing, M. (2011), 'Inferring Motives in Psychology and Psychoanalysis', *Philosophy, Psychiatry, Psychology*, forthcoming.

Laitinen, A. and Sandis, C. (eds) (2010a), *Hegel on Action* (Basingstoke: Palgrave Macmillan).

—— (2010b), 'Hegel and Contemporary Philosophy of Action', in Laitinen and Sandis (2010a: 1–21).

Lehrer, J. (2009), *How We Decide* (Boston: Houghton Mifflin Co).

Lenman, J. (1996), 'Belief, Desire and Motivation: An Essay on Quasi-Hydraulics', *American Philosophical Quarterly*, 33, 3(July), 291–301.

—— (2009), 'Reasons for Action: Justification vs. Explanation', *Stanford Encyclopedia of Philosophy*, http://plato.stanford.edu/entries/reasons-just-vs-expl/.

Lennon, K. (1990), *Explaining Human Action* (London: Duckworth).

Lepore, E. and McLaughlin, B. P. (eds) (1985), *Actions and Events: Perspectives on the Philosophy of Donald Davidson* (Oxford: Blackwell).

Levin, P. F. and Isen, A. M. (1972), 'Effects of Feeling Good and Helping: Cookies and Kindness', *Journal of Personality and Social Psychology*, 3, 384–8.
—— (1975), 'Further Studies on the Effect of Feeling Good on Helping', *Sociometry*, Vol. 38, No. 1 (Mar.), 141–7.
Levine, C. G. (1997), *Ella Enchanted* (London: Harper Collins).
Lewontin, R. (2001), *It Ain't Necessarily So: The Dream of the Human Genome and Other Illusions, 2nd edition* (New York: New York Review of Books).
Lippmann, W. (1922), *Public Opinion* (Harcourt Brace & Co: New York).
Louch, A. R. (1966), *Explanation and Human Action* (Oxford: Blackwell).
Lowe, E. J. (2010), 'Action Theory and Ontology', in O'Connor Sandis (2010: 3–9).
Lucas, J. R. (1970), *The Freedom of the Will* (Oxford: Oxford University Press).
Maasen, S., Prinz, W. and Roth, G. (eds) (2003), *Voluntary Action: Brains, Minds, and Sociality* (Oxford: Oxford University Press).
MacIntyre, A. (1958), *The Unconscious* (London: Routledge).
—— (1999), *Dependent Rational Animals: Why Human Beings Need the Virtues* (Chicago: Open Court).
Macmurray, J. (1938), 'What is Action?', *Proceedings of the Aristotelian Society*, Supplementary Volume XVII, 69–85.
Malcolm, N. (1967), *Wittgenstein: A Memoir* (Oxford: Oxford University Press).
—— (1968), 'The Conceivability of Mechanism', *Philosophical Review*, 77: 45–72.
Malle, B. (2006), *How the Mind Explains Behavior: Folk Explanations, Meaning, and Social Interaction* (Boston: MIT Press).
Malle, B. F., Moses, L. J. and Baldwin, D.A. (eds) (2001), *Intentions and Intentionality: Foundations of Social Cognition* (Cambridge MA: The MIT Press).
Mandelbaum, M. (1961), 'The Problem of "Covering Laws"', originally published under the title 'Historical Explanation: The Problem of "Covering Laws"' in *History and Theory* I, 3. Reprinted under the present title in Gardiner (1974: 51–65), to which any page numbers given refer.
Martin J., Sugarman S., and Thomson, J. (2003), *Psychology and the Question of Agency* (New York: SUNY Press).
Maslow, A. H. (1954), *Motivation and Personality* (New York: Harper & Row).
Mayr, E. (1961), 'Cause and Effect in Biology', *Science*, 134, 1501–06.
McCann, H. (1972), 'Is Raising One's Arm a Basic Action ?', *Journal of Philosophy*, Vol. 64, No. 9, 235–49.
—— (1974), 'Volition and Basic Action', *Philosophical Review*, 83, 451–73.
—— (1975), 'Trying, Paralysis, and Volition', *Review of Metaphysics*, 28, 423–42.
—— (1979), 'Nominals, Facts, and Two Conceptions of Events', *Philosophical Studies: An International Journal for Philosophy in the Analytic Tradition*, Vol. 35, No. 2 (Feb), 129–49.
—— (1998), *The Works of Agency* (New York: Cornell University Press).
McDowell, J. (1978), 'Are Moral Requirements Hypithetical Imperatives?', *Proceedings of the Aristotelian Society*, Supplementary Vol. 52, 13–29. Reprinted in McDowell (1998: 77–95) to which any page numbers given refer.
—— (1979), 'Virtue and Reason', *Monist* , 62: 331–50. Reprinted in McDowell (1998: 50–73) to which any page numbers given refer.
—— (1995), 'Might there be External Reasons?', in (eds) J. E. J. Altham and R. Harrison, *World, Mind, and Ethics: The Philosophy of Bernard Williams*

(Cambridge: Cambridge University Press). Reprinted in McDowell (1998: 95–111) to which any page numbers given refer.

—— (1996), *Mind and World*, 2nd edition (Cambridge MA: Harvard University Press).

—— (1998), *Mind, Virtue and Value* (Cambridge MA: Harvard University Press).

McNaughton, D. (1988), *Moral Vision* (Oxford: Blackwell).

Melden, A. I. (1956), 'Action', *The Philosophical Review*, LXV. Reprinted in Care and Landesman (1968, 27–47), to which any page numbers given refer.

—— (1961), 'Willing', *Philosophical Review*, Vol. 69, 475–84. Reprinted in White (1968: 70–8), to which any page numbers given refer.

—— (1961), *Free Action* (London: Routledge & Kegan Paul).

—— (1962) 'Reasons for Action and Matters of Fact', *Proceedings and Addresses of the American Philosophical Association*, 35, 45–60.

Mele, A. R. (1992), *The Springs of Action* (Oxford: Oxford University Press).

—— (ed.) (1997a), *The Philosophy of Action* (Oxford: Oxford University Press).

—— (2007b), 'Reasonology and False Beliefs', *Philosophical Papers*, Vol. 36, No. 1, 91–118.

—— (2010), 'Motivational Strength', in O'Connor and Sandis (2010: 259–66).

—— (forthcoming), 'Actions, Explanations, and Causes', in (ed.) G. D'Oro, *Reasons and Causes: Causalism and Non-Causalism in the Philosophy of Action* (Basingstoke: Palgrave Macmillan).

Mellor, D. H. (1995), *The Facts of Causation* (London: Routledge).

Merrill, K.R. (2008), *Historical Dictionary of Hume's Philosophy* (Lanham MD: The Scarecrow Press).

Milgram, S. (1963), 'Behavioral Study of Obedience',*Journal of Abnormal and Social Psychology*, Vol. 67, No. 4, 371–8.

Mill, J. S. (1843/1973), *A System of Logic, Ratiocinative and Inductive* (London: Longman, Green, and Co.). Reprinted in his *Collected Works* Vols. 7–8 (Toronto: University of Toronto Press); references are to page numbers given in the latter, followed by original by book, chapter, and section number.

—— (1865/1976), *An Examination of Sir William Hamilton's Philosophy and of the Principle Philosophical Questions Discussed in his Writings* (Boston: William V. Spencer). Reprinted in his *Collected Works* Vol. 9 (Toronto: University of Toronto Press); references are to page numbers given in the latter, followed by original by book, chapter, and section number.

Millgram, E. (2009), *Hard Truths* (Oxford: Wiley-Blackwell).

—— (2010), 'Pluralism About Action', in O'Connor and Sandis (2010: 90–6).

Millican, P. (2011), 'Hume, Causal Realism, and Free Will', in Allen and Stoneham (2011: 123–65).

Mischel, T. (ed.) (1969), *Human Action: Conceptual and Empirical Issues* (New York and London: Academic Press, Inc.).

Mook, D. G. (1986), *Motivation* (New York : W. W. Norton).

Moore, G.E. (1903), *Principia Ethica* (Cambridge: Cambridge University Press).

—— (1953), *Some Main Problems of Philosophy* (London: Harper Collins).

—— (1966), *Lectures on Philosophy* (London: Allen & Unwin).

Mourelatos, A. P. D. (1978), 'Events, States, and Processes', *Linguistics and Philosophy*, Vol. 2, No. 3, 415–34.

Moyar, D. (2010), 'Hegel and Agent-Relative Reasons', in Laitinen and Sandis (2010: 260–80).

Nagel, E. (1960), 'Determinism in History', *Philosophy and Phenomenological Research*, Vol. 20, No. 3, 291–317. Reprinted in Gardiner (1974: 187–215), to which any page numbers given refer.

Nagel, T. (1970), *The Possibility of Altruism* (Princeton, NJ: Princeton University Press).

—— (1986), *The View From Nowhere* (Cambridge: Cambridge University Press).

—— (1997), *The Last Word* (Oxford: Oxford University Press).

Nestroy, J. N. E. A. (1847) *Der Schützling* (The Protégé), April 9 (Vienna: Theater in der Leopoldstadt).

Nietzsche, F. (1868/1973), *Beyond Good and Evil*, trans. R. J. Hollingdale (London: Penguin).

Nisbett, R. E. and Wilson, T. D. (1977), 'Telling More Than We Can Know: Verbal Reports on Mental Processes', *Psychological Review*, Vol. 84, No. 3, 231–259.

Norman, R. (1971), *Reasons for Actions* (Oxford: Blackwell).

Nowell-Smith, P.H. (1956), 'Are Historical Events Unique?', in *Proceedings of the Aristotelian Society*, 57, 107–60.

O'Brien, L. (2007), *Self-Knowing Agents* (Oxford: Oxford University Press).

O' Connor, T. (2000), *Persons & Causes* (Oxford: Oxford University Press).

O'Connor, T. and Sandis, C. (eds) (2010), *A Companion to the Philosophy of Action* (Oxford: Wiley-Blackwell).

Ogilvy, D. (1963),*Confessions of an Advertising Man* (New York: Atheneum).

O' Hear, A. (ed.) (2003), *Minds and Persons* (Cambridge: Cambridge University Press).

O' Shaugnessy, B. (1972), 'Processes', *Proceedings of the Aristotelian Society*, New Series, Vol. 72 (1971–72), 215–40.

—— (1973), 'Trying as the Mental "Pineal Gland"', *Journal of Philosophy*, 70, 365–386. Reprinted in Mele (1997: 53–74) to which any page numbers given refer.

—— (1980), *The Will* (Cambridge: Cambridge University Press).

Packard, V. (1957/2007), *The Hidden Persuaders*, new (50th anniversary) edition (New York: IG Publishing).

Papineau, D. (2011), 'What is X-phi Good For?', *The Philosophers' Magazine*, No. 51 (First Quarter), 87–8.

Parfit, D. (1997), 'Reasons and Motivation', *Proceedings of the Aristotelian Society*, Supplementary. Vol. 71, 99–130.

—— (2011), *On What Matters*, Vols. I and II (Oxford: Oxford University Press).

Pascal, B. (1670/1966), Pensées, trans. A. J. Krailsheimer (London: Penguin).

Passmore, J. (1958), 'Review Article: Law and Explanation in History', *Australasian Journal of Politics and History*, Vol. 4, No. 2, 269–75.

Peacocke, C. (2008), *Truly Understood* (Oxford: Oxford University Press).

Peters, R.S. (1958), *The Concept of Motivation* (London: Routledge and Kegan Paul).

—— (1969), 'Motivation, Emotion, and the Conceptual Schemes of Common Sense' in Mischel (1969:135–66).

Pettit, P. (1987), 'Humeans, Anti-Humeans, and Motivation', *Mind*, 96, 550–3.

Pettit, P., Sylvan R., and Norman, J. (1987), *Metaphysics & Morality: Essays in Honour of J.J.C. Smart* (Oxford: Blackwell).

Pietroski, P. M. (2000), *Causing Actions* (Oxford: Oxford University Press).

Pigden, C. (ed.) (2009), *Hume on Motivation and Virtue* (Basingstoke: Palgrave Macmillan).

Pink, D. H. (2009), *Drive: The Surprising Truth About What Motivates Us* (New York: Riverhead Books).
—— (2010), *Drive: The Surprising Truth About What Motivates Us* (Edinburgh: Canongate Books).
Pinker, S. (2002), *The Blank Slate* (London: Penguin).
Plato (1952), *Phaedo*, trans. by R. Hackforth (Cambridge: Cambridge University Press) and by D. Gallop (Oxford: Oxford University Press).
—— (1977), *Phaedo*, trans. by D. Gallop (Oxford: Oxford University Press).
Pope, A. (1734), *Essay on Man* (London: Cassel & Company).
Popper, K. R. (1957), *The Poverty of Historicism* (London: Routledge & Kegan Paul).
—— (1959), *The Logic of Scientific Discovery* (London: Hutchinson & Co.).
Priestley, J. (1777), *Disquisitions Relating to Matter and Spirit* (London: J. Johnson); references are to section and objection number, followed by the original page number(s).
Prichard, H. A. (1949), *Moral Obligation* (Oxford: Clarendon Press). Reprinted in its entirety in Prichard (2004), to which any page numbers refer.
—— (2004), *Moral Writings*, ed. J. MacAdam (Oxford: Clarendon Press).
Prior, A. N. (1963), 'Oratio Obliqua', *Proceedings of the Aristotelian Society*, Supp. Vol. xxxvii, 115–26.
—— (1971), *The Objects of Thought*, ed. P.T. Geach and A. J. P. Kenny (Oxford: Oxford University Press).
Pyle, A. (ed.) (1999), *Key Philosophers in Conversation: The Cogito Interviews* (Routledge: London).
Quine, W. V. O. (1960), *Word and Object* (Cambridge MA: MIT Press).
Quinn, W. (1993), 'Putting Rationality in its Place', in (eds) R. Frey and C. Morris, *Value Welfare and Morality* (Cambridge: Cambridge University Press), 26–50.
Railton, P. (1978), 'A Deductive-Nomological Model of Probabilistic Explanation', *Philosophy of Science*, 45, 206–26.
Ramsey, F. P. (1925), 'Universals', in Ramsey (1931), to which any page numbers given refer.
—— (1931), *The Foundations of Mathematics and Other Logical Essays*, ed. R. B. Braithwaite (Patterson: Littlefield Adams & Co.).
Rawls, J. (1955), 'Two Concepts of Rules', *The Philosophical Review*, LXIV. Reprinted in Care and Landesman (1968: 306–40), to which any page numbers given refer.
Raz, J. (1986), *The Morality of Freedom* (Oxford: Clarendon Press).
—— (1999), *Engaging Reason: On the Theory of Value and Action* (Oxford: Oxford University Press).
—— (2009), 'Reasons: Explanatory and Normative', in Sandis (2009a: 184–202).
Reeves, R. (1962), *Reality in Advertising* (New York: Alfred A. Knopf).
Ricœur, P. (1990/1992), *Oneself As Another*, trans. K. Blamey (Chicago: University of Chicago Press).
Rorty, A. O. (1988), *Mind in Action: Essays in the Philosophy of Action* (Boston: Beacon Press).
Rorty, R. (1998), *Truth and Progress: Philosophical Papers Volume 3* (Cambridge: Cambridge University Press).
Rorty, R. and Engel, P. (2007), *What's the Use of Truth?* (New York: Columbia University Press).

Rose, A. M. (ed.) (1962), *Human Behavior and Social Processes: An Interactionist Approach* (London: Routledge & Kegan Paul).

Rose, S. (1997), *Lifelines: Biology, Freedom, Determinism* (London: Penguin).

Ross, L. (1977), 'The Intuitive Psychologist and his Shortcomings: Distortions in the Attribution Process' in Berkowitz (1977).

Ross, W. D. (1930), *The Right and the Good* (Oxford: Clarendon Press).

Ruben, D. H. (1990), *Explaining Explanation* (London: Routledge).

—— (2003), *Action and its Explanation* (Oxford: Clarendon Press).

—— (2009), 'Con-Reasons as Causes', in Sandis (2009a: 62–74).

Rumi (1995), *Selected Poems*, trans. Coleman Banks (London: Penguin).

Rundle, B. (1979), *Grammar in Philosophy* (Oxford: Clarendon Press).

—— (1993), *Facts* (London: Duckworth).

Russell, B. (1919), 'On Propositions: What They are and How They Mean', *Proceedings of the Aristotelian Society*, Supplementary Vol. II, 1–43.

—— (1948), *Human Knowledge: Its Scope and Limits* (London: Routledge).

Russell, P. (1995), *Freedom & Sentiment: Hume's Way of Naturalizing Responsibility* (Oxford: Oxford University Press).

Ryan, A. (1970), *The Philosophy of the Social Sciences* (London: Macmillan).

——(ed.) (1973), *The Philosophy of Social Explanation* (Oxford: Oxford University Press).

Ryle, G. (1949), *The Concept of Mind* (London: Hutchinson).

Salmon, W. (1975), 'Theoretical Explanation', in Körner (1975: 118–45).

Sandis, C. (2004a) 'Review of Psychology and the Question of Agency' by J. Martin et al., *Metapsychology*, Vol. 8, No. 45 (1 Nov.).

—— (2004b), 'Review of Problems of Rationality -Philosophical Essays', Vol. 4 by Donald Davidson, *Philosophical Writings*, No. 27, Autumn, 63–5.

—— (2006), 'When Did the Killing Occur?: Donald Davidson on Action Individuation', *Daimon Revista de Filosofía*, 37, 179–86.

—— (2007), 'Review of Ethics and the A Priori' by Michael Smith, *Metapsychology*, Vol. 11, No. 10 (March 6).

—— (2008), 'How to Act Against Your Better Judgement', *Philosophical Frontiers*, Vol. 3.2, 111–24.

—— (2009a), (ed.), *New Essays on the Explanation of Action* (Basingstoke: Palgrave Macmillan).

—— (2009b), 'Gods and Mental States: the Causation of Action in Ancient Tragedy and Modern Philosophy of Mind', in (ed.) C. Sandis (2009: 358–85)

—— (2009c), 'Hume and the debate on "Motivating Reasons"', in (ed.) C. Pigden, *Hume on Motivation and Virtue: New Essays* (Basingstoke: Palgrave Macmillan), 142–54.

—— (2010a), 'Basic Actions and Individuation', in O'Connor and Sandis (2010: 10–7).

—— (2010b), 'The Man Who Mistook his Handlung for a Tat: Hegel on Oedipus and Other Tragic Thebans', *Bulletin of the Hegel Society of Great Britain*, No. 62, 35–60.

—— (2010c), 'For X to Have a Desire', *Times Literary Supplement*, 12 March.

—— (2010d), 'The Experimental Turn and Ordinary Language', *Essays in Philosophy*, Vol. 11. No. 2 (July), 181–96.

—— (2010e) 'Animal Ethics' in (eds) R. Corrigan and M.E. Farrell, *Ethics: A University Reader* (Gloucester: Progressive Frontiers Press), 21–40.

—— (ed.) (2011a), Special Issue of *Essays in Philosophy* on *Love and Reasons*, Vol. 12. No. 1 (Jan).

—— (2011b), 'Hume on the meaning of "necessity"' in Allen and Stoneham (2011: 166–87).

—— (2011c) 'Animal Minds', in (ed.) J. Garvey, *Continuum Companion to the Philosophy of Mind* (London: Continuum).

—— (2011d), 'Action, Reason, and the Passions' in (eds) Alan Bailey and Dan O'Brien, *The Continuum Companion to Hume* (London: Continuum)

—— (2011e), 'A Just Medium: Empathy and Detachment in Historical Understanding', *Journal of the Philosophy of History*, Vol. 5, No. 2, 179–200.

Schiller, F. C. S. (1921), 'Discussions of the Symposium "The Meaning of Meaning"', *Mind*, 30 (July), 185–90 and 444–7.

Schor, J. (1998), *The Overspent American: Upscaling, Downshifting and the New Consumer* (New York: Basic Books).

Schreirer, F. T. (1957), *Human Motivation* (Illinois: The Free Press, Glencoe).

Schroeder, M. (2007), *Slaves of the Passions* (Oxford: Oxford University Press).

Schroeder, S. (2001a), 'Are Reasons Causes: A Wittgensteinian Response to Davidson' in Schroeder (2001b: 150–70).

—— (ed.) (2001b), *Wittgenstein and Contemporary Philosophy of Mind* (Basingstoke: Palgrave Macmillan).

—— (2001c), 'The Concept of Trying', *Philosophical Investigations* 24, 3 (July), 213–27.

—— (2010), 'Wittgenstein' in O'Conner and Sandis (2010: 554–61).

Schroeder, T. (2009), 'Desire', in (ed.) E. N. Zalta, *The Stanford Encyclopedia of Philosophy* (Winter Edition), http://plato.stanford.edu/entries/desire/.

Schueler, G. F. (1995), *Desire: Its Role in Practical Reason and the Explanation of Action* (Cambridge MA: The MIT Press).

—— (2001) 'Action Explanations: Causes and Purposes', in Malle, Moses and Baldwin (2001: 251–64)

—— (2003), *Reasons and Purposes* (Oxford: Clarendon Press).

Searle, J. R. (2001), *Rationality in Action* (Cambridge MA: The MIT Press).

Sehon, S. R. (1997), 'Deviant Causal Chains and the Irreducibility of Teleological Explanation', *Pacific Philosophical Quarterly*, 78, 195–213.

Selby-Bigge, A. (1897) (ed.), *British Moralists*, Vols. I and II (Oxford: Clarendon Press).

Sellars, W. (1966), 'Fatalism and Determinism', in (ed.) K. Lehrer (1966).

Gardner, J. and Jorder, J. (eds) (1993), *Action and Value in Criminal Law* (Oxford: Clarendon Press).

Setiya, K. (2007), *Reasons Without Rationalism* (New Jersey: Princeton University Press).

Shakespeare, W. (1603–6/1996), *King Lear*, ed. G. K. Hunter (London: Penguin).

Shinn, E. (1924), *Tightrope Walker*, Oil on Canvas, 23–1/2 x 18 inches (Ohio: The Dayton Art Institute).

Silber, J. R. (1964), 'Human Action and the Language of Volitions', *Proceedings of the Aristotelian Society*, NXV. Reprinted in Care and Landesman (1968: 68–92), to which any page numbers given refer.

Skinner, Q. (1972), '"Social Meaning" and the Explanation of Social Action' in (eds) P. Laslett, W. G. Runciman, and Q. Skinner, *Philosophy, Politics and Society*, 4th series (Oxford: Basil Blackwell); slightly revised version reprinted in (1974: 106–26), to which any page numbers given refer.

Skorupski, J. (2010), *The Domain of Reasons* (Oxford: Oxford University Press).

Smith, A. (1759), *The Theory of Moral Sentiments* (London: A. Millar).

Smith, M. (1983), 'Actions, Attempts and Internal Events', *Analysis*, 43, 142–6.

—— (1987), 'The Humean Theory of Motivation', *Mind* , 96: 36–61.

—— (1988), 'On Humeans, Anti-Humeans, and Motivation: A Reply to Pettit', *Mind*, 97, 589–95.

—— (1991), 'Realism' in (ed.) P.Singer, *A Companion to Ethics* (Oxford: Blackwell), 399–410.

Smith, M. (1992), 'Valuing: Desiring or Believing?', in (eds) D. Charles and K. Lennon, *Reduction, Explanation, and Realism* (Oxford: Oxford University Press), 323–60.

—— (1994), *The Moral Problem* (Oxford: Blackwell).

—— (1998), 'The Possibility of Philosophy of Action' in Bransen and Cupyers (1998: 17–41). Reprinted in Smith (2004: 155–77), to which any page numbers given refer.

—— (2000), 'Moral Realism' in (ed.) H. LaFollette, *The Blackwell Guide to Ethical Theory* (Oxford: Blackwell), 15–27.

—— (2003),'Humeanism, Psychologism, and the Normative Story', *Philosophy and Phenomenological Research*, Vol. LXVII, No. 2 (September), 460–7. Reprinted in Smith (2004: 146–54), to which any page numbers given refer.

—— (2004), *Ethics and the A Priori: Selected Essays on Moral Psychology and Meta-Ethics*(Cambridge: Cambridge University Press).

—— (2010), 'Humeanism About Motivation', in O'Conner and Sandis (2010: 153–58).

Smith M. and Pettit, P. (1997), 'Parfit's "P"' in Dancy (1997: 71–95).

Steward, H. (1997), *The Ontology of Mind* (Oxford: Clarendon Press).

Stout, R. (1996), *Things That Happen Because They Should* (Oxford: Oxford University Press).

—— (1997), 'Processes', *Philosophy*, Vol. 72, No. 279 (Jan.),19–27.

—— (2005), *Action* (Chesham: Acumen).

Stoutland, F. (1968), 'Basic Actions and Causality', *The Journal of Philosophy*, Vol. LXV, No. 16 (22 August), 467–75.

—— (1976), 'The Causation of Behaviour', in *Esssays on Wittgenstein in Honour of G. H. von Wright Acta Philosophica Fennica*, 28: 286–325.

—— (1998), 'The Real Reasons' in J. Bransen and S. E. Cuypers (eds), *Human Action, Deliberation and Causation* (Dordrecht: Kluwer Academic Publishers), 43–66.

—— (1999), 'Intentionalists and Davidson on Rational Explanation' in (ed.) G. Meggle, *Actions, Norms, Values* (Berlin: Walter de Gruyter), 191–208.

Strawson, G. (1986/2010), *Freedom and Belief*, 2nd revised edition (Oxford: Clarendon Press).

Strawson, P. F. (1950), 'Truth', *Proceedings of the Aristotelian Society*, Supplementary Vol. xxiv, 129–57.

—— (1985/2005), *Scepticism and Naturalism: Some Varieties*, 2nd edition (London: Routledge).

Stueber, K. (2006), *Rediscovering Empathy: Agency, Folk psychology, and the Human Sciences* (Cambridge MA: MIT Press).

—— (2009), 'Intentionalism, Intentional Realism, and Empathy', *Journal of the Philosophy of History*, Vol. 3, No. 3, 290–307.

Sutherland, S. (1992), *Irrationality* (London: Constable & Co.).

Taleb, N. N. (2007), *The Black Swan* (London: Penguin).
—— (2010), *The Bed of Procrustes* (London: Penguin).
Taleb, N. N. and Blyth, M. (2011), 'The Black Swan of Cairo: How Suppressing Volatility Makes the World Less Predictable and More Dangerous', *Foreign Affairs*, Vol. 90, No. 3 (May/June), 33–9.
Taleb, N.N. and Pilpel, A. (2010), 'The Prediction of Action' in O'Connor and Sandis (2010: 410–6).
Tanney, J. (1995). 'Why Reasons May Not Be Causes', *Mind & Language, 10*, 103–26.
—— (2009), 'Reasons as Non-Causal, Context-placing Eplanations', in Sandis (2009a: 94–111).
Taylor, C. (1964), *The Explanation of Behaviour* (London: Routledge & Kegan Paul).
—— (1979), 'Action as Expression' in (eds) C. Diamond and J. Teichman, *Intention and Intentionality*: Essays *for G.E.M. Anscombe* (Sussex: Harvester Press), 73–89.
—— (1983), 'Hegel and the Philosophy of Action' in (eds) L. S. Stepelevich and D. Lamb, *Hegel's Philosophy of Action* (New Jersey: Humanities Press), 1–18. Reprinted in Laitinen and Sandis (2010a: 22–41), to which any page numbers given refer.
Taylor, G. (1976), 'Love', *Proceedings of the Aristotelian Society*, LXXVI (1975/6), 147–64.
Taylor, K. (2004), *Brainwashing: The Science of Thought Control* (Oxford: Oxford University Press).
Taylor, R. (1966), *Action and Purpose* (New Jersey: Prentice-Hall, Inc.).
Teichmann, R. (2008), *The Philosophy of Elizabeth Anscombe* (Oxford: Oxford University Press).
Thalberg, I. (1977), *Perception, Emotion and Action: A Component Approach* (Oxford: Blackwell).
—— (1985), 'Questions About Motivational Strength', in LePore and McLaughlin (1985: 88–103).
Thaler, R. H. and Sunstein, C. R. (2008/9), *Nudge:Improving Decisions About Health,Wealth and Happiness*, revised edition (London: Penguin).
Thompson, D.W. (1917), *On Growth and Form* (Cambridge: Cambridge University Press).
Thompson, M. (2008), *Life and Action: Elementary Structures of Practice and Practical Thought* (Cambridge MA: Harvard University Press).
Thomson, J. J. (1977), *Acts and Other Events* (Ithaca NY, Cornell University Press).
Tierney, J. (2008), 'In Bias Test, Shades of Gray', *New York Times*, 17 November.
Thierry, B. (2004), 'Integrating Proximate and Ultimate Causation: Just One More Go!', *Current Science*, Vol. 89, No. 7 (Oct), 1180–3.
Tuomela, R. (1977), *Human Action and its Explanation* (Dordrecht: Reidel).
Toates, F. (1986), *Motivational Systems* (Cambridge: Cambridge University Press).
Tolman, E. C. (1932), *Purposive Behavior in Animals and Men* (Berkeley: University of California Press).
Toulmin, S. (1964), *Reason in Ethics* (Cambridge: Cambridge University Press).
—— (1969), 'Concepts and the Explanation of Human Behaviour', in Mischel (1969b: 71–104).
—— (1970), 'Reasons and Causes', in Borger and Cioffi (1970: 1–26).

Urmson, J. O. (1952), 'Motives and Causes', *Proceedings of the Aristotelian Society*, Supplementary Vol. 2, 179–94. Reprinted in White (1968: 153–65) to which any page numbers given refer.

Velleman, D. J. (1989), *Practical Reflection* (Princeton: Princeton University Press).

—— (1992), 'What Happens When Someone Acts?', *Mind*, 101, 461–81. Reprinted in Velleman (2000: 123–43), to which any page numbers given refer.

—— (2000), *The Possibility of Practical Reason* (Oxford: Oxford University Press).

—— (2006) *Self to Self* (Cambridge: Cambridge University Press).

Vendler, Z. (1962), 'Effects, Results and Consequences' in (ed.) R. J. Butler, *Analytical Philosophy* (New York: Barnes & Noble), 1–14.

—— (1967), 'Causal Relations', *The Journal of Philosophy*, 64, 704–13.

—— (1984), 'Agency and Causation', *Midwest Studies in Philosophy*, IX, 371–84.

—— (1984), *The Matter of Minds* (Oxford: Clarendon Press).

Vermazen B. and Hintikka M. B. (eds) (1985), *Essays on Davidson: Actions and Events* (Oxford: Oxford University Press).

Vesey, G. N. A. (ed.) (1971), *The Proper Study* (London: Macmillan).

Vogler, C. (2002), *Reasonably Vicious* (Cambridge MA: Harvard University Press).

von Wright, G. H. (1963), *Norm and Action* (London: Routledge & Kegan Paul).

—— (1971), *Explanation and Understanding* (London: Routledge & Kegan Paul).

—— (1988), 'An Essay on Door Knocking', *Rechtstheorie* 19. Reprinted in von Wright (1998: 83–96) to which any page numbers given refer.

—— (1998), *In the Shadow of Descartes: Essays in the Philosophy of Mind* (Dordrecht: Kluwer Academic Publishers).

Wallace, R. J. (2003), 'Explanation, Deliberation, and Reasons', *Philosophy and Phenomenological Research*, Vol. 67 , No. 2, 429–35.

Wallace, R. J., Pettit, P., Scheffler, S., and Smith, M. (2004), *Reason and Value: Themes from the Moral Philosophy of Joseph Raz* (Oxford: Clarendon Press).

Ward, K. (2007), *Divine Action: Examining God's Role in an Open and Emergent Universe*, 2nd edition (Philadelphia: Templeton Foundation Press).

Watson, G. (1975), 'Free Agency', *Journal of Philosophy*, 72, 205–20.

—— (2004), *Agency and Answerability* (Oxford: Oxford University Press).

Watson, J. B. (1919), *Psychology from the Standpoint of a Behaviorist* (Philadelphia: Lippincott).

—— (1924), *Behaviourism* (New Jersey: Transaction).

Weber, M. (1975), *Roscher and Knies: The Logical Problems of Historical Economics* (New York: Free Press).

Weiner, B. (1972), *Theories of Motivation – From Mechanism to Cognition* (Chicago: Markham Publishing Company).

—— (1992), *Human Motivation: Metaphors, Theories and Research* (California: Sage Publishers Inc).

White, A. R. (1967), *The Philosophy of Mind* (New York: Random House).

—— (ed.) (1968), *The Philosophy of Action* (Oxford: Oxford University Press).

—— (1970), *Truth* (London: Macmillan & Co.).

—— (1972), 'What We Believe' in (ed.) N. Rescher, *Studies in the Philosophy of Mind*, APQ Monograph Series No. 6 (Oxford: Blackwell), 69–84.

Williams, B. A. O. (1980), 'Internal and External Reasons', in (ed.) R. Harrison, *Rational Action* (Cambridge: Cambridge University Press). Reprinted in Williams (1981: 101–13) to which any page numbers given refer.

—— (1981), *Moral Luck* (Cambridge: Cambridge University Press).

Winch, P. (1958), *The Idea of a Social Science* (London: Routledge and Kegan Paul).

Wittgenstein, L. (1921/1961), *Tractatus Logico-Philosophicus*, revised trans. D. F. Pears and B. F. McGuiness (London: Routledge).

—— (1953/2009), *Philosophical Investigations*, 4th edition, trans. G. E. M. Anscombe, P. M. S. Hacker, and J. Schulte (Oxford: Wiley-Blackwell).

—— (1974), *Philosophical Grammar*, ed. R. Rhees, trans. A Kenny (Oxford: Blackwell).

—— (1975), *Philosophical Remarks*, ed. R. Rhees, trans. R. Hargreaves and R. White (Oxford: Blackwell)

—— (1980), *Wittgenstein's Lectures: Cambridge 1930–32*, ed. D. Lee [from the notes of John King and Desmond Lee] (Oxford: Blackwell).

Werther, D. (2007), 'Everything Happens for a Reason' in (ed.) S. Kaye, *Lost and Philosophy: The Island Has Its Reasons* (Oxford: Wiley-Blackwell), 221–30.

Wollaston, W. (1722/1750), *The Religion of Nature Delineated*, 7th edition (London: J & P. Knapton).

Young, P. T. (1961), *Motivation and Emotion* (New York: Wiley).

Index

Page numbers in **bold** denote entries of particular importance

215